The Psychology of Female Violence

D1460476

'. . . an intellectually substantial and highly readable contribution to our clinical knowledge of the complex roots of female violence.' Estela Welldon, in her Foreword.

The Psychology of Female Violence explores the psychology of violent and criminal women. Drawing upon psychodynamic and criminological perspectives of female offending, the link between childhood experience and adult behaviour is expounded.

The book is divided into three parts focusing upon violence against children, violence against the self, and violence against others. Major topics include:

- self-harm
- eating disorders
- physical and sexual abuse of children
- infanticide
- Munchausen's Syndrome by Proxy
- battered women who kill.

The Psychology of Female Violence will be valuable to students studying clinical psychology, women's studies, sociology, counselling, psycho-analysis and criminology as well as all practitioners involved in mental health and the criminal justice system.

Anna Motz is a chartered clinical and forensic psychologist working within the Forensic Directorate of Ealing, Hammersmith and Fulham Mental Health NHS Trust. She has extensive experience of psychological assessment and treatment of perpetrators and survivors of violence. She is the Secretary of the International Association of Forensic Psychotherapy.

The Psychology of Female Violence

Crimes Against the Body

Anna Motz

BRUNNER-ROUTLEDGE
ALERE FLAMMAM
Taylor & Francis Group

First published 2001 by
Brunner-Routledge
27 Church Road, Hove, East Sussex BN3 2FA

Simultaneously published in the USA and Canada
by Taylor & Francis Inc.
325 Chestnut Street, 8th Floor, Philadelphia, PA 19106

Brunner-Routledge is an imprint of the Taylor & Francis Group

Typeset in Times by
Keystroke, Jacaranda Lodge, Wolverhampton
Printed and bound in Great Britain by
TJ International Ltd, Padstow, Cornwall

British Library Cataloguing in Publication Data
A catalogue record for this book is available from the British Library

Library of Congress Cataloging in Publication Data
Motz, Anna, 1964–
    The psychology of female violence : crimes against the body / Anna Motz.
      p. cm.
    Includes bibliographical references and index.
    1. Female offenders—Psychology. 2. Child abuse. 3. Self-destructive
behaviour. I. Title.

HV6046 .M64 2000
616.89′0082—dc21   00-042499

ISBN 0–415–12675–4 (pbk)
      0–415–12674–6 (hbk)

To the memory of Hans and Lotte Motz

Contents

Foreword

I have to declare a special interest in this book as I met Anna Motz when she joined one of the first Diploma Courses in Forensic Psychotherapy which I inaugurated at the Portman Clinic. One always has high hopes for all one's students, and almost all of them go on to do difficult and demanding work with courage and integrity. But relatively few produce books that make a significant advance in our understanding of our chosen field. Anna Motz is one of those few.

As a clinician of genuine brilliance and courage, Motz provides us, her colleagues, with much that is valuable and new in our work with violent women. In her view, women who fail to express feelings of frustration and anger use their bodies 'as their most powerful means of communication and their greatest weapon' and she adds a new insight in her assertion: 'Self-harm is a defence against intimacy, binding a woman to her own body to the exclusion of others.'

The case histories offered in this book are of women who have either been assessed or who are in treatment for crimes of violence against their own bodies, or their children or their partners. Motz's description of the forensic settings and working relationships of the staff involved in those institutions is a key part of the contribution that she makes to our understanding of this most painful area of forensic psychotherapy.

In purely numerical terms, there are only a few hundred documented examples of perverse motherhood. But the impact of perverse mothers is enormously powerful: on their innocent and helpless victims, on the growing numbers of families and communities corrupted and demoralised, on whole societies in shock, disbelief and bewilderment. These are not just clinical concerns. They are social, moral, cultural, penal, legal and bureaucratic, and as such touch almost everyone in society.

As a professional colleague, I am grateful for the way that Motz describes the psychodynamics of the battered wife who becomes a husband-killer and how both partners re-enact their own unconscious wishes to swap roles. The long-term emotional and behavioural consequences of the children being witnesses and victims of parental abuse and the vulnerability of the abuser herself are delineated in a fine, delicate way.

Motz provides us, her fellow-clinicians, with case studies, theoretical discussions and professional insights that are all excellent. But her concerns and conclusions go beyond those of our profession. Counter-pointing the calm professional voice is an angry and urgent call for attention from the clinicians with whom we have to work.

We have now begun to understand that female violence has been with us in many different forms throughout human history. But it is only in the past twenty years or so that it has found a place on the psychological, social and political agenda. Even now, the whole topic is surrounded by extreme confusion and not only for tabloid journalists and the general public. Motz shows that, all too often, the professionals, who make the decisions about the future of perverse mothers and their child-victims, are driven by their own unconscious expectations, prejudices, political imperatives and professional inadequacies.

For these reasons, I wish I could give a copy of this book to every MP, social worker, tabloid editor, local councillor, caring professional, lawyer and police-person.

Obviously, a book that is intended mainly for clinicians cannot begin adequately to deal with the issues that Motz so eloquently and sensitively documents. But by placing the case histories in the context of inter- and intra-agency decision-taking, she opens up the field of forensic psychotherapy in a new and important way.

As forensic psychotherapists, we are required to provide professionally objective clinical assessments of the risks that perverse mothers present to their children, to themselves and to society at large. And, like many of us, Anna Motz is keenly aware of her own femaleness, her own body, her own emotional response to the perpetrators and their tragic victims. Thus, the future lives of severely abused and damaged children are at the centre of her concern, and it is to her credit that she allows us to share in her dismay and anger at the inadequacy of the thinking of the decision-takers, and of the strategies that are available for the care and protection of these tragic innocents.

The case studies show that these violent and perverse mothers have themselves been severely sexually and/or physically abused. Without exception, these are women whose perverse violence results from their own early experiences of deprivation and abuse. Hence, the importance of designing and implementing comprehensive and sensitive treatment programmes for such women is incontestable.

Existing treatment programmes tend to fail because they are fraught with the consequences of the prejudices derived from the difference in our attitudes towards victims and perpetrators. Lip service is generally paid to the inevitable cycle of violence and abuse applicable to both genders, but the victims are still thought to be women, and the perpetrators men. This book breaks new ground by providing us with new and brave insights into the suffering of small children inflicted by many generations of women who were themselves early victims of abuse, deprivation and despair.

Apart from the inadequacy of the available treatment programmes for perpetrators, there is the question of the failure of existing programmes of care and protection for the victims who, without proper and comprehensive understanding, may easily become victimisers.

When social workers and psychiatrists so often have no choice but to perpetuate, or even intensify, the pattern of abuse and deprivation, the dilemmas of the clinicians and decision-makers are indeed horrendous. They may have no choice but to consign a 10-year-old, who has been severely abused by her own mother, to a local authority's care and protection system, But how do they cope with the knowledge that it is in that very system that the perverse mother has herself been abused and perverted?

That is why she points us finally towards the need for 'the system', of which we are all a part, to 'learn' how to respond to the tragic dilemmas with which we are all confronted.

In that context, all of us should have a part to play in deciding and implementing the strategies that our society develops to respond to this very new issue on its agenda. It is a challenge to all of us in the clinical and caring professions. And, especially, to those with responsibility for determining our society's attitudes towards and strategies for dealing with these rare but appalling perversions.

In conclusion, we, her colleagues in forensic psychotherapy, have cause to be grateful to Anna Motz for making such an intellectually substantial and highly readable contribution to our clinical knowledge of the complex roots of female violence.

But she has done much more than her professional duty. She has highlighted the systemic dilemmas that perverse mothers, in particular, reveal in our clinical, social, penal and caring programmes. In so doing, she has done a substantial service to society as a whole.

Estela V. Welldon, MD, DSc (Hon), FRCPsych
Consultant Psychiatrist in Psychotherapy, Portman Clinic
Honorary Senior Lecturer in Forensic Psychotherapy
at University College London

Acknowledgements

My desire to write this book comes from my clinical work with the many women who have allowed me to hear about their experiences, both as victims and perpetrators of violence. I am indebted to these women, whose candour, resilience and eloquence led me to try to understand this violence.

I was assisted in this understanding by the forensic psychotherapy course at the Portman Clinic and particularly by Estela Welldon, Donald Campbell, Robert Hale, Marianne Parsons and Anne Zachary.

I am grateful to clinical psychologists Helen Liebling and Caroline Lovelock, whose sensitive understanding of female violence has been illuminating.

For their close reading and thoughtful comments I want to thank Tina Baker, Joanna Burrell, Jackie Craissati, Paul van Heeswyk, Kate Iwe, Sally Lane, Sheila Redfern, Maya Turcan, Jane Ussher, Elyse Weiner and Estela Welldon. I am very grateful to my mother, the late Lotte Motz, whose interest in my work and perceptive, intelligent and honest comments on the early chapters were invaluable; her involvement and interest in this research have been greatly missed. I am most indebted to my husband, Nigel Warburton, for his support, enthusiasm and the many insightful comments which have helped me greatly at all stages of writing. I also owe much to my uncle, Herbert Edlis, for his support and interest throughout this project. I would also like to thank Paul Valentine, Librarian, Coombes Medical Library, Ealing, Hammersmith and Fulham Mental Health NHS Trust, for his great help in obtaining numerous journal articles for this research.

I thank the following people for their moral support and intellectual participation in this project: Jean Burrell, Gavin and Margaret Cartledge, Susan Edlis, Margaret Fishman, Kate Harris, the late Kate Hill, David Kirkby, Mrs Mills Burton, Ben Ross, David Shelton, Marian Wassner and Saskia van der Zee. I am grateful to Sean Hand for his insights into the link between violence and sentimentality. I owe special thanks to my daughter Hannah for her love and patience.

The Routledge editorial team including Imogen Burch, Alison Dixon, Joanne Forshaw, Kate Hawes and Vivien Ward have been of great help in this project as well as Frank Pert who compiled the index.

I am particularly grateful for the inspiration and encouragement of Estela Welldon, whose illuminating work and personal support have been invaluable.

I am especially indebted to my parents, Lotte and Hans Motz, both of whom were inspirational and passionate scholars.

Introduction

'Some of us use the body to convey the things for which we cannot find words.'

(Hornbacher, 1998:125)

In this book I explore the psychology of violent women, outlining the link between childhood experience and adult behaviour. I highlight the psychological and social functions and meanings of violence and provide a psychodynamic perspective on female violence, using case material throughout to illustrate theory. I describe acts of violence committed by women and identify those features which are unique to women. The pioneering work on female perversion by Estela Welldon in *Mother, Madonna, Whore: The Idealisation and Denigration of Motherhood*, first published in 1988, is central to this task as it provides a conceptual framework for understanding how female development and biology affect the evolution of perverse and violent behaviour.

In this book I present a psychological model for understanding female violence, emphasising its function and the meaning of the violent act, and, where appropriate, the implications for treatment. The unique situation of women demands that their experiences be considered separately, with emphasis on the perversions and crimes that women typically commit. A woman uses her body as her most powerful means of communication and her greatest weapon. In a sense she writes on her body in a gesture of protest and in order to elicit help, to communicate her sense of crisis. This book is intended to be an introduction to this largely unexplored area and to the model of forensic psychotherapy which provides a theoretical and clinical approach to understanding the dynamics of violence and criminality.

DEFINING VIOLENCE

It is important to understand what is meant by violence. Violence can be seen 'as a loss of control of aggressive impulse leading to action' (Shengold, 1999:xii). Central to the definition of violence is the act of causing physical harm. In this book I focus on violence directed against individuals, not against objects.

The roots of violence have been linked to a developmental failure to conceptualise one's own and other people's states of mind. What is too painful to be thought about may be enacted. It has been suggested that this difficulty is created by the mother's hostility towards the infant which makes it difficult for the infant to think about her mother's state of mind, and how the mother views her (Fonagy and Target, 1999). This is clearly linked to violence:

> Violence, aggression directed against the body, may be closely linked to failures of mentalisation, as the lack of capacity to think about mental states may force individuals to manage thoughts, beliefs, and desires in the physical domain, primarily in the realm of body states and processes.
>
> (Fonagy and Target, 1999:53)

I am particularly interested in exploring the inner unconscious conflicts which may be reflected in the outward manifestation of violence; my main focus is on the inner world of the violent woman. Throughout the book I distinguish between offending and non-criminal acts of violence. I use the word 'crimes' both literally and metaphorically.

CLINICAL CONTEXT

I am a clinical psychologist working within the forensic psychiatry and psychology services, based at a regional secure unit. I assess and treat inpatients and outpatients. The women with whom I have clinical contact have been referred from both criminal and civil courts, social services, and the probation or psychiatric services. The group of women described may reflect extremes: as female violence is largely unexplored, however, it is valuable to study extreme examples of violent behaviour to shed light on the phenomenon in general. Although many of the women I see have come through the criminal justice system, not all are offenders, and some may have committed crimes for which they have never been convicted. Rather than focusing on criminal women specifically I have addressed the general area of female violence, with reference to violent crimes which women typically commit. Not all types of violence discussed in this book are against the law, e.g. self-harm and anorexia nervosa, but I consider these to be metaphorically crimes against the body, acts of violence against the self.

I have illustrated theory with case material throughout, drawn from my clinical contact with women, both as inpatients and outpatients of the psychological and psychiatric services. I consider clinical case material to be an invaluable source of instruction about the nature of female violence. The case material is drawn from a wide range of assessments and treatment of women seen over a ten-year period. In addition to working within the National Health Service, I work independently and see women for assessment in child-care proceedings cases who may have no previous contact with psychological or psychiatric services. I have included material drawn from these contacts in the case discussions. Although I have disguised the individual women and some aspects of their circumstances, I have attempted to retain the essential features which illustrate the nature of female violence. I have changed the clients' details in order to preserve confidentiality and anonymity.

The nature of the treatment I offer is short term compared to the traditional length of psychoanalytic psychotherapy: the maximum treatment undertaken is approximately two to three years and consists of once weekly therapy. Although my work is informed by psychoanalytic ideas, I am not a psychoanalytic psychotherapist and do not intend to suggest to the reader that the clinical work described here is analytical psychotherapy in the traditional sense. I use the tools of forensic psychotherapy, as developed at the Portman Clinic, in which a psychodynamic understanding of the internal world of the offender guides clinical practice. While my background is in clinical psychology, I am informed by concepts like transference, countertransference, part-object, and the psychological defences like projection, projective identification and identification with the aggressor, to which I will refer in this text. For anyone unfamiliar with the terminology, Laplanche and Pontalis's *A Dictionary of Psychoanalysis* provides a clear definition and explanation of psychoanalytic terms.

CENTRAL AIM OF THE BOOK: CHALLENGE TO THE DENIAL OF FEMALE VIOLENCE

Although this book focuses on the violence committed by women, it is also essential to recognise the violence which is done to them through the denial of their capacity for aggression, and the refusal to acknowledge their moral agency. It is possible that the envy which this idealisation by others creates is also responsible for the denigration of women, particularly mothers, when they do not fulfil the expectations created by sentimentalised notions of motherhood and femininity.

Two important reasons for ignoring female violence are, on the one hand, the widespread denial of female aggression and, on the other, the idealisation of motherhood. A further reason is the secretive or personal nature of much female violence, perversity or deviance. 'Most violence is perpetrated by men, whether directed at men or women' (Mayhew *et al.*, 1992) but when women do commit acts of violence they are likely to do so in the private sphere, in the home, against themselves or their children. These may be considered hidden crimes and will not necessarily show up in the criminal statistics. Female violence is often committed in the private, domestic arena as opposed to the traditionally male arena of public life, highlighting important issues about the demarcation of spheres of power in society.

Welldon's (1991, 1992, 1993, 1994, 1996) work on female violence and perversion has outlined the psychodynamic processes which shape this behaviour, and the intergenerational transmission of perverse and abusive mothering. Dinora Pines (1993) describes the ways in which unconscious conflicts are expressed through pregnancy, childbirth and sexuality in women. These processes are evident in the women with whom I have clinical contact, many of whom are psychologically disturbed, and manifested in the violence that they inflict on their own bodies and those of their children.

PARAMETERS OF THE BOOK

There are many expressions of female violence which demand careful analysis and exploration. In this text I have chosen to discuss those manifestations of female violence with which I have had most clinical contact, and this tends to be in the areas of maternal abuse, self-harm, and the experience of women who have been the victims of male violence, some of whom have eventually retaliated. Because of the depths of disturbance and deprivation of the women I describe here, it is possible that the case material will appear dramatic and shocking; I must emphasise that I see a highly selective group of patients, some of whom have been convicted of serious crimes and sentenced to hospital treatment.

I have also included material drawn from my assessments of women for use in care proceedings cases. I have almost always been asked to assess these women because of known or suspected abuse of their children, and the concerns of the local authorities that these mothers either pose an actual risk to their children or have serious difficulties in protecting them from abuse inflicted by violent partners. It is undeniable that I see very disturbed women in the inpatient population, and only assess those mothers about whom concern has been expressed, and who may often have been known to social services even before they became mothers. There is therefore an important sense in which I am describing women in this book whose violence and deprivation is on the extreme end of a continuum; nonetheless, these women dramatically illustrate processes and experiences shared by other, non-offending women.

I am aware that there are important manifestations of violence in women including arson, lesbian partner violence, gang violence, and serial murder which I have not addressed here. This study should not be considered a comprehensive account of the vast and neglected area of female violence but rather an introduction to it.

THE MODEL OF FEMALE PERVERSION: CONCEPTUAL FOUNDATIONS

The notion of perversion as sexualised aggression is relevant to understanding female aggression. I consider many varieties of self-harm, including anorexia, to be female perversions, that is, the sexualised expression of aggression which serves to defend the person against depression or even psychosis, and in the case of women is not directed towards an objectified other but towards their own or their children's bodies. The notion that there is a special, unique category of female perversion was developed by Welldon and eating disorders, self-cutting and maternal incest can all be conceptualised as such. Welldon argues:

> The reproductive functions and organs are used by both sexes to express perversion. Perverse men use their penises to attack and show hatred towards symbolic sources of humiliation, usually represented by part-objects. If perversion in the man is focused through his penis, in the woman it will similarly be expressed through her reproductive organs and the mental representations of motherhood.
>
> (Welldon, 1991:85)

Unlike Freud's definition of perversion, this conceptualisation need not be used in an exclusively sexual context. Throughout the book I have described female perversion: I hope it is clear to the reader that the term 'perversion' is used descriptively rather than pejoratively or morally, though many of the acts described are at the extreme of morality.

THE LANGUAGE OF THE BODY

I consider the acts of violence typically committed by women, against their own bodies and against their children, to be essential tools of communication. The work of McDougall (1989) addressing the psycho-analysis of psychosomatic disorder is relevant to an understanding of how the body can manifest conflicts and traumas which cannot be accessed or articulated consciously. While acknowledging the privileged position accorded to language in structuring the psyche and therapy in traditional psychoanalysis, she stresses the importance of paying attention to the complaints and disorders of the body. She argues that such psychosomatic illnesses reflect significant psychological distress and are both meaningful and potentially analysable, with some hope that these conditions can become articulated, and verbalised, gradually diminishing in lethal force. She states:

> not all communications use language. In attempting to attack any awareness of certain thoughts, fantasies or conflictual situations apt to stir up strong feelings of either a painful or overexciting nature, a patient may for example produce a somatic explosion instead of a thought, a fantasy, or a dream.
>
> (McDougall, 1989:11)

I see a woman's unconscious use of her body in pregnancy, and its symbolic use in self-harm, anorexia and its engagement in acts of violence against children as analogous to psychosomatic illnesses. These acts of violence serve a psychic function for the woman who perpetrates them just as the symptoms of psychosomatic illness 'are childlike attempts at self-care and were created as a solution to unbearable mental pain' (McDougall, 1989:8). She relates the development of these disorders to early infancy, where the psychic structures are pre-linguistic and the earliest representations of the self are related to bodily experiences, and where the body is the primary medium for communication.

I consider the most plausible model for understanding female violence to be one in which the violent act is conceptualised as a solution to a psychological difficulty and a bodily expression or communication of distress and anger, analogous to the psychosomatic complaint described by McDougall. The link between violence and perversion, as a defence against underlying psychological distress, is an essential one, which underpins the model of female violence suggested in this book.

ALTERNATIVE MODELS OF FEMALE VIOLENCE

There are alternative models of understanding female violence. These include a feminist understanding of female violence as a response to oppression and social conditioning, the biological model which places emphasis on the role of hormonal factors related to reproduction, a cognitive behavioural model of understanding the development and maintenance of psychological disturbance, and attachment theory, which offers a paradigm for understanding how patterns of parenting and early relations can lead to difficulties in psychological and social functioning in later life. Attachment theory is closely related to the psychodynamic model and developed both within ethology and within psychoanalytic paradigms. In this book I focus on a psychodynamic understanding of female violence, which I believe is the most powerful model for understanding its genesis and manifestation.

Although I draw on feminist research, particularly in relation to self-harm and domestic violence, I do not use this model exclusively, favouring a psychological model in which psychodynamic processes are elucidated. My main aim is to understand the communicative function of the acts of violence discussed, and the psychological motivation which generates them. I view the acts of violence and offences as symbols and expressions of earlier conflicts, many of which can be traced to very early experiences in relation to the violent women's own experience of mothering. Other models leave important aspects of female violence unexplained.

Attachment theory offers insights into the intergenerational transmission of abuse. I accept the significant insight offered by Fonagy and Target (1995) relating to disturbed early attachment patterns and the resulting failure of infants to develop the capacity to mentalise: this difficulty appears to be manifested in some of the women I describe, whose bodies are used unconsciously as their main tools of communication. De Zuleta's (1993) work has contributed significantly to the understanding of how disturbed attachment systems and traumatic events can lay the foundations for later perversions, which develop as a defence against psychic pain; she has made explicit the link between attachment theory, trauma, and the development of pathological defences in the perverse or violent individual.

STRUCTURE OF THE BOOK

The book is divided into three parts: violence against children, violence against the self, and violence against others. I have ordered these types of violence according to a conceptual progression, from the most hidden to the most public forms of violence. I consider maternal violence, both sexual and physical, the most hidden crime, often occurring in the private realm of the home. There may be no obvious physical signs on the victims as bruises may be hidden and the fact of sexual abuse concealed; the traces are most often psychological.

These acts of violence may become public when the child is brought to hospital with non-accidental injuries or the symptoms of illnesses, which, in the case of Munchausen's syndrome by proxy, may turn out to have been either fabricated or induced. At this point the public arena is entered and the intervention of the social services and the Courts may become necessary. Maternal abuse may be hidden because of the absolute power which mothers have in relation to their children, whom they care for within the private realm of the home. Violence against the self may also reflect a private crime which can be perpetrated in secret, away from public view, but its effects are more readily seen in the scars of self-mutilation or the emaciated bodies of anorectic women than the hidden scars of emotional or sexual abuse in children.

I link the aims of violence in self-harm and maternal abuse, using the notion of female perversion, with its emphasis on attacking the body, and the bodies of children. In the third part of the book I explore the phenomenon of women who kill their violent partners. It is in this chapter that violence is most clearly seen in the context of wider social issues related to power imbalances between men and women; the legal defences of these women are analysed in some detail.

I Violence against children

This is a major part of the book and discusses the often hidden crimes of child sexual and physical abuse, Munchausen's syndrome by proxy, and the tragic crime of infanticide. I explore the idealisation of motherhood, the myth of 'The Great Mother', a universal mother goddess (Motz, 1997), and the pathological process in which unconscious conflicts are resolved through pregnancies and abusive parenting. The symbolic function of the child is also explored.

In chapter 1 I describe Welldon's model of perverse mothering in my exploration of female sexual abuse of children, a taboo subject, which has only relatively recently become the subject of media and professional interest. In order to do this I outline the theoretical basis for the model of female violence, and the roots of disturbed mothering. For some disturbed young women with impoverished experiences of being mothered themselves, their children are narcissistic extensions of themselves. The baby can be seen as the good object which the 'bad' woman desperately needs as a receptacle for her projections. In her mother's fantasy the unborn infant is the embodiment of a loving creature who confirms the mother's regenerative power and the existence of some good in her: this idealisation can lead to disappointment and depression when the infant is actually born, awakening rage in the mother. Pines' (1993) analysis of the experiences of pregnancy and mothering, and their disturbances, and Welldon's (1992) work on perverse mothering, underpin this thesis.

I outline intergenerational patterns of deprivation and abuse which may predispose some women to repeat abusive behaviour with their children. This model draws upon early experience of mothering as well as later social stresses and traces the path from abused girl to partnership with an abuser, the intensification of loss of control, learned helplessness and eventually a repetition of the abuse cycle. I provide examples of 'pathological pregnancies' as well as violence towards children to illustrate how women may direct their aggression on to their own bodies or those of their children to provide 'solutions' to psychological problems. This is related to early experiences of abuse, deprivation or neglect and mirrors the earlier trauma.

It is crucially important to recognise the phenomenon of female sexual abuse of children and to offer assessment and treatment to female perpetrators of sexual abuse against children, many of whom will also have been victims of intrafamilial abuse themselves. The denial of female sexuality, and the idealisation of motherhood, are evident in the refusal to 'think the unthinkable' – to recognise the existence of maternal perversion. The notion of perverse mothering elucidates the causes, manifestations and psychic functions of maternal sexual abuse.

Chapter 2 outlines how physical and emotional abuse of children can be manifested in Munchausen's syndrome by proxy. In this chapter I consider the physical and emotional abuse manifested in mothers who display the characteristics of Munchausen's syndrome by proxy, which, although a rare disorder, graphically illustrates how women may use their children perversely, continuing the theme of female perversion. I provide a case illustration and theoretical discussion of this dangerous and complex condition. In this hidden form of abuse mothers may induce or fabricate symptoms in their children, sometimes with fatal consequences. This syndrome appears perverse and unbelievable to those who encounter it, and is sometimes only detected through the use of covert video surveillance, raising ethical difficulties (Cordess, 1998). It is essential to understand the syndrome and to outline risk factors and signs which can help professionals to identify it.

Chapter 3 addresses physical abuse of children by their mothers. Physical abuse of a child can reflect the tremendous social stresses and personal losses that many young mothers face, as well as stemming from the reactivation of their own experiences of abuse or neglect. The symbolic significance of care proceedings in cases of child abuse is discussed. In care proceedings private violence becomes a public issue.

In chapter 4 I discuss infanticide, one of the most shocking expressions of maternal violence. Again the mother uses her own body, as represented in the body of her child, to carry out an act of intense and irrevocable violence. The remorse and grief experienced by women who kill their children is understandably profound. I discuss the association of infanticide with hysterical denial of pregnancy which also features in one of the two case illustrations provided in this chapter.

2 Violence against the self

Female violence is often directed against the self in depression, self-mutilation or voluntary starvation. Although these manifestations may reflect unconscious violence, directed against the self, they are not commonly considered to be crimes, and are certainly not prohibited legally. Because these manifestations of female violence are directed against women's own bodies, or the bodies of their children, they are often hidden from the public. The book's subtitle 'Crimes against the body' refers to the self-directed nature of much of female violence; the term 'crimes' is used metaphorically. The women I describe here appear to identify themselves strongly with their bodies, reflecting not only their own inner, psychic difficulties, but also the tremendous cultural emphasis placed on women's bodies, and their reproductive capacities. Their notion of selfhood is interwoven with their physical bodies: attacking their own bodies has a multiplicity of meanings which require articulation. These women attack themselves, and, in fantasy, the body of their own mothers, through self-injury, using the concrete experience of pain to express psychological anguish and communicate unconscious conflicts.

This part has two chapters, one on self-harm and one on anorexia nervosa. Each is illustrated with case material to complement the theoretical understanding of violence against the self. My aim is to provide some understanding of the complexity and development of the behaviour, the underlying distress it signifies, its symbolic meaning and its impact on those working with these women.

Chapter 5 focuses on deliberate self-harm, emphasising its communicative function and elucidating the model of female perversion developed by Welldon. Women harm themselves primarily to express their distress and anger, in the hope, often unconscious, that others will respond to this. Likewise, the violence which women inflict on their children's bodies often reflects a communicative need, and may be seen as a symptom of other conflicts. They choose to manage the intense internal pain they feel by directing it on to themselves, to externalise it in an attack on the body. The violence of self-injury is often minimised and it is viewed by others as simply annoying or manipulative rather than as a powerful communication. The majority of those who self-harm are not actually dangerous to others although a minority are, particularly those who have themselves experienced very severe sexual, physical and emotional abuse.

In chapter 6, I discuss anorexia nervosa. Self-injury, including anorexia, may appear to offer a means of obtaining control, albeit temporarily, over the self through the body. Anorexia nervosa is a life-threatening condition in which the body is deliberately starved, expressing tremendous aggression turned against the self. A proportion of anorectics binge and then purge, engaging in a cycle of indulgence and self-punishment in which the abuse of their own bodies is evident. The act of purging can be viewed as a symbolic defence against retaining painful thoughts and memories, and can also be manifested in therapy as the inability to take in and digest the material. Issues for therapists in working with anorexic women are explored, with reference to the psychoanalytic work of Williams (1997) and Birksted-Breen (1997). While anorexia nervosa and bulimia nervosa are two distinct clinical conditions, anorectic women can sometimes use the purging methods that characterise bulimia. The chapter focuses on anorexia nervosa, but I provide some discussion of bulimia nervosa, particularly in relation to the psychic meaning of purging.

3 Violence against others

This part is devoted to the exploration of battered women who kill, which is discussed in chapter 7. Women who are subjected to sustained physical abuse can become psychologically damaged, sometimes to the point of extreme passivity, a process which has been termed 'learned helplessness' (Seligman, 1975; Browne, 1987) and features in the 'battered woman syndrome' (Walker, 1984). I describe what happens to women during periods of sustained abuse by their violent partners and then describe the process which can lead such women to kill their abusive partners. Case illustrations are provided, one of which demonstrates the impact of sustained violence on a woman, the other describing how the experience of domestic violence led to her killing her abusive partner. I discuss the psychological processes using psychodynamic terms, and evaluate the validity of the legal defence of 'battered woman syndrome'.

Conclusion

The conclusion ties together the themes of the preceding chapters and points the way forward for future research. It describes the role of forensic psychotherapy in understanding female violence and offering a treatment model in which the meaning of the violent act can be explored, with the hope that such understanding can lead to reflection, and render the violence obsolete. The ultimate goal of such therapy is to enable the violent woman to find another voice and to be less confined to using the language of the body, painful as this achievement may be.

Part I

Violence against children

Chapter 1

Female sexual abuse
of children

So Ruth rose up and out of her guileless inefficiency to claim her
bit of balm right after the preparation of dinner and just before the
return of her husband from his office. It was one of her two secret
indulgences – the one that involved her son – and part of the pleasure
it gave her came from the room in which she did it . . . She sat in the
room holding her son on her lap, staring at his closed eyelids and
listening to the sound of his sucking. Staring not so much from
maternal joy as from a wish to avoid seeing his legs dangling almost
to the floor . . .

In the late afternoon, before her husband closed his office and came
home, she called her son to her. When he came into the little room she
unbuttoned her blouse and smiled. He was too young to be dazzled by
her nipples, but he was old enough to be bored by the flat taste of
mother's milk, so he came reluctantly as to a chore, and lay as he had
at least once each day of his life in his mother's arms, and tried to
pull the thin, faintly sweet milk from her flesh without hurting her
with his teeth.

She felt him. His restraint, his courtesy, his indifference, all of
which pushed her into fantasy. She had the distinct impression that
his lips were pulling from her a thread of light. It was as though she
were a cauldron issuing spinning gold. Like the miller's daughter –
the one who sat at night in a straw-filled room, thrilled with the secret
power Rumpelstiltskin had given her: to see golden thread stream
from her very own shuttle. And that was the other part of her pleasure,
a pleasure she hated to give up.

(*Song of Solomon*, Morrison, 1977)

Mothering, whether in the home or on the hospital floor, is a much
more common route to power for psychopathic women than is
commerce or sex.

(Pearson, 1998:107)

INTRODUCTION

The site of female perversion is the whole body and, by extension, the bodies of children. When women attack their own bodies, through self-mutilation, self-starvation or bingeing, they are symbolically wreaking revenge on their own internalised, often cruel and perverse mothers. They identify their own body with the body of the mother. Likewise when they attack their children, they express violence towards a narcissistic extension of themselves:

> The main difference between male and female perverse action lies in the aim. Whereas in men the act is aimed at an external part-object, in women it is against themselves: either against their bodies or against objects of their own creation – that is, their babies.
>
> (Welldon, 1992: 72)

These mothers have typically been used as extensions of their own mothers, who have treated them narcissistically: they repeat this pattern in the way they relate to their own babies. Early experience of maternal abuse or neglect increases the likelihood that in adulthood these women will be exposed to other situations of risk, including relationships with sexually and physically abusive men, leading to further distortions in their self-image, and psychological functioning; this will, in turn, adversely affect their own capacity to mother.

In this chapter I will explore disturbances of pregnancy and motherhood, addressing the specific problem of female sexual offending against children. I illustrate the chapter with three case studies of women who sexually abused children: in two cases their own children, in another, other people's children as an accomplice to a male paedophile. I also present case material which demonstrates the psychic processes of a highly disturbed pregnancy, in which a young mother displayed physical rather than sexual violence towards her own pregnant body, and later towards her infant. These cases illustrate Welldon's model of female perversion. In order to understand the phenomenon of sexual abuse of children it is essential to consider the nature of female perversion, and its roots in disturbed parenting. I begin this chapter with a discussion of female perversion, and psychological disturbances in pregnancy and mothering in general, before moving on to explore sexual abuse of children in particular.

THE NATURE OF FEMALE PERVERSION

Estela Welldon's radical thesis challenged the assumption that perversion was related to the phallus, and thus the province of men, as Freud had established. In her preface to the 1992 edition of Welldon's book, *Mother, Madonna, Whore: The Idealisation and Denigration of Motherhood* (first published in 1988), Juliet Mitchell writes:

> Men are perverse; women neurotic; Estela Welldon was one of the first – perhaps in her field, the first – to question the status of this psychosocial truism . . . women could not be seen to be perverse because the model for perversion was male. . . . Welldon sets out her argument that female psychophysiology gives a completely different pattern to perversion. At the centre of female perversion is the perversion of motherhood. The source of both male and female perversion may lie in a disturbed infant/mother relationship but the aims of subsequent adult perversion in the two sexes differ. Both attack the mother who abused, neglected or deprived them but women will attack this mother as she is internalised in her own female body or found within her own mothering. The hated one is identified and lies thus within or in the baby who extends the self as once the perverse woman was her own mother's extension. Consequently the typical perversions of women entail self-mutilation or child abuse . . . Perversion of motherhood is the end product of serial abuse or chronic infantile neglect. The reproduction of mothering is also the reproduction of perverse mothering.
>
> (Mitchell, 1992:iv)

Welldon argues that female perversion has generally been overlooked by psychoanalytic authors who have identified perversion with male sexuality and the castration complex which results from Oedipal longings. Freud essentially neglected the study of female sexuality and the possible perversions of women's maternal desires, attributing to women strong feelings of inferiority about being female and a compensatory craving to be impregnated with sons. For Freud the penis is symbolically equated with babies; girls resolve their Oedipus complex by transferring the object of sexual desire from mother to father, and then changing the wish for a penis to a wish to be impregnated by their fathers. Having babies fulfils a woman's needs, related to her penis envy and the compensatory craving for babies by the father. There was no indication by Freud that pregnancy or childhood could afford disturbed women opportunities for perversion and that motherhood itself might provide such a rich source of perverse and destructive power.

Welldon was the first to describe explicitly how, for women, perversion is not simply located in the genitals. The whole functioning female body, and the babies which it produces, provide the focus for the manifestation of female perversion.

> I believe the term 'body' in the definition of perversion has been mistakenly identified exclusively with the male anatomy and physiology, specifically with the penis and genital orgasm. How could we otherwise have overlooked the fact that women's bodies are completely taken over in the course of their inherent functioning by procreative drives, sometimes accompanied with the most perverse fantasies whose outcome materialises in their bodies?
>
> (Welldon, 1992:7)

Perversion as the erotic form of hatred

Perverse behaviour enables women to project their own experience of childhood victimisation on to someone else, namely a child or children entrusted to their care. This process illustrates an important psychological function of a perversion. In the psychoanalytic sense perversion is a term used not pejoratively but descriptively, referring to a particular kind of erotic activity which does not have as its aim genital sexuality, thereby avoiding the intimacy that full sexual intercourse involves. Analysts differ in their understanding of the defining characteristics of perversion. Stoller (1975) describes it thus:

> Perversion, the erotic form of hatred, is a fantasy, usually acted out but occasionally restricted to a daydream (either self-produced or packaged by others, that is, pornography). It is a habitual, preferred aberration necessary for one's full satisfaction, primarily motivated by hostility. By 'hostility' I mean a state in which one wishes to harm an object; that differentiates it from 'aggression', which often implies only forcefulness. This hostility in perversions takes form in a fantasy of revenge hidden in the actions that make up the perversion and serves to convert childhood trauma to adult triumph. To create the greatest excitement, the perversion must also portray itself as an act of risk taking. While these definitions remove former incongruities, they impose on us the new burden of learning from a person what motivates him. But we are freed from a process of designation that

does not take the subject's personality and motivation into account. We no longer need to define a perversion according to the anatomy used, the object chosen, the society's stated morality, or the number of people who do it.

(Stoller, 1975:4)

Key characteristics of perversion include risk-taking, deceit, objectification of the victim, secrecy and ritualised behaviour. Perversions also appear to psychically engulf the person who enacts them, providing the central meaning to their existence. One is struck by the importance of the sexual behaviour for the perverse woman, who seems almost wholly preoccupied by it, as though there were nothing else of meaning or value in her life. This indicates the extent to which perversion may mask an underlying emptiness and sense of flatness, or depression, and helps us to understand how it assumes a life of its own, in that keeping the perverse behaviour secret, and employing elaborate strategies to preserve its existence become a governing principle of life. For mothers, presenting the facade of ordinary, devoted maternal care provides an invaluable subterfuge for sexual abuse, as the quality of the contact will then rarely be questioned.

THE ROOTS OF DISTURBED MOTHERING

The ideas of Dinora Pines and Estela Welldon in relation to women's unconscious use of their bodies are complementary and make significant contributions to the understanding of female experience. The psychoanalyst Dinora Pines eloquently describes how women's bodies, in particular their reproductive systems, can become the vehicles for the expression of unconscious conflicts. She explores the many ways in which unconscious conflicts may be expressed through pregnancy, miscarriage, childbirth and sexuality. Her work differs from Welldon's in that she does not specifically focus on perverse or criminal women, although the processes that she describes can also be seen in extreme forms in these women.

Through her pregnancies and the babies which she produces, the perverse mother is able to re-create the destructive patterns of her own birth and childhood, inhabiting a domain within which she has power, where she can wreak vengeance and gain compensation for her own abuse and deprivation. While these motivations may be unconscious, their conscious expression can be manifested in a woman's apparently benign, but overwhelmingly powerful, desires to have a baby inside her body, and to produce a child who will finally give her unconditional love and affirmation of her own vitality and power. The baby may in fact be a potential receptacle for her own unacceptable feelings of helplessness and deprivation.

The notion of the separateness of the baby is difficult for such mothers to conceptualise. Their understanding of the needs of the children for welfare and protection is limited, as their main concern is their own need to feel cherished and loved. They may describe feeling 'empty' inside and wanting a baby to make them feel filled up, and whole. This emptiness may relate to and mirror an earlier experience of emotional deprivation and depletion: the absence of an internalised good object. The birth of children for these women is inevitably a tremendous disappointment, as the demands of the infants reawaken their awareness of their own unmet needs, making the situation persecutory and, at times, unbearable. 'Mature object love, in which the needs of self and object are mutually understood and fulfilled, cannot be achieved, and the birth of a real baby might be a calamity' (Pines, 1993:103).

Pines (1993) identifies an essential distinction between the experiences of pregnancy and motherhood; this differentiation is crucial in both practical and psychodynamic terms. The disappointment that women may feel when the pregnancy ends and the baby is born, the baby who not only fails to compensate them for their deprivation, but who also stirs up memories of frustrated needs and infantile rage, can lead to renewed feelings of anger, abandonment and isolation. The unbearable nature of the reactivated pain can lead to violent or perverse assaults on the baby.

In the following case illustration I describe the psychic processes which give rise to violent assaults on an infant, both in the womb and following her birth. These attacks are not sexual ones, but stem from the disturbed constellation of experiences which I suggest could also give rise to maternal incest. Both physical and sexual assault on children can be considered manifestations of female perversion. I have described this young woman, Kate, in order to illustrate the discussion of unconscious fantasies and terrors in pregnancy and their link with maternal abuse. She graphically illustrates Welldon's notion of women's 'perverse fantasies whose outcome materialises in their bodies' (1992:7).

Case illustration: Pregnancy and unconscious fantasies

Kate, an 18-year-old woman, was seen for assessment of her capacity to care for and protect her 7-month-old daughter, who was currently placed in foster care and was the subject of care proceedings. The local authority was exploring the possibility of placing the child for adoption as an alternative to returning her to Kate's care. Kate presented as a vulnerable young woman with difficulty in understanding the nature and purpose of the assessment and an overall sense of confusion and distractedness. She was slight and dishevelled, wearing ill-fitting and dirty clothes. She chose to keep her heavy jacket on throughout the initial interview, despite the warmth of the room, conveying a sense that she needed the protection of her clothing, and was not fully aware of how to take care of herself or how to respond to her environment. Her unwashed and unkempt appearance and red-rimmed eyes evoked the image of a neglected child, or an adolescent runaway sleeping on the streets. She was twelve weeks pregnant with her second child when I met her and had recently separated from the violent partner, the father of her first child. She was unsure who the father of her second baby was, having had casual sexual relationships with several men over the past year. I was asked to provide a report for the Court in which I considered her parenting capacity and expressed an opinion about her general psychological presentation, particularly in relation to her mothering and any work which could be undertaken to help her in this.

Kate looked several years younger than her actual age, appearing ill at ease and awkward. Her face and voice were almost expressionless, aside from the occasion when she burst into tears as she described the extreme violence to which her mother, father and eventually stepfather had subjected her throughout her early life. At age 12 she had come to the attention of social services because of bruising to her face and arms and disturbed behaviour at school. Her parents had separated the previous year and her mother had formed a new relationship with a man who had been charged with, but not eventually convicted for, sexual offences against children two years before he had met Kate's mother. Kate referred to this man as her 'stepfather' and disclosed that she had been 'terrified of him'. She had eventually been removed from her mother's care and placed in a children's home when she was 13. She had two younger brothers, who still lived at home with her mother.

Kate's own mother had been classified as having learning disabilities and had suffered with depression since her early 20s; her first depressive episode had occurred when Kate was three weeks old. Kate said she 'could not remember' if she had been subject to sexual violence in early childhood but she had been seriously indecently assaulted by a stranger when she was 14. She had been willing to give evidence against her assailant but he had died before the case came to court.

Kate gave the impression of being someone vulnerable and traumatised, who had been emotionally, physically and sexually damaged to the extent that she did not believe anything good or alive could survive inside of her. In conflict with her fear of what was inside of her was her overwhelming desire to continue with her pregnancy and become a mother, although she did not appear to have a real sense of what either experience involved.

Kate vividly described her sense of confusion and fear during her first pregnancy, 'I didn't know what was inside of me' she explained, and went on to relate how she had used coat hangers and other sharp instruments to try to dislodge the unborn baby from 18 weeks on, eventually giving birth at 36 weeks to a girl. She had presented at casualty frequently during her first pregnancy and the medical reports gave a graphic picture of her: 'the patient presented as a young woman screaming to have the baby taken out of her.' She experienced her pregnancy as filled with horror, describing a powerful sense of invasion. She had vivid images throughout her pregnancy of a monstrous creature, growing inside of her. She had wondered whether the baby was fully human and felt desperate for it to be born so that she could find out whether it was, in fact, a human baby.

Once her daughter had been born, following Kate's repeated, unsuccessful and violent attempts to induce labour, she had found it increasingly difficult to cope with her demands. When the baby was nine days old Kate had shaken and thrown her, finding it unbearable to hear her crying, which she could not stop, and which powerfully reawakened her own memories of deprivation. Her assault on the baby brought her to the attention of the social services once again, this time as a mother; she had only recently been discharged from a care order herself. When care proceedings were instigated on her newborn child Kate reported a sense of relief, because she was aware that she was not able to cope with motherhood. In this sense the relief and her desire to protect the baby from suffering as she had reflected a healthy and protective aspect of her maternal capacity. Although she had an intellectual awareness, at times, about her potential to damage the baby, at another level she was able to deny her own murderousness and felt bereft and furious about having to lose care of her. She revealed how desperately she had wanted someone to love her, hoping that the baby would meet this need.

Following the assault, the baby had been removed from Kate's care and she soon became pregnant with her second child, having conceived approximately five months after the first was born. She appeared wholly unaware of the fact that she was considered to be a severe risk to a child in her care and thought she was seeing me to get 'some ideas about how to look after two babies'. Although I had clearly and repeatedly explained my actual function, which was to prepare an assessment report for the Court in care proceedings, she did not seem to understand this, and related to me with a degree of trust and hope that was both moving and distressing, in light of the fact that she did not seem to have the capacity to meet the needs of her children, and in fact proved to be someone with a significant degree of learning difficulty, revealed by formal cognitive assessment carried out by my colleague as part of the assessment. The risk that she would pose to a child of neglect or physical injury was significant and it appeared that the only hope for rehabilitation of her daughter to her care would be if the two were jointly fostered, with an experienced foster mother who might also be able to provide Kate with an experience of being cared for and contained. This had, in fact, been attempted when the baby was three weeks old but the placement had broken down because of Kate's extreme envy about the foster mother's attention to the baby, which she had found intolerable. Her low sense of self-esteem left her feeling devastated by criticism, to the extent that even minor suggestions about how to improve her sensitivity to her baby's needs enraged her.

I referred Kate to the local learning disability team and recommended that she receive supportive psychotherapy to help her cope with the trauma of her recent loss of her daughter, and to enable her to discuss how to manage her overwhelming feelings of distress and rage, which she had directed both at herself and her child. It appeared unlikely that she would be able to cope with the demands of her second baby unless she were placed in a highly supportive and structured environment with the baby on a long-term basis, and it was possible that she would also have this child removed from her care. This would be another devastating loss.

Both pregnancy and motherhood had proved to be deeply disturbing and persecutory experiences which stirred up unbearable memories and feelings for this vulnerable and violent woman. Her sense of alienation from her own body, which the pregnancy created, seemed to be a graphic illustration of how her own impoverished experience of being mothered had left her without a secure sense of her own female body. She perceived her own pregnant body as an unreliable and frightening object, mirroring her experience in infancy of her own mother's depression and emotional unavailability. There was a sense in which she unconsciously identified with the murderous and inhuman infant, whose desires for her mother threatened the mother's identity, and would, inevitably, remain unmet. Kate seemed to be tortured by an almost psychotic sense of unreality and fear about what was happening to her body during pregnancy. For this woman, who had so few inner resources and no sense of an internalised mother, the experience of pregnancy was one of unbearable violation and persecution.

DISCUSSION

Unconscious fantasies in pregnancy

In pregnancy a woman narcissistically identifies with the foetus inside her and this revives infantile fantasies about herself as the baby in her mother's body, which may result in the reactivation of intense ambivalent feelings towards her own mother, her internalised representation of her own mother and herself as a baby. If the hostility inherent in these ambivalent feelings is too great, she may not feel able to allow the actual baby inside her to live. Alternatively, she may not feel able to allow this baby a separate psychic life, viewing it as a narcissistic extension of herself. The notion of perverse motherhood described by Welldon is clearly consistent with Pines' delineation of the psychic processes by which a young woman with an impoverished or disturbed experience of parenting may find the tasks of motherhood difficult, if not impossible.

For women who have not experienced 'good enough' mothering in their own childhood, with the experience of internalised and integrated bodily experiences, the inevitable regressions involved in pregnancy may be very threatening, and the 'infantile wish to merge with the mother and the opposing fear of it which occasioned a partial failure of self/object differentiation may be revived' (Pines, 1987:99). The child's separation–individuation is also influenced by her mother's relationship with the father, and her capacity to enjoy her own adult sexual body. Pregnancy offers the woman a form of biological identification with her own mother, which may be extremely frightening for her, depending on her own experience of being mothered and social circumstances.

The tasks faced by pregnant young women and adolescent girls, moving away from their prepubertal state, involve changing their relationship to themselves and identifying with their own mother. These tasks may reawaken earlier difficulties and produce symptoms as a defence against psychic pain, particularly where separation from the mother at earlier developmental phases has not been achieved. Laufer (1993) relates this difficulty to the Oedipus complex and the requirement that must be resolved in order for the little girl to identify with her mother, and to view herself as having a body without a penis. This further requires her to give up the fantasy of possessing and fulfilling her mother as a man could; she must relinquish the fantasy of being able to give her mother sexual fulfilment. The loss of this omnipotent fantasy may generate serious anxieties in the child.

> What has impressed me most has been the capacity of some women to deny the reality of the changes taking place in their compelling need physically to attack their own bodies, or later that of their babies during these critical developmental periods.
>
> (Laufer, 1993:69)

This was clearly the case with Kate, who described her pregnancy as 'terrifying', saying, 'I just didn't know what was inside me'; this may also have been an expression of her fear about her unconscious murderous feelings towards her mother, her baby and, ultimately, herself. Throughout her pregnancy she had made violent attacks on her body in order to force the infant out, because she found the terrors of pregnancy unbearable and her unconscious and conscious fears about what creature or forces were inhabiting her intolerable. It was possible that her experience of sexual violence had also made her highly sensitive to perceived intrusion and violation of her internal space: the unborn baby became a persecutory and terrifying object. Her violence could be understood as a response to her own sexual and violent traumatisation in childhood, underpinned by an inadequate attachment to her own mother, which led to perverse defences, such as the reliance on physical violence and powerful identification with a murderous infant (De Zuleta, 1993).

The combination of bodily and emotional states of first pregnancy provides the young woman with an alternative means of resolving psychic conflict, as Pines describes:

> the young woman may become aware of primitive, previously repressed fantasies and conflicts, arising from childhood sexual theories about her own conception, intrauterine life, and birth. It follows that positive and negative aspects of the self and of the object may be projected onto the unseen fetus as if it were an extension of them.
>
> (Pines, 1993:100)

Pines explores the interplay between a young woman's relationship to her body, herself, her own mother as an object, and her own experience of being mothered, in relation to her experience of pregnancy and, later, to the baby. She identifies the process whereby the little girl who has not felt satisfied by her mother at the pre-Oedipal stage, where she can introject feelings of bodily satisfaction, is left with a sense of being incomplete, empty. This contributes to a feeling of deprivation in adulthood where the woman longs for and seeks an experience which provides this sense of satisfaction. This deprived state, in which the adult woman is left feeling incomplete, can result in deep-seated problems with separation and individuation, as the achievement of an adult identity requires the prior internalisation of a sense of being mothered. Such a woman may 'never make up for this basic loss of a primary stable sense of well-being in her body and with her body image . . . Narcissistic injury, giving rise to narcissistic rage, envy of the mother and lack of self esteem, may be painful and add to the difficulties of separation' (Pines, 1987:101). This is an extension of the Kleinian notion of the basis of the feeling of integration and security which is the consequence of the introjection of, or taking in, an object who is loving and protective of the self and who is, in turn, loved and protected by the self (Klein, 1932). This is the introjected object, the internalised mother. Introjection has strong links with the first feeding experience, in which something is taken inside the infant, from the mother. Without this successful introjection the process of separation in relation to the mother may become highly disturbed and create tremendous psychological difficulties.

These difficulties may be repeated in the woman's relationship with her baby, where separation and individuation become particularly problematic. Her own psychic state is vulnerable to becoming over-whelmed when memories and feelings related to her own deprivation are reawakened. This may be persecutory, leading to powerful feelings of anger and fear about the development of the baby. These fears may be expressed as preoccupations about giving birth to deformed or damaged babies, illustrating the extent to which guilt about the murderous and destructive impulses towards the baby shapes fantasies. These fears may also coexist with fantasies of narcissistic fulfilment, that the unborn baby will offer the mother unconditional love and nurturance: this hope was clearly expressed by Kate, who said she wanted to have a baby so that she could have 'something of my own . . . someone who loves me'.

While pregnancy might fuel a woman's fantasies of wholeness and creativity, or, alternatively, terrify her with thoughts of invasion, con-tamination and murder from within, the experience of being responsible for another person, a helpless and demanding infant, involves a com-pletely different set of fantasies and experiences. This was clearly illustrated in Kate's disturbances both in her pregnancy and in mothering, resulting in her violent assaults on the baby, both during and after the pregnancy, within and without her body.

Promiscuity and pregnancy

Promiscuous sexual intercourse, with the unconscious aim of establishing pregnancies, may reflect a young woman's desperate and unmet need for mothering, for the sense of fulfilment and 'wholeness' of which she feels deprived.

A young woman's physiologically mature and sexually alive body establishes adult status but also enables her to split off and deny painful emotional states by substituting bodily sensations. In this way, feelings of love or hate towards the self or towards the object can be concretely expressed, depression avoided and self-esteem raised. It follows that a sexual act, which, to the outside world, appears to be an act of adult, genital sexuality, may unconsciously become a means of satisfying unfulfilled pregenital longings for the mother and for being mothered. The mother is to her child the symbol both of the maturational environment and of motherliness itself. Her physical presence and emotional attitudes towards her child and its body are integrated with the child's experience and her conscious and unconscious fantasies. The representation of an internal mother created in this way is a lifelong model for her daughter to identify with and also to differentiate herself from.

(Pines, 1987:102)

Pines, unlike Freud, does not believe that pregnancy and birth gratify every woman's basic wish to receive compensation for the deprivation of a penis. She states:

There is a marked distinction between the wish to become pregnant and the wish to bring a live child into the world and become a mother. For primitive anxieties and conflicts arising from a woman's lifelong task of separation–individuation from her own mother may be unexpectedly revealed by the emotional experience of first pregnancy and motherhood.

(Pines, 1987:98)

The importance of her work is in tracing the development of disturbed mothering, through a woman's fantasies during her pregnancy, to her own identifications with the internal representation of her own mother, that is 'bodily reinforced' in pregnancy. For perverse mothers this internalised mother will also be a perverse object.

TRANSMISSION OF DISTURBED ATTACHMENT PATTERNS

Important empirical research about the intergenerational transmission of disturbed parenting has come from attachment theory, based on the seminal work of John Bowlby. The experience of a disturbed early environment and particular styles of parenting, which are not attuned to the infant's needs and desires, has been associated with difficulty in later social functioning. Disturbances in attachment in childhood may lead to problems in forming trusting and stable relationships with partners and in parenting children in a way which fosters secure attachment (Fonagy, 1991, Fonagy *et al.*, 1995). The lack of trust and security in early life may have long-term consequences for attachment patterns in later life. Insecure early attachment is associated with personality disorders in adulthood and has been studied in adulthood using the Adult Attachment Interview (AAI), a semi-structured psychodynamic interview schedule which provides rich qualitative data about the nature of parenting in childhood, from which particular parenting styles can be identified. Participants are asked to describe their early attachments, their feelings about their parents, and significant losses or traumatic experiences in childhood. They are then classified into four different attachment categories, largely based on their style in describing their early attachments: 'free to evaluate attachment', 'dismissing of attachment', 'enmeshed in attitude towards attachment' and 'unresolved/disorganised/disorientated' (Holmes, 1993).

Classification of these types of attachment in adults based on the AAI has been shown to predict particular styles of parenting relating to their own children, as demonstrated by observing the children's response to temporary separations from their mothers or caregivers using the Ainsworth 'strange situation' experiment (1978). When pregnant mothers were given the AAI it predicted the attachment status of their infants at one year with 70 per cent accuracy (Fonagy *et al.*, 1991).

FEMALE SEXUAL ABUSE OF CHILDREN

For some women, their own histories of neglect, deprivation and sexual abuse lead them to sexually abuse their children. Having considered the roots of disturbed attachment, and the model of female perversion, it is now possible to apply this understanding to female sexual abuse of children. This abuse can be understood by reference to the development of perverse defences against pain, which arise when attachment has been disrupted. In dynamic terms, a reliable internal object has not been introjected, that is, a containing mother has not been internalised; the internal representation of mother is of a frustrating, cruel or fragile object. A central function of sexual abuse of children is to ward off depression and temporarily rid the self of unbearable feelings of helplessness. The abusers may genuinely confuse sexual pleasure and affection, related to the confusion of their own sexual victimisation in childhood: this is re-created with their children. There may also be a psychic pressure to repeat the abuse; the defence of identification with the aggressor is a powerful method for dealing with intolerable feelings, allowing former victims of abuse to project their own experiences of helplessness and humiliation on to child victims.

Defining sexual abuse of children

Clinical definitions of sexual abuse of children tend to centre on three dimensions: an age difference of five years or more between perpetrator and child; specific sexual behaviours such as digital penetration, oral sex, penetration of the vagina or anus using the penis or objects, exhibitionism, pornographic photography, kissing, fondling the genitalia or breasts, and coercing the child to masturbate or touch the adult (Craissati, 1998). There are grey areas, relating to issues like the extent of nudity in the family, at what age, if any, parents and children become modest about nudity, sleeping naked in bed with children and exposing children to sexual affection between adults: 'There is little consistent agreement on the way in which familial and cultural norms can influence the decision to define behaviour as abuse' (Craissati, 1998:3).

Prevalence of female sexual abuse of children

While criminal statistics indicate that the vast majority of sex offenders against children are male, it is nonetheless evident that female sexual abuse does occur, and it is likely that it is vastly under-reported, possibly because of the complex emotional attachment of children to their mothers or carers, and also out of a fear, in many cases justified, that they will not be believed. The notion that some mothers, or women of child-bearing age, abuse children sexually is an unacceptable one which powerfully challenges idealised constructions of motherhood and femininity. The difficulty in accepting the existence of maternal sexual abuse appears greater than that of acknowledging maternal physical abuse, notwithstanding that when 'battered baby syndrome' was first identified there was a sense of outrage and disbelief. The failure to recognise the possibility of female sexual abuse may reflect a general tendency to deny female sexuality in general, and female perversion in particular.

The taboo of maternal incest remains strikingly powerful, making it difficult for female sexual abuse to be conceptualised: 'secrecy and denial about sexual abuse are still common, particularly when the perpetrator of that abuse is a woman' (Saradjian, 1996:xiii). The easy access that women have to children as mothers, child-minders, nannies, nursery nurses and au pairs and the intimate nature of their ordinary contact, i.e. bathing, dressing, feeding, changing nappies, applying creams and lotions, may make it particularly easy to abuse children in their care, and also allow the abuse to be concealed, affording many opportunities for perverse handling of children. The abuser herself may confuse sexual contact with children with genuine affection for them, mirroring her own experiences in childhood; the early experience of sexual abuse may predispose a woman to later sexual offending against children.

Criminal statistics reveal that in 1995 in England and Wales, 4,600 men and 100 women were sentenced for indictable sexual offences against children and a further 2,500 cautioned (Home Office, 1995). When these were further analysed to cases where the victims of sexual abuse were under 16 there were 1,350 cautions, of which 34 were against female offenders, 3,284 prosecutions, of which 30 were female offenders, and 2,554 convictions, of which 19 were against female offenders. The most recent *Criminal Statistics*, relating to recorded crime in England and Wales in 1997, published by the Home Office in 1998, indicated that of 6,500 offenders found guilty at all courts of sexual offences, only 100 were females, again pointing to the great discrepancy between the recorded crime rates of male and female sexual offenders.

Grubin's 1998 study for the Home Office on sex offending against children notes that the recorded offence for child sexual abuse by women is relatively uncommon. According to *Criminal Statistics* (1998), less than 1 per cent of sexual offences are committed by women, although offender samples cite higher figures, i.e. Craissati and McGlurg (1996) reported that 7 per cent of the sexual abuse reported by adult male sex offenders was perpetrated by females, and in the United States, 22 per cent of male adolescent offenders with a history of sexual abuse claimed that their abuser was female (Ryan *et al.*, 1996). The lower figure found in *Criminal Statistics*, which is drawn from recorded crimes, may, as the author acknowledges, be an artefact of the difficulty in defining and detecting child sexual abuse in relation to women offenders:

> The issue of women as perpetrators of child sexual abuse has been taken seriously only over the past 15 years and the actual extent of the problem is even more difficult to determine than it is for male offenders. Part of the difficulty, of course, is in the definition of sexual abuse, as in western societies women are permitted greater freedom than men in their physical interactions with children. In addition, overt sexual activity between an adult female and a boy may not be conceptualised by the boy as 'sexual abuse' even if he is emotionally unprepared for it and psychologically destabilised as a result

(Johnson and Shreier, 1987). Indeed, in spite of his confusion the child may be encouraged to view the event as proof of his virility.

(Grubin, 1998:28)

This suggests another reason for the low rate of reporting maternal sexual abuse, which is the degree of ambiguity in the nature of the act, as illustrated in the passage from Morrison's *Song of Solomon*, which opened the chapter. As the passage illustrates, there can be a powerful narcissistic element to breastfeeding, which may become an intoxicating experience for a mother, to the extent that she continues to suckle her child for her own gratification. Morrison beautifully describes the secrecy of this breastfeeding mother, in search of a 'balm' against the drudgery of her daily life. She so loves the power of her own lactation and the sensual pleasure of the experience that she tries to avoid recognition of how old her child is, so as not to spoil her fantasy, or inhibit her behaviour. Is this sexual abuse or simply a retreat to a maternal fantasy of feeding an infant? The mother appears aware that there is something wrong in her treatment of her son, but cannot bear to give up her 'secret indulgence'. The ambiguity of this passage, its sympathy coupled with its hints of maternal perversion, exemplify the complexity of conceptualising maternal sexual abuse.

THE PSYCHOLOGICAL IMPACT OF MATERNAL SEXUAL ABUSE

The emotional impact of sexual abuse on children is profound, and the experience confusing. In sexual abuse a child's needs for physical attention and handling have been met in a sexualised way, intricately connecting their experiences of care and sexual arousal. This makes it impossible for them to differentiate between Oedipal fantasy and reality, as their unconscious sexual desires for their mother or father have actually been fulfilled. As well as being physically intrusive, female sexual abuse may also be emotionally damaging to the child; the invitation to get inside mother's body is a frightening and alarming perversion of a wish, and offers the child a degree of power and responsibility which he or she cannot manage. It may be terrifying, particularly confusing in the sense in which it is this perverse enactment of a wish, or a repetition of an infantile activity, e.g. sucking mother's breasts. The child cannot feel certain that there is a strong barrier separating fantasy and reality. It is clear that the infant's unconscious longings for mother, to be back inside her, to suckle at her breasts, to kill off father, are fantasies which need to be resisted in order for the child to feel that she is not omnipotent, cannot destroy either her father or the parental couple, in order to transcend these pre-Oedipal and Oedipal longings. Being encouraged to enact these fantasies wreaks considerable psychological damage on the child, introducing a confused, perverse model of care.

Kirsta (1994) describes both the widespread difficulty in accepting the fact of female perversion and its consequences for victims:

> One of the enduring myths surrounding female sexual abuse is that because of women's essentially caring, gentle natures – as well as their physical and sexual characteristics – the word 'abuse' must be a misnomer, a contradiction in terms, and what we are really talking about are loving expressions of intimacy and caring that may border on the erotic or be mistaken by the child as sexual behaviour or abuse, such as mothers caressing and fondling their children in ways that inadvertently include genital contact with the capacity to arouse. This is one misconception of which we must rid ourselves entirely if the full horror of certain types of abuse is ever to be acknowledged and victims genuinely helped to recover from their trauma.
>
> (Kirsta, 1994:281)

A child's body as well as her mind is violated through sexual involvement with an adult. This is experienced as highly intrusive, sometimes physically painful, and, if coupled with her own sexual arousal, highly confusing, particularly when the child becomes old enough to appreciate the significance of the abusive behaviour. In maternal sexual abuse of children the most basic relationship, in which trust and containment are paramount, has become subverted into an intrusive, frightening and demanding seduction and/or rape.

Where the victims of child sexual abuse are male, there may often be a belief that the boys must have enjoyed the interaction and did not feel used or violated by it, which conception misses the point that sexual abuse of children is not defined by reference to whether or not the child felt that he or she was exploited and abused. This notion is clearest in cases where the victim of female sexual abuse is an adolescent boy who is not related to the perpetrator: the case of Mary Kay Letourneau, a teacher who had sexual intercourse with her 13-year-old pupil is one such example (Fualaau, 1998). It was initially very difficult for those around her, including her husband, to recognise that she was having a sexual relationship with her teenage victim. The trivialising response of tabloid journalists and photographers, who appeared titillated by the idea of an attractive woman 'seducing' her student, illustrates this type of prejudice about the sexually voracious nature of adolescent boys and the power of the seduction myth – i.e. that an adolescent male would *necessarily* find it emotionally rewarding and sexually fulfilling to have sexual relations with an older woman. In the *Panorama* television special 'investigating' this case, it is striking that the only person who explicitly describes Letourneau as a sex offender is a female police officer, who identifies the 'grooming' techniques used by Letourneau, including granting her student the privilege of starting her car, singling him out as special, and using her powerful position to her advantage.

Female sexual abuse is explored in the following case illustration, which draws upon notions of female perversion and the transmission of disturbed parenting.

Case illustration: Laura: Child sexual abuse with a male accomplice

Laura was referred to the forensic clinical psychology service for assessment of her capacity to protect and provide for the welfare of her young daughter, Elizabeth, following her 18-month period of incarceration in custody for a conviction of two counts of indecent assault on a 7-year-old boy and a 10-year-old girl who were not her own children. They had both been made to masturbate Laura's husband in her presence and she had taken part in coercing the children into posing for pornographic pictures, in which they were touching his genitals. She had been released from custody three months before seeing me. Once she had been convicted for criminal offences against children, Elizabeth had been placed on the Child Protection Register under the category of 'at risk of sexual harm'. Her daughter's social worker had requested an assessment of Laura's risk to her and asked for an opinion about her suitability for psychological treatment addressing her sexual offending.

Laura presented at the clinical interview as an obese, affable middle-aged woman with no obvious symptoms of major mental illness, or learning difficulties. She expressed great apprehension about attending an outpatient clinic attached to a notorious psychiatric hospital, and asked whether I had been asked to see if she were 'bonkers'. She wore a voluminous dress and slippers, with bare legs displaying extensive varicose veins. She walked very slowly and appeared breathless when she entered the consulting room. Her manner was almost aggressively jocular, and her laughter at frequent points throughout the interview was quite incongruous, given the disturbing and distressing events that she was relating. She frequently impersonated her former husband in the interview, making graphic sexual statements in imitation of his voice. It appeared as though her jocular manner was a form of bravado, a defence against her underlying anxiety and discomfort. Indeed, Laura cancelled the following two assessment appointments saying that she had found the first meeting too upsetting. She eventually attended the final assessment appointment offered to her.

Laura described her childhood as 'ordinary' but presented a clear picture of a controlling, rejecting mother and distant, emotionally unavailable father. He was often away from the family home for weeks at a time, working as a long-distance lorry driver. During his long absences from home Laura's mother would have sexual relationships with several male friends, all of whom the children regarded as 'uncles'. Her own mother had herself experienced periods of depression during Laura's childhood and had identified Laura as 'a bad one', treating her with a degree of contempt and showing her little affection or concern.

Laura was the eldest of five children and had spent much of her childhood acting as surrogate mother to her younger siblings. Between the ages of 8 and 14 Laura had been sexually abused by a friend of her mother's, a man in his 50s whom she had always considered her 'uncle'. One aspect of the abuse involved his taking photographs of her naked, which involved elaborate planning and great secrecy. He would also ask Laura to stimulate and masturbate him and would stroke her hair and face during this. He would masturbate her manually and she had occasionally experienced orgasm. Laura had tried to tell her mother about the abuse to which her mother responded that she was not to 'make up stories'. In retrospect she herself described this abuse as 'lovely' and had seen it as a form of affection and avuncular interest. She had mainly felt unwanted by her parents and it appeared that the sexual interference was the only form of attention that she had received from adults which she could construe as 'affectionate and caring'.

She had felt that her abuser had genuinely liked and cared for her, complimenting her and generally paying her attention. She had been very hurt when he lost contact with her family and her, feeling that he had 'dropped' her, but did not view this as evidence that his interest in her had been primarily exploitative and abusive.

Laura had attended mainstream schooling and had left education at age 16 with three GCSEs, going on to work in a food packaging factory until she married her first husband at age 19. He had been physically abusive to her for many years; the violence had started when she was pregnant with their first child at age 20. She had three children by this husband, a daughter now aged 21, a son aged 19 and another son aged 17. She had separated from this man when she was 41 and become involved with the man who was to become her second husband, and who had been her co-defendant in the criminal proceedings. Her daughter, Elizabeth, was the product of this marriage. At the time of the assessment Laura's second husband was completing his prison sentence for the indecent assaults. Her eldest three children had been interviewed by social services and had denied that they had ever been subject to sexual abuse, expressing shock at their mother's criminal conviction for sexual offences and attributing blame to her second husband.

Observations

It was striking that Laura only described the sexual offences that she had committed by speaking in her husband's voice, as though she was unable to bear ownership of her own role in the offence, and denied her own excitement and gratification. She was unable to describe the victims' experience with any real sense of empathy or compassion, finding it difficult to imagine how they had felt during and after the abuse. She perceived herself as the victim of her husband's bullying, viewing herself as without any independent agency or volition, recalling the contemptuous names that she had been called by her husband, and how his constant belittling of her had reduced any sense of autonomy or pride. She remembered how he had publicly insulted her, calling her 'the fat cunt', and inviting others to engage in denigration of her. She thought that he had an excessive interest in masturbation and reported that he would treat her sadistically, forcing her to masturbate him and hitting her brutally if she failed to give him satisfaction. Her imitations of him were chilling and highly detailed, as though she were wholly 'in role'.

Laura blamed her sexual offending on her ex-husband's coercion and bullying; she denied having instigated the abuse or deriving any gratification from it. She had encouraged the 7- and 10-year-old victims to accompany her husband and herself on a camping holiday, where she had taken indecent photographs of the two children while they were masturbating her husband. She acknowledged, in retrospect, that this had been wrong, but repeatedly asserted that she had not herself been 'turned on' by taking the pictures. She claimed that these pictures had remained in the possession of her husband who had used them when he masturbated. She acknowledged that the children had looked 'beautiful' but denied that she had found them sexually stimulating. She minimised the extent to which the children had been coerced into masturbating her husband and expressed little awareness that they might have felt afraid, confused and unhappy.

Laura seemed to have almost no sense of herself, suffering from low self-esteem, a significant degree of emotional dependency, and a highly distorted conception of childhood sexual abuse, to which her own experience of sexual victimisation in the context of an emotionally barren childhood had significantly contributed. Her role in sexually abusing young children indicated both her emotional dependence on her husband, who appeared to have instigated the abuse, and her own unmet needs for comfort and control, which appeared to have been satisfied through this offence. She seemed to view the sexual activities with the children as non-abusive: this reflected her identification with the abused child who had actually enjoyed sexual relations with an adult, and illustrated the extent of her denial of her own exploitation of the children's trust in her. She had little empathy for the confusion and vulnerability of young children. Her descriptions of her husband's sexual preoccupations were so vivid and passionately delivered that I was left with the strong impression that she herself was excited by the behaviour but could only experience this pleasure vicariously.

The power and control that she exerted over the children were aspects of the pleasure that she derived from the perverse activity.

The element of deceit involved, in that both parents and children were 'tricked' into agreeing to a camping trip, was an important aspect of the abuse, and revealed the extent to which Laura was quite consciously and deliberately involved in criminal behaviour and saw the children as objects to be manipulated for the pleasure of adults.

Laura's description of her marriage revealed strong elements of a sadomasochistic relationship in which issues of power, control, subjugation and humiliation were central. At times, others, the children, would be brought into this relationship and she and her husband would join forces, becoming joint aggressors. Within this partnership Laura would take on the seductive and protective role, encouraging children to come away with the couple, assuring both the children and parents that her role as mother would ensure the children's safety. Her strong maternal presence and heavy, middle-aged, unglamorous appearance served as apparent safeguards that any activities with children would be innocent. In this way a massive deception was facilitated and two young children were abused. Her social worker expressed serious concerns that Laura's daughter Elizabeth had also been abused by her parents in sexual activities; she demonstrated sexualised behaviour at school and suffered from headaches, stomach aches, thrush infections and bed-wetting.

Laura remained able to deceive herself about the extent of her own role as offender, presenting herself clearly as victim rather than aggressor and projecting her sexual perversions and desires on to her husband, then identifying him as perverse and voracious in his sexual appetites. Her animated impersonations of him, and the sense in which she 'became him' in these imitations, indicated the power of the projective identification with him. Her animation in these impersonations contrasted dramatically with her general depression and self-deprecation, mirroring something of the function of perversion in temporarily defeating an overwhelming sense of flatness, emptiness and depression.

I considered her to be a risk to children in her care and felt that she should be engaged in treatment addressing her sexual offending. She was highly ambivalent about such treatment despite having asked for help herself, deciding that she could not face continued attendance at the outpatient clinic after beginning therapy. She clearly found therapy destabilising and became increasingly depressed, appearing unwilling or psychically unable to attend her appointments. It was therefore not possible to engage her in treatment, and we agreed to terminate therapy.

Although her daughter, Elizabeth, had made allegations that her father had sexually abused her, neither criminal nor civil proceedings were instigated against him and Laura remained sole carer for the child; her status as a Schedule One offender did not appear relevant to the decision-making process in the Civil Courts. It appeared difficult, if not impossible, for the professionals to bear in mind the possibility that Laura herself, independently of her violent and sexually abusive partner, could pose a risk of sexual, emotional or physical abuse to children.

DISCUSSION

Perversion as a defence against depression

Various defence mechanisms can be identified in female sexual offenders including identification with the aggressor, i.e their own sexual abuser, identification with the child victim, by, for example, choosing a victim the same age as they were when they were abused, identification with their non-protective mothers, denial and projection, in that female abusers may attribute sexual motivations or seductiveness to their child victims. For many female sexual offenders, sexual abuse of children represents a powerful solution to a psychic problem.

In the case described the sexual offences appeared to ward off Laura's underlying sense of inadequacy, powerlessness and depression and clearly expressed her perverse sexuality. Laura's behaviour could be considered a perversion, as defined by Welldon, demonstrating the characteristics of dehumanisation, repetition and an element of compulsion, and the fact that the aim of her perversion was not simply genital stimulation or orgasm. She achieved sexual gratification through the reduction of object to part-object; the child was not seen as wholly human, as a subject, but was reduced to being a conduit of sexual pleasure for the adult, whose gratification came partially from the degree of control and manipulation which the abuse affords (Green and Kaplan, 1994:958). Laura appeared to be able to ward off a considerable degree of depression through her perversion.

For Laura the child, or children, involved also represented her own child-self, who enjoyed the experience of sexual abuse or, at least, the aspect of the abuse which she construed as expressing attention and affection. It seemed as though Laura's sense of herself was almost wholly sexualised and relational, in that she existed only in so far as she was desired or desirous; interacting sexually with children was a way of asserting her existence and engaging with others, devoid though it was of genuine intimacy. She identified both with the victims, the children, who she thought may have enjoyed the abuse, and with the perpetrator, becoming the aggressor in her relation to the child victims.

Glasser's (1979) notion of the core complex of perversion is relevant to an understanding of female as well as male sexual abuse of children, in its emphasis on the fear of annihilation and the terrors of actual intimacy. The roots of these fears inhere in early maternal deprivation and neglect; the manifestation of the psychopathology in adulthood is the constant struggle between closeness and distance with others and the narcissistic complex which precludes genuine intimacy with others. It is this lack of intimacy and the failure of genital sexuality which characterise perversion.

Her difficulties seemed to reflect what Glasser termed the 'core complex' of perversion, in which a fear of intimacy results in keeping the object of sexual desire at bay, and treating it sadistically. There is a fundamental narcissism in the core complex and a central fear of being either engulfed or annihilated by another, as the result of early experience with a mother perceived to be potentially overwhelming and destructive. The roots of Laura's maternal perversion could be traced to her own emotionally deprived and sexually abusive childhood. Her distorted view of appropriate boundaries between children and adults reflected not only her participation in sexual behaviour with an adult in her own childhood but also her mother's use of her as a surrogate parent to her younger siblings and her mother's failure to acknowledge and respond to Laura's needs. Laura's mother appeared to have herself been depressed and isolated and she sought comfort through sexual liaisons with various partners, one of whom had abused her own daughter. Her neglect of Laura and lack of concern about her safety and her emotional development had clearly contributed to her daughter's sense of being unwanted, worthless and without any sense of identity.

In Laura's case her mother had been elusive and rejecting, an object that she wanted to 'get hold of' and possess, who had powerfully resisted these attempts. She had a strong desire to fuse with a maternal object, to become part of an idealised union, but this longing was very threatening to her fragile sense of herself and she feared that she might completely lose her identity through such a fusion without any possibility of recovery. Glasser describes the major component in the 'core complex' as 'a deep-seated and pervasive longing for an intense and most intimate closeness to another person, amounting to a "merging", a "state of oneness", a "blissful union"' (Glasser, 1979:278). It seemed that her underlying sense of emptiness, deadness and depression was temporarily alleviated through voyeuristic sexual activity; her fear of being wholly lost in, psychically annihilated by, someone else meant that only perverse sexuality was safe for her. She needed to keep the objects at bay and control the sexual interaction: child sexual abuse allowed her this control. She described hating sexual intercourse with her husband and 'going through with it' simply in order to be touched and cuddled. She had never had orgasms from sexual intercourse.

It is significant that Laura had eaten compulsively ever since she was a young child in what appeared to be a desperate attempt to comfort and provide nurturance for herself. She had developed what could be classified as an eating disorder and was very obese, which in turn contributed to her negative self-image and her vulnerability to abusive, sadistic men, whom she seemed to attract and who taunted and humiliated her. She wanted to be filled up with something good and it appeared likely that food, which she ate compulsively, served this function symbolically, although this bingeing could never actually fulfil her craving for emotional sustenance. She was both victim and victimiser, using children sexually to rid herself, temporarily, of intolerable feelings of self-loathing and depression. She had herself been the abused child whose emotional deprivation made her ripe to be targeted by an adult sex offender and had internalised this wholly distorted model of sexual behaviour. She abused children as she abused her own body: both were acts of violence as well as expressions of terrible, unmet need.

In abusing children Laura was able to escape from a sense of torment, subdue what Glasser calls 'annihilation anxiety'. According to her own description, Laura used her abuse of children to feel less awful about herself and was able to avoid intimacy with the objects of her desire. She was essentially a grotesque parody of a mother who could comfort children with her enormous breasts and welcoming lap: instead of offering this protection to the children she became an abuser who, at some level, was sexually aroused by stimulation and manipulation of them. She acknowledged that she had been aroused by the pictures of the children, but only indirectly, in that her husband had used the pictures to 'excite himself' and had then encouraged her to masturbate as well. She admitted to experiencing sexual pleasure during these activities and had also enjoyed the occasions of 'relaxing' the children and encouraging them to pose for the camera, although she did not consider that this constituted sexual abuse of them.

It seemed that Laura's maternal status, her appearance of being an ordinary, middle-aged mother, was deeply confusing to those who knew that she had been convicted of sexual assaults of children. This was clearly a case of thinking the unthinkable. Ironically, Laura's sexual abuse of children was seen as antithetical to motherhood, rather than an expression of perverse motherhood (and her own perverse mothering). This made it difficult for professionals to see her as a risk to children. The frightening result was that the outcome of the care proceedings relating to her daughter was to allow her to continue to care for her daughter without any shared care with the local authority and without any requirement that Laura engage in therapeutic work addressing her offending. It was impossible for the system to accept the notion of perverse motherhood and respond with an appropriate degree of protection for the child in this case.

Once again, a dangerous and highly disturbed woman and mother was refigured as a victim of male aggression and tyranny. Once again, her female sexuality and its perversion were overlooked and her subjectivity denied. Her wrongdoing, her perversion, was located in her association with a violent and sexually avaricious man. This splitting enabled the professionals to locate 'evil' safely outside of the woman who had greatest access to children, and whose activities with them afforded the easiest and least visible avenues to child abuse.

Relevance of this case to empirical research on female sex offenders

The reluctance to address the fact of maternal sexual abuse has been reflected in the relative paucity of literature related to female offenders. Saradjian's study of women who sexually abuse children is a significant attempt to describe and classify women who have been convicted of sexual offences against children. According to the classificatory system used by Saradjian in her 1996 study, women who sexually abuse children can be divided into three groups:

- women who initially target young children;
- women who initially target adolescent children;
- women who were initially coerced into sexually abusing by men.

Laura could best be classified as falling into the last group although the degree to which she had been coerced is unclear, as she appeared to have derived considerable gratification from the sexual activities with children, and demonstrated little evidence of concern for them, or awareness of the harm that she was inflicting on them.

Saradjian makes the following observations about the characteristics of women who sexually abuse children, based on her own study:

- Women of any age, social class group, intellectual ability, type of employment and marital status can sexually abuse children.
- The children they target are most likely to be children to whom they are in a maternal role.
- When they abuse very young children, the sex of the child does not appear to be crucial in the choice of target child.
- When adolescents are abused, the gender of the child appears to be an important aspect of the decision as to which child is targeted.
- Women tend to use similar tactics to men in grooming the child for compliance and disclosure; threat, coercion, care-giving, attribution of responsibility onto the child, fear of abandonment, etc.
- Women are likely to sexually abuse children in all the ways that a man does, except they have to penetrate the child with digits or objects instead of a penis. *Women are capable of obtaining sexual satisfaction from sexual sadism with children.* [my italics.]
- Women of any age can and do sexually abuse children. It is proposed that age difference is not the key issue but that some aspects of the woman offender are developmentally fixated, leading to emotional congruence with the child.
- Women tend to sexually abuse children over a long period of time particularly if the target children are their biological children. This may be because of the increased dependency of children on the women who sexually abuse them and/or because the children have less conviction that they will be believed if they say that their abuser was a woman, and therefore are less likely to disclose abuse.

(Saradjian, 1996:38)

According to a somewhat different classificatory scheme proposed by Green and Kaplan (1994), Laura could be identified as someone who committed a 'non-contact offence' in which women coerce children into sexual activity with an adult, usually a male accomplice, or allow the co-defendant to molest the child in their presence. Their research demonstrated that incarcerated female child molesters had both greater psychiatric impairment and more intrafamilial physical and sexual abuse than a comparison group of incarcerated women who had not committed sexual offences (Green and Kaplan, 1994). This was evident in Laura's case, in that she had herself experienced intrafamilial physical abuse, although her sexual victimisation had occurred through her contact with her mother's boyfriend. She believed that her mother had been aware of the abuse but failed to stop it, just as Laura herself had allowed, and encouraged, the children to be sexually abused both through involvement in pornography and through genital contact with her husband.

Laura had taken an active part in enticing children to leave their homes and participate in sexually abusive activities. Additionally, her own childhood experiences and consequent construction of sexual activity between children and adults as affection, comfort and excitement had created her own desire to engage in sexual relations with children. She identified strongly with children and displayed a high level of emotional congruence, i.e. she felt that she could empathise with and relate to children better than to adults, with whom she felt inadequate and clumsy. Her voyeurism was evident when she encouraged the children to pose for pornographic pictures. She seemed to gain vicarious sexual excitement by allowing her husband to express her desire for her, enabling her to remain in control of what threatened to be overwhelming and confusing feelings of sexual excitement and to abnegate responsibility for it.

Mothers who abuse their children can be seen as treating them as narcissistic extensions of themselves and inflicting violence on them in a perverse attempt to rid themselves of underlying feelings of inadequacy, guilt and depression. The sexual interaction provides a temporary release from these feelings, an escape from their self-loathing and unhappiness, but after an initial euphoria the depression and guilt return and a vicious cycle is established. The guilt reinforces the depression, which, in turn, creates a greater need to escape from powerful negative feelings. Sexual fantasies provide a means of release and comfort. The desire to act on the fantasies gradually increases and, once acted on, the crucial boundary between thought and action has been crossed: the mother has become an active agent, perpetrating sexual violence against her child. Welldon gives an account of this cycle in her description of the female abuser:

> Clinically, the female abuser demonstrates a perversion of the 'maternal instinct' in which she, at times of stress, experiences strong and powerful physical sensations including sexual attraction towards

children; her own and/or others. She tries to stop herself from acting out the thought, since she knows it is wrong, but the urge physically and/or sexually to attack the object of her desire/hate proves irresistible, and hence she succumbs. When committing the action there is a sense of elation and release of sexual excitement, but these feelings are immediately superseded by shame, self-disgust, and depression.

(Welldon, 1996:178)

In understanding the roots of perverse mothering it is crucial to explore the mother's own experience of childhood, of being mothered. The intergenerational transmission of abusive patterns of parenting is a phenomenon of such importance that it cannot be overestimated. The repetition of such patterns can be identified clearly in the histories of women who present at the forensic outpatients' clinic, either under accusation of committing acts of sexual or physical abuse against children or because they did not protect their children from such abuse. These women may form relationships with sexually and physically violent men and become part of incestuous and chaotic families in which boundaries between children and adults are absent or perverted. Sexual abuse of their own children, echoing their own experiences of sexual abuse in their own childhood, may become the norm within these unsafe families. This is illustrated in the following clinical material.

Case illustration: Monica: Maternal abuse by a 62-year-old woman

Monica was referred for assessment to evaluate the risk which she posed to her granddaughter, who was the first child of Monica's youngest daughter. This daughter had been abused by Monica sexually, in the context of gross abuse within the entire family, in which all of the ten children had been involved in sexual activities, with each other, with their parents, and with two middle-aged lodgers. Monica had herself been charged with two counts of indecent assault on the two youngest girls, whom she had penetrated digitally and whose breasts she had fondled. She had also been charged with indecent assault on her youngest son, whose penis she had touched in an attempt to masturbate him.

In interview she was timid, with a marked speech impediment and a cleft palette. She wept when discussing the possibility that she might lose contact with her granddaughter, but seemed unconcerned about having no relations whatsoever with any of her other children, all of whom appeared to have disowned her following their disclosure of the widespread and deeply perverse abuse, which had included exposure of the children to hard-core pornography.

My first contact with this family had been through one of the older sons, who had been beaten and sodomised by his eldest three stepbrothers, and by a lodger, from the age of 7. He had subsequently gone on to assault a 3-year-old girl when he was aged 15 and had been active in abusing his younger sisters by having sexual intercourse with them: the youngest girl was 6 when the abuse started. He came to me for assessment when he was 19 following his release from custody and his partner of 18 months was expecting their first child. He had served a custodial sentence for the indecent assault and had made several serious suicide attempts in prison. He engaged in treatment related to his sexual offending and I saw him for approximately nine months, during which time he related details of his own childhood, including the degree to which his mother had interfered with him sexually. She would come into his bedroom at night and fondle his penis, until it became erect, and would sometimes masturbate him until he had an orgasm. He also had vivid memories of the violence and sadism with which his stepbrothers would have anal sex with him, often in front of his parents and other siblings. He and his younger brothers would both be buggered by the older boys and then encouraged to have sexual intercourse with their younger sisters. All the abuse was common knowledge within the family and would often take place in communal places. Pornographic material was freely available and often used in the household, including child pornography involving animals, and videos showing adults and children having group sex.

This family was one of the most abusive, sadistic and disturbed families I had ever encountered, and the extent of the abuse and cruelty was very difficult to bear. Perhaps most distressing was the clear illustration of the transmission of abuse seen as brothers raped sisters, under the instruction of their parents and elder siblings. The abuse often involved sadism, including violent assaults on the victims. An example of the nature of the sadism and humiliation was that the stepbrothers would make the younger children drink their own urine. The mother whom I was asked to assess had not only been aware of this extreme, almost unbelievable abuse, but had actively participated in it, appearing to derive both emotional and sexual gratification from the control and power that she exerted over these desperately damaged children.

Monica's youngest daughter, then aged 10 described her experience of maternal abuse in her police statement. A lesser form of abuse involved washing her mother in the bath, and being made to wash her breasts. This would follow the apparently ordinary activity of being bathed by Monica. In a perversion of the usual role of mothering Monica ordered the girls to wash her breasts, and then asked them to put talcum powder on them. This had an infantile and desperate quality, as though Monica was asking her young daughters to provide her with the kind of physical contact of which she had been deprived in her own infancy. At the same time as revealing this deprivation and pathos it demonstrated a complete disregard for the feelings of the girls, who were used as objects for her gratification. She forbade the girls to tell visiting social workers about any aspect of the sexual abuse which they experienced on a daily basis, by brothers, sisters and by Monica herself.

Another daughter, then aged 12, the other main victim of the abuse, corroborated the description of her involvement in being made to bathe and fondle her mother's breasts, going on to describe how Monica would rub her and her sisters' genitals. She described how Monica would come into their shared bedroom and ask if their vaginas were sore, indicating her full awareness of the extent of the girls' sexual victimisation by members of the family. This question also appears to be a perverse parody of ordinary maternal concern. If the girls said yes, because they quite often were, she would insert her finger into their vaginas in a rough way, before removing her finger and rubbing talcum powder into their genitals. This child described this behaviour as 'rude' and said it had 'hurt'. Her statement is painful to read, particularly when she says 'When mum had done this she would say not to tell anyone or she would put me away.' The pain, confusion, fear and cruelty of the sexual abuse is vividly presented in the descriptions provided by these children.

Unfortunately, many of the criminal proceedings against the siblings were discontinued owing to difficulties in gathering evidence from the other children. It was therefore extremely important that findings of fact in relation to sexual abuse were made in the Civil Court. In the care proceedings case regarding five of the children the Judge stated in his summing up: 'so much of this is almost incredible that I repeatedly warn myself to be on guard and to be cautious but, however frequently I give myself that warning, I am driven to conclude not just on a balance of probabilities but with a quite saddening, frightening certainty that the children of the family have been sexually abused . . . They have been sexually abused by the members of the family on a scale and over a length of time that even those who did not actively participate in that abuse must have known of it and must have failed to protect the younger children who were members of their own family.'

Although it was initially surprising that there should even be a question about Monica's risk to children, the request for an assessment revealed the extent to which her participation in the sexual abuse of her own children could not really be borne by the professionals involved. It could not fully be understood or thought about. Her elderly, infirm appearance, her own psychological vulnerabilities, and the fact that she was the grandmother of an infant seemed to obscure the fact that she was a convicted Schedule One offender. In my report to the Court I repeated the central facts of the case and the allegations which had been made about her systematic sexual abuse of her children, strongly emphasising the risk that she posed to any child with whom she had contact. The local authority care plan, which did not allow her contact with the child, was eventually accepted. The fact that the baby's mother, the girl who had been aged 12 in her original statements to the police, and who had been one of the worst victims of abuse within the family, might also pose a risk of sexual abuse to her child, was also an important consideration, which needed to be brought to the attention of the social workers involved in this distressing case. The extent of the traumatic sexualisation and violence within this family created a significant risk that the abuse would continue to be transmitted from one generation to the next.

Kaplan (1991) describes the link between the strategies of the perverse woman and the social constructions which govern how her behaviour will be understood: 'Since deception is so crucial to perversion, unless we lay bare the lies that are hidden there we will be deceived at once' (Kaplan, 1991:9). The issue of deceit, including self-deception, is a crucial one, which can powerfully interfere with the offenders acknowledging their responsibility for sexually abusing a child, and reduce the chances of engagement in treatment. The problem of denial in male sex offenders, for whom well-researched treatment programmes exist, has been well-described by clinicians, and applies equally to female sex offenders (Beckett, 1994).

The following case illustration describes both the difficulty of confronting denial in the female offender, particularly in the context of care proceedings where the future placement of the child hangs in the balance, and the powerful countertransference feelings which can interfere with the therapist's capacity to engage the client. The greater shame of child abuse by mothers is a burden both to victims of maternal sexual abuse and to women themselves, as this is the crime which is probably thought most perverse and unacceptable to others, in its direct challenge to cherished notions about motherhood. The possible attraction of mothers to their children, even their adolescent sons, is still a highly taboo subject, and the potential for sexual contact can usually only be acknowledged if, like Jocasta, the woman is unaware that she is actually committing incest.

Case illustration: Allison: Maternal sexual abuse and deception

Allison was a 39-year-old woman who was referred to the outpatients' department for assessment of her suitability for psychological treatment related to her feelings of depression. She had recently lost custody of her baby daughter Samantha following a Court Hearing. The local authority had won their appeal for a care order to be granted on Samantha and the care plan they had submitted had identified adoption as the aim for her. Five years earlier Allison had voluntarily placed her 6-year-old daughter Jennifer into local authority care because she had felt unable to cope with her. This child had made extensive allegations that Allison had abused her sexually, which had resulted in her eventually being placed in long-term care under a full care order. Allison denied the allegations of sexual abuse but admitted that she had rejected her daughter and neglected her needs. At the time of the assessment

Allison lived alone with her 13-year-old son Luke, who was not subject to a child care order.

Allison was an anxious woman in her thirties who was apprehensive about attending the outpatient clinic, having had unhappy experiences with psychologists, one of whom had assessed her for the previous care proceedings, relating to Jennifer, and had concluded that she was a risk to children. She had found this hurtful and deeply unfair, expressing anger about this conclusion and pointing out apparent factual inaccuracies in the report which had been presented to the Court. The documentation related to the case revealed, however, that Allison habitually changed factual details for no obvious reasons, leading to inconsistent and contradictory statements about such apparently straightforward facts as birthday and address. She admitted that she sometimes forgot things and found her situation confusing and overwhelming, not always being sure of 'what was going on'. Her distracted and nervous manner conveyed her overwhelmingly chaotic life and disorganised personality, revealing her unstable sense of herself and her environment. She strongly disagreed with the observations of the child psychologists who had assessed Jennifer and concluded that it was highly probable that she had been abused by her mother. The child psychologists had assessed Jennifer extensively and found her allegations very plausible in the light of her many consistent statements and the degree of disturbance that she had displayed. Jennifer had made suicide attempts and graphically described the maternal abuse that she had experienced.

The descriptions of the sexual abuse which Allison was alleged to have perpetrated on Jennifer were graphic and the behaviour highly perverse. She reported that Allison had painted her own genital and nipple area prior to the abuse. She was alleged to have forced Jennifer to perform oral sex on her and would also penetrate her vaginally using her fingers and other objects. Jennifer reported that this abuse occurred frequently, sometimes up to three or four times a week and that physical violence had also taken place. Luke had told a social worker that his mother 'did rude things' to his sister, but asked her not to tell his mother that he had said so. Jennifer displayed very disturbed and sexualised behaviour at school and was eventually brought into local authority care by her mother who found her 'impossible' to cope with. She consistently demonstrated very sexualised behaviour with other children, including Luke, with whom she was seen kissing and cuddling in an intimate 'adult' way, saying that she was just 'snogging him'.

It was during her first placement with foster carers that Jennifer had made the serious allegations of sexual abuse. Jennifer had presented great difficulties for her foster carers because of her sexually disinhibited and aggressive behaviour, particularly in relation to her younger foster sister. Allison attributed these allegations to Jennifer's anger at being rejected by her. Shortly after being taken into foster care Jennifer had stood in the middle of the road, pulled her skirt up, her underpants down, and said that she was 'waiting for a car to come'. This appeared to be a highly sexualised suicide attempt, indicating the extent to which the child felt objectified and desperate. Allison understood this to reveal how rejected Jennifer had felt when she had been placed in care, asking why she would have placed her in care if she had wanted to abuse her, and becoming furious when I suggested that sometimes parents recognise that their children may be at risk at home. Allison disclosed that she herself had been sexually abused by her elder sister. She became highly distressed and angry when I suggested that she might have wanted to protect Jennifer from going through the same abuse which she herself had experienced, and that a healthy part of her wanted to ensure that the child was placed out of harm's way. It was evident that Allison found it far easier to discuss her experiences of sexual victimisation than her own sexually abusive fantasies and activities. She tended to attribute blame for Jennifer's disturbed behaviour, which included stealing and fighting, to the child herself, describing her as 'canny', 'manipulative', 'a wind-up merchant' and 'attention-seeking'.

It was very difficult to take a clear history of Allison's life to date, and to glean a coherent picture of recent events. She had lived in numerous places, moving frequently and impulsively following the break-up of sexual relationships with men. She was unclear about times and dates of moves, and gave a confusing account of her current residence, indicating that she had moved, but providing me with her previous address, only then to accuse me of getting her address wrong when I cited this address in my report to the Court.

She reported that she had not used drugs in recent years, but had, in the past, been a regular cannabis user, with occasional use of harder drugs including Ecstasy and cocaine. She described general feelings of depression, victimisation, hopelessness generally and a profound sense of injustice, particularly in relation to being considered a sexual risk to her infant daughter.

It emerged during the first interview that Allison had herself been sexually abused by her older sister when she was a child. She had been 6 years old and her sister 11 when her sister had begun to force her to perform oral sex on her, and had also penetrated her digitally. Allison was the youngest of three girls. Her natural father had left her mother before she was born: she had never known him. When she was 8 her mother had married an American, after having a series of brief relationships with other men, one of whom had sexually interfered with Allison on one occasion. Her mother had herself been a depressed woman with a violent temper who would frequently assault her children with any available weapons, including, on one particularly frightening occasion, a fire poker. She had also failed to provide adequate protection of Allison, with the consequence that Allison had been sexually assaulted by her own sister for several years during her latency. Her older sister, Rachel, had abused Allison sexually from the ages of 6 to 10, when she would tie her to the bed and perform oral sex on her, also forcing Allison to reciprocate. Allison clearly remembered the sexual violence and the 'treats' which she would be given after the sexual activity took place. She became visibly distressed as she related these details to me. Although Allison stated that she now hated her older sister she had repeatedly left Jennifer in Rachel's care, denying concern about the possibility that she would also be abused by her. She had some contact with her sister in adult life but did not see her parents or middle sister, whom she described as a 'waste of space'.

It appeared easier for Allison to view her son, Luke, as a separate person than it was for her to disentangle herself psychically from her daughter. It seemed possible for her to differentiate herself from him, perhaps because giving birth to him had not evoked her own feelings and memories about her own relationship with her mother as powerfully. He was allowed some kind of individuation, although

I bore in mind the possibility that Allison was sexually provocative and confusing with him, even if she did not actually engage him in incestuous activity. She spoke about Luke in terms of his capacity to care for and protect her, reflecting her wholly distorted boundaries and indicating the depths of her own dependence and egocentricity. Interestingly, he was not viewed as vulnerable by the child protection professionals, despite his disturbed and sexualised behaviour at school and some indication that he may have been involved in the sexual abuse of Jennifer. It was as though it was inconceivable that a (now adolescent) boy could be at risk of sexual abuse by his mother, even though his sister had made clear allegations of such maternal abuse.

Although there had been no criminal proceedings regarding the sexual abuse allegations, the Judge in the civil case concerning Jennifer had made findings of fact regarding them and had determined that the sexual abuse had been perpetrated by Allison on her daughter. This was based, in part, on the evidence of several child-care professionals who had assessed Jennifer, and on the evidence of the forensic clinical psychologist who had assessed Allison and produced a report for the Court. The Judge had found Allison to be a woman who posed a risk to children in her care, with little regard for their emotional and physical welfare, describing her sexual abuse and rejection of Jennifer as showing 'callous disregard for her interests'.

Allison attended the three assessment appointments offered to her but declined the offer to engage in psychological treatment because of my links with the forensic services, saying that she was not a criminal, she was simply depressed because she had lost two children, and had been a victim of childhood sexual abuse by her sister. She felt that she was 'the accused' and that everyone was 'against' her. The fact that seeing me would have involved exploration of her relationship with Jennifer and the sexual aspects of her mothering, her deep identification with her daughter, and her difficulty in establishing clear boundaries between children and adults, made the task far too threatening for her. She complained that I had 'not really been listening' and felt she was left completely isolated and helpless. There was an adamant refusal to acknowledge the hatred that she had felt towards her daughter and the hostility with which she had treated her. She eventually lost care of the baby, who was made the subject of a care order and placed for adoption. Once again, she had lost care of a daughter, and was left feeling furious and bereft.

My intense countertransference feelings made it difficult to retain a therapeutically neutral stance in relation to Allison because of the depths of her denial and her cruelty towards her daughter. I understood the cruelty to reflect her own murderous impulses towards herself and her own unprotective mother. I wondered whether Allison might lie compulsively about seemingly insignificant details in order to create a sense of identity and to convince herself that she had an internal, private space into which others could not easily enter. Through lying about apparently insignificant events and facts she could create a distance between herself and others and preserve a sense of separateness, as though the boundaries of her personal identity were so fragile as to engender in her a fear of being wholly engulfed and lost. I was left with a sense of being tricked or deceived by the many contradictions in Allison's narratives, with the result that I felt quite persecutory towards her, wanting to challenge her about these inconsistencies. When I did ask about the discrepancies in her statements I was met with hostile denial of any such differences, and was accused, instead, of 'not listening' and 'getting things wrong'. This led to my confusion and I found myself questioning my own understanding of the interviews and the accuracy of my notes. I was put in the role of being an unreliable witness, a position which alerted me to the significance of Allison's own experience of deception and abuse. The person who listened and tried to make sense of her experience became persecutory and unreliable just as Allison had experienced her mother as being an unprotective, negligent figure who had both allowed sexual abuse to occur and had herself inflicted physical violence on her. It seemed to mirror her experience in childhood of being lied to and made to feel that her perceptions were inaccurate. In addition, Allison felt furious that her own 'victimhood' was not being addressed, identifying herself as victim not perpetrator and feeling confused and desperate when her role as victimiser was explored. She could not manage to hold both these aspects of herself in mind, and found it intolerable when I attempted to do so.

The intensity of the countertransference feelings seemed to relate to the cruelty of Allison's own impulses towards herself, as expressed in her sexual abuse of her daughter. Through sexually abusing Jennifer, Allison was unconsciously enacting her own experiences, attacking the body of the little girl as her own had been attacked. She had made a serious suicide attempt during the time of the final hearing regarding Jennifer, which she described as motivated by guilt about having placed the child in foster care. In her mind Jennifer stood for her, and was the repository of her self-hatred and the target for her murderous impulses. The sexual sadism she directed towards her represented a kind of psychic murder:

> the sexual abuse of children amounts to no less than the enactment of a symbolic form of murder, since the only way to kill someone, in the psychic sense, yet not literally take their life, is to penetrate their body via its orifices.
>
> (Kirsta, 1994:289)

By refusing to enter therapy Allison was also killing me off. She could trust me only in so far as I could nurture her and respond sympathetically to her as a victim of sexual abuse by a woman, and physical and emotional abuse by both her mother and stepfather. She could not bear me to acknowledge the sense in which she was also an aggressor, and a victimiser of children. Her unhappiness and desperation appeared genuine and her defensive attitude seemed to relate to her guilt feelings and her underlying sense of her own worthlessness. The fact that I was aware of the allegations which Jennifer had made, and which her son had corroborated, indicated to her that I would ultimately reject and condemn her.

Allison had defended against intolerable psychic pain by splitting off her aggressive impulses, projecting them on to her daughter through her sexual manipulation of her. She appeared to have an emotionally, if not sexually, over-involved relationship with her son, whom she described as the 'man in my life'. She had little capacity to recognise her own aggression, projected it on to others, saw it reflected back at her in the rest of the world, and therefore inhabited a paranoid world where she was repeatedly rejected, humiliated and, ultimately, abandoned. Her sexual abuse of Jennifer had temporarily afforded her an avenue of escape from her depression and fear.

The origins of Allison's anger seemed to lie in her experiences in infancy and childhood, which had left her with a sense of abject self-loathing and undiluted, infantile fury towards her own depriving, unprotective and violent mother and her sexually exploitative sister. She had not had the experience of integrating her angry unacceptable feelings in childhood, and had developed no safe repository for them, either in the external world or in her internal world. For Allison her mother had been a barren, cruel object, unable to respond to her needs or her attempts to engage with her. Becoming the sexual aggressor against her own daughter enabled Allison to rid herself of the profound feelings of helplessness and victimisation that she had experienced by projecting them. She had internalised and identified with both her sister and her mother as aggressors and could re-create this dynamic with her own female child.

CONCLUSION

These perversions of motherhood reflect the overwhelming sense of powerlessness and low self-esteem which create such difficulties for these women during pregnancy and motherhood. Motherhood may become an avenue for compensation and a forum for revenge, a sphere of authority, power and control. 'Female sexual abuse, particularly maternal incest, represents the most tragically grotesque misuse and abuse of that power' (Kirsta, 1994:295).

In these offences there is a re-enactment by the mothers of earlier trauma in which they identify both with the child-victims and with the aggressor: these defences, and those of denial, minimisation and emotional detachment from the child, enable such mothers to be freed, temporarily, from the psychic pain of remembering their own abusive histories. They are acting out, through their children's bodies, experiences which are too difficult to think about. What cannot be borne mentally becomes enacted through this sexualised violence.

As well as becoming more receptive to the possibility of maternal sexual abuse in child protection cases, clinicians have a responsibility to identify and classify the types of sexual abuse which have been perpetrated, and to heighten awareness of risk factors in women's backgrounds which may predispose them to sexually offend against children. Additionally, assessment measures and treatment programmes specifically for the female sex offender need to be devised. There has been growing attention to this area, and some attempts to modify assessment measures for female offenders, but this remains a largely unexplored area of research, which requires urgent attention, both in terms of adequate child protection assessments and in relation to the unmet therapeutic needs of the female sex offender. An important new body of research on female sexual abusers, relating to the findings of three US studies on female sex offenders has recently been published (Davin *et al.*, 1999). This literature represents a serious attempt to begin to recognise, explore and treat this problem. It is crucially important that this problem is identified and that attempts are made to develop treatment programmes whose success can be evaluated.

While it has been argued that there are intrinsic as well as culturally determined characteristics of women which might disincline them to abuse children sexually, such as their tendency not to sexualise relationships to the extent that men do, their preference for more powerful sexual partners, stronger bonding with children and disinclination to initiate sexual contact, it is clear that these factors may not operate in women with serious histories of childhood victimisation experiences within their own families (Finklehor, 1984). To cope with the trauma of this victimisation the women have developed certain pathological defences which make sexual abuse of children possible, and even likely. Furthermore, their own experience of sexualised behaviour by their family members may have desensitised them to the potentially traumatic effects of sexual abuse, distorting their understanding of children's behaviour, and the importance of clear boundaries between children and adults. The experience of a neglectful or abusive mother may create a perverse 'blueprint' for abusive behaviour, which these women re-enact with their own, or other people's, children.

Further research into female sexual abuse of children must be based on a comprehensive model of analysis, and a sensitive understanding of the complexity of the problem. It is essential for good practice that sensitive supervision is provided for clinicians working in this disturbing area, since they are likely to experience strongly negative countertransference feelings to female sex offenders. Understanding the female sex offender requires the capacity to suspend stereotypes about 'maternal instincts' and the ability to hear, from the offender herself, the story of her own mothering: this will enable clinicians to gain a clear picture of the development of the psychopathology and to feel less shocked by, and punitive towards, the perverse mother, allowing them to address the crucial task of child protection.

Chapter 2

Munchausen's syndrome by proxy

INTRODUCTION

Munchausen's syndrome by proxy (MSBP) provides one of the most disturbing and dramatic examples of a female perversion, in which women use the ostensibly caring role of mother, nurse or nanny to inflict harm on children. I consider the roles of nurse and nanny to be symbolic maternal roles, which are idealised in such a way as to mask the opportunity for cruelty and perversion that they afford. In this chapter I discuss the theoretical literature relating to this relatively rare but highly dangerous condition and provide a case illustration of the difficulties inherent in the identification of MSBP and the complexity of its manifestation. The difficulty in understanding and detecting MSBP may relate to professionals' blind spots in recognising female violence, particularly when it involves maternal abuse. A recent epidemiological study has indicated that in 85 per cent of 128 cases of MSBP, non-accidental poisoning and non-accidental suffocation, the perpetrator was the child's mother (McClure *et al.*, 1996). The reluctance to recognise this syndrome reflects the strength of idealisations of motherhood and the denial of its potential danger.

This emotional and intellectual difficulty in recognising MSBP is well described in the accounts of the trial of Beverley Allitt, provided by Hunt and Goldring, barristers for the defence and for the Crown Prosecution Service in the case (1997). Ms Allitt, though vilified, was ultimately sentenced to psychiatric treatment in a Special Hospital under section 37/41 of the Mental Health Act. James Hunt, QC, leading Counsel for the Defendant, described the difficulty of the case:

> we were presented with a defendant who insisted that she had done nothing to harm anyone and continued to do so after she was

sentenced. She was a nurse, she was a member of a profession dedicated to caring and saving life. On the face of it, an unlikely candidate. . . . From our research into the defendant's background we also knew of the diagnosis, or, at least to begin with, a possible diagnosis of Munchausen's syndrome, both *simpliciter* and by proxy . . . we knew that many of those diagnosed as Munchausen's by proxy cases were nurses, 20 per cent, most being the mothers of the children they abused.

(Hunt and Goldring, 1997:189)

In describing two previous cases of MSBP, one in Canada and in the United States, he writes:

In each case, it is worth noting that not just detection, but a realisation of what was happening, took months because *those in charge would not think the unthinkable, and even when they started to think it wouldn't believe it*, a nurse killing a patient and particularly babies.

(Hunt and Goldring, 1997:190; my italics)

In the cases which he cites of Susan Nellis, Janey Jones and Beverley Allitt, the combination of being a woman in the caring professions, particularly a nurse, and the victims being babies, made accurate understanding of what had happened 'unthinkable'. It appeared that when these factors combined they rendered understanding of the problem impossible. Too many taboos and idealisations were challenged simultaneously, resulting in a paralysis in the system and an inability to think about or recognise what was happening. This attack on thinking interfered with the capacity of the organisation, i.e. the hospital in which Beverley Allitt worked, to take protective action even after acknowledging her dangerousness.

The failure to see the obvious, and the resulting tragedy of further deaths, then had a profound backlash in terms of the vilification of Ms Allitt and the outrage and horror that greeted her crime. While she was, no doubt, highly disturbed and dangerous, the degree to which her offences were treated with disbelief and moral panic reflected the extent to which she, as a nurse caring for children, had shattered the images of womanhood held most sacred by the general public. Little was understood about the link between her need for destructive power and her attraction to the role of nurse, to be seen as an 'angel of mercy' when she leapt to the aid of the injured or ill child. Most seriously, failure to consider her potential for harm earlier contributed to the institutional failure to protect vulnerable children in her care.

THE LINK BETWEEN MUNCHAUSEN'S SYNDROME AND MSBP

In his original paper coining the phrase Munchausen's syndrome by proxy, Meadow (1977) described the great similarity between Munchausen's syndrome proper and MSBP. In MSBP mothers use their children to generate the attention and care which they craved for themselves, whereas in Munchausen's syndrome itself people present themselves for medical attention for fabricated injuries and illnesses, even to the extent of undergoing unnecessary operations and other medical interventions. Munchausen's syndrome can be understood as a form of self-harm, which both creates a situation of self-injury and, in a sense, victimises the medical professionals, who are tricked into being active agents of this self-mutilation. Approximately 20 per cent of people diagnosed with MSBP have also displayed signs of Munchausen's syndrome (Adshead, 1997) and 10–25 per cent of the MSBP perpetrators produce or feign illness in themselves (Rosenberg, 1987). Of great interest in considering the phenomenon of female violence is the finding that while sufferers of Munchausen's syndrome are equally divided between men and women (Hyler and Sussman, 1981) it has been estimated that 98 per cent of MSBP perpetrators are female (Rosenberg, 1987). The victims, however, are equally divided between male and female children (Rosenberg, 1987). Additionally, some mothers continue to exhibit signs of Munchausen's syndrome preceding their MSBP and following discovery of their abuse and removal of their children (Parnell, 1998).

There are significant actual differences in terms of the nature of MSBP abuse compared to the self-injury and deception of Munchausen's syndrome, and there are dramatically different legal consequences between injuring a child and harming oneself. Parnell suggests that

> there seems to be a fundamental difference between the psychopathology of an individual who is willing to make herself suffer and that of one who is willing not only to watch but to create suffering in another human being, particularly her own helpless child.
>
> (Parnell, 1998:19)

I argue, in contrast to this view, that, for perverse mothers, the motivation is, in fact, very closely linked. In psychodynamic terms, however, there is clear identification for the mother between her child and herself, the two become fused for her and her own somatisation is extended to include her child, viewed as part of herself.

CLASSIFICATIONS OF MSBP

It is helpful to distinguish between different types of MSBP rather than viewing it as a unitary diagnostic category. Libow and Schreier (1986) attempt to refine the concept of MSBP and distinguish between its presentations through providing the following categories of MSBP:

Help seekers

The production of symptoms in the child is seen infrequently, usually as a result of stresses in the mother such as depression or anxiety. She presents the child as an expression of her own distress when her maternal competence is overwhelmed as a result of these stresses.

Doctor addicts

These mothers seem genuinely convinced that the child is ill, to the extent that this belief approaches delusional intensity. Such mothers may also hold paranoid, suspicious beliefs and may have personality disorders.

Active inducers

It is this last category of women who commit dramatic and often highly complex and secretive physical assaults on their children, and who also demonstrate extreme denial, projection and affective dissociation in their presentation. They frequently injure their children and/or fabricate mysterious symptoms. They are most characteristic of MSBP perpetrators (cited by Barker and Howell, 1994).

The last two categories describe those individuals most clearly representative of MSBP, and whose diagnosis as suffering with the disorder is most valid. It has been suggested that these two groups are motivated more by unconscious than conscious needs and secondary gain.

In the second classification of MSBP, the doctor addicts, the mother is one step removed from actually abusing the child directly but brings her child to medical professionals under false pretexts, with the intention that they will proceed with intervention. In such a case the mother has fabricated symptoms which require medical intervention. In other cases, those of the active inducers, the mother herself harms the child, in order to induce apparent symptoms of illness which require medical treatment; for example, subjecting her child to laxative poisoning which causes severe diarrhoea, for which no obvious organic cause is detected, leading to high levels of concern and further investigation.

Although the illnesses of children who have been subject to MSBP abuse often involve respiratory, neurological, infectious, gastrointestinal and haematological difficulties, there are more than 100 symptoms which have been associated with this syndrome (Schreier and Libow, 1993; Parnell and Day, 1998). The most common factitious symptoms associated with MSBP are seizures, bleeding, apnoea, diarrhoea, vomiting, fever, rash (Rosenberg, 1987) and lethargy (Schreier and Libow, 1993). It has been noted that such mothers can be very creative and deceptive, falsifying symptoms in ways which a physician might find it difficult to imagine. Attempting to cross-reference the current presentation of a child with their previous medical records may provide important clues about the nature of the apparently inexplicable illness, pointing to an extensive history of medical consultation and even evidence of fabrication and induction of symptoms in the past:

> The written medical records may contain evidence of false medical history of the child or family, exaggeration of the child's medical condition, exaggeration of physician statements regarding the child's medical condition, reports of symptoms that never occurred, faked or simulated symptoms, and actual induction of symptoms. The distinction between exaggeration and fabrication is difficult to make, as is a determination of simulation versus induction, through consideration of the symptom presentation or report alone. Induced symptoms are generally much more difficult to detect, especially because induction tends to create actual physiological conditions.
>
> (Parnell and Day, 1998:78)

The risk for professionals of failing to take seriously the mother's presentation of an apparently ill child is great: a sick child might be left untreated and suffer serious harm. The professional has a duty to take action. In those instances where the mother fabricates symptoms, leading to unnecessary and intrusive medical intervention, she entices neutral professionals into a destructive game where the tools of treatment become the weapons which injure vulnerable children. This has clear parallels with the type of self-harm evident in Munchausen's syndrome, where the patient deceives medical professionals into conducting painful interventions, sometimes including surgical procedures. The patient is passive in terms of directly injuring themselves but manipulates a third party into doing so.

The current diagnostic criteria for MSBP suggested by Meadow (1995) are:

1   The illness is fabricated by the parent or carer.
2   The child is presented to doctors, usually persistently.
3   The perpetrator (initially) denies causing the child's illness.
4   The illness clears up when the child is separated from the perpetrator.

BACKGROUND FACTORS IN WOMEN DIAGNOSED WITH MSBP

Both mental health professionals and specialists in child health require basic information about the backgrounds of women diagnosed with MSBP so that they may have a clearer idea about how such individuals may present. One important link is between those who have displayed Munchausen's syndrome themselves and have gone on to develop the syndrome by proxy, using their children's bodies as they have used their own, as tools for violence and deception, possibly with the unconscious aim of being 'found out' and prevented from continuing in this abuse.

Women with somatic disorders have been found to represent a high proportion of MSBP mothers; this has been described as 'maternal somatisation disorder' (Livingstone, 1987) based on clinical interviews and examination of available medical records. Livingstone linked the complex medical histories of MSBP mothers with multiple unexplained symptoms and repeated hospitalisations and surgical procedures without evidence that their own symptoms had been voluntarily produced and noted that these medical histories were consistent with diagnosis of somatisation disorder as described in the *Diagnostic Statistical Manual*, Third Edition (DSM III), which is retained in the Fourth Edition of DSM. The description of these mothers as suffering from somatisation disorder rather than factitious illness such as Munchausen's syndrome was first described in the literature by Livingstone (1987).

Background features in women diagnosed with MSBP include delinquency and criminal convictions in adolescence, eating disorders, self-harm, parental abuse or neglect, including sexual abuse, and a history of self-harm (Adshead, 1997). For women who have undergone experiences of abuse, their conception of the value and use of their own bodies may be heavily distorted and they may use their bodies to express their pain and despair, as well as their anger at the parents whom they feel have let them down and betrayed them. Their sense of identity may reside in their bodies, as their early experiences have not allowed them the opportunity to develop a clear sense of themselves as separate from their bodies, which have been treated as objects to be punished or sexually exploited by adults. The domain of control and of the sense of self are located firmly in the body which therefore assumes a central importance and expressive function for these women.

There are significant commonalities in women who self-harm and women who perpetrate injuries upon and/or fabricate illnesses in their children. The development of these forms of violence can be understood in the context of both social and individual factors. There are important communicative functions of self-harm and MSBP: both are clear expressions of a distorted and damaged sense of self, often related to a history of abuse. Women with MSBP may also have eating disorders and histories of depression, as well as self-harm. In these manifestations of female violence, aggression is turned against the self or against children, the central domains of power and control. The body of the woman herself, or, by extension, her child's body, is the focus of female violence (Welldon, 1988).

It has been suggested that vulnerability to developing MSBP may have its roots in women's own attachments in childhood and in their relationship to the world, in their excessive susceptibility to taking on socially prescribed roles of mother or caretaker:

> The ultimate role of caretaker is that of the mother figure. Women are expected to be the primary nurturing figures for their children and to attach to them protectively. However, MSBP mother-perpetrators clearly display a disorder of empathy and attachment with their children. They harm their children without feeling the children's pain. The children become objects used horribly by the mother-perpetrators in order to have their own needs met. The reasons attachment fails to develop are diverse, but they grow from disturbed object relationships beginning in childhood with experiences of physical, sexual, and emotional abuse.
>
> (Day and Parnell, 1998:163)

Case illustration: Grace, a 24-year-old woman with suspected MSBP

Harriet, a 10-month-old baby, was presented at her general practitioner's (GP's) surgery with breathing difficulties by her mother, Grace, a 24-year-old woman who had worked as a nursing assistant in a surgical ward three years earlier, for approximately 15 months. She appeared highly distressed by the baby's condition and was well informed about the possible implications of the difficulties, such as asthma or bronchiolitis. The GP found no clear organic cause of the baby's difficulties, nor did he observe any signs of chest congestion or wheezing in the infant. He was initially impressed by the mother's intelligence, concern and apparent medical awareness, but noted that he could not detect any physical signs in the infant to corroborate her observations.

A few weeks later Harriet was again presented at the surgery by her mother who expressed concern about bruising around the baby's eyes. This bruising was not easily explained. At this point the GP developed some concern about the welfare of the child as such bruising can be associated with suffocation or strangulation attempts but did not feel that he had sufficient evidence to contact social services to alert them to the possibility of child abuse. Although Grace had requested that a referral be made to a specialist breathing unit this referral had not been made. She was insistent that the bruising around the eyes be investigated thoroughly by a specialist but the GP offered her an appointment at the surgery the following week to check on the baby's condition. At this appointment Grace, appearing calm and composed but very adamant and assertive in her views, complained that Harriet had been vomiting, that the rash around the eyes was persisting and that she continued to have fits in which she found it difficult to breathe. She expressed the fear that Harriet suffered from asthma, which she insisted must be diagnosed and treated as a matter of urgency. The GP felt alarmed by what he considered to be an over-insistent approach by Grace and he was disturbed by the extent of Harriet's crying and irritability of mood. He examined Harriet thoroughly at this third appointment and found swelling and tenderness of her arm; he had her referred immediately for X-rays which demonstrated that she had a spiral fracture of her left arm as well as other bruises indicative of earlier injuries. He now strongly suspected that the injuries were non-accidental and contacted social services who placed Harriet's name on the Child Protection Register in the category of at risk of physical abuse.

Grace denied that she had played any role in perpetrating the injuries, or that her husband could have caused them as he had been away on business several days a week for the past few months, and had not been at home at the time the spiral fracture was believed to have occurred. There was still no evidence or direct observation of Harriet's breathing difficulties or vomiting, despite Grace's assertion that these had occurred on an almost daily basis when she was at home with her.

Grace and her husband, Mick, were subsequently assessed by social services and by the consultant psychiatrist based at the child and family psychiatry services. The psychiatrist concluded that Grace had low self-esteem and difficulty in asserting herself but detected no evidence of mental illness. She evaluated Mick as being less articulate and intelligent than Grace but perceived that he had a strong need to assert his control over his wife. Grace had reported that he had physically assaulted her on one occasion, after she had gone out with friends, and that he tended to be jealous and possessive of her, encouraging her to stay at home and have minimal contact with friends and family.

Although the consultant child psychiatrist did not report the extent of her grave concerns about the mother's deceptiveness and the dangerous family dynamics in her report, as some of her views were matters of speculation, she stated that the spiral fracture was an almost classic case of battered baby syndrome. In an informal discussion with me she expressed her opinion that Grace had several risk factors indicative of maternal abuse and that she retained serious concerns about the welfare of a child in her care. She considered it highly likely that Grace was suffering from MSBP, but said that she did not feel that she could make this diagnosis in a report for the Court.

I was requested to assess the risk which Grace posed to Harriet in the light of the occurrence of non-accidental injuries for which both parents denied responsibility. I was aware that the psychiatric opinion was that the injuries were very likely to have been perpetrated by the mother and that her presentation was of a woman with long-standing psychological difficulties in self-esteem and self-expression. The psychiatrist had also concluded that there was no evidence of formal mental illness or personality disorder in the husband. The parents' understanding of child development appeared relatively sophisticated and Grace had been described by her husband as 'an ideal mother'. There was a history of sexual difficulties in the marital relationship, dating back to Grace's pregnancy with Harriet, who was their first child. Her husband said that he had been 'delighted' to learn that Grace was expecting a girl, as he came from a family of three boys; Grace had said she didn't mind what the baby's sex was.

Harriet had been born four weeks early and her delivery, by Caesarean section, had not been easy. Grace had been looking forward to a natural birth but was diagnosed with placenta praevia at 36 weeks. Harriet had weighed 5lbs 1oz when she was born and had developed jaundice, which had required photo therapy. Grace described the sense of loss and worry that Harriet's removal from her care to be placed under lights had generated, and her fear that the jaundice reflected a serious liver condition rather than simply a common and easily treated complication of preterm birth. Harriet was slow to gain weight and Grace said that she had also worried about this, particularly as she felt upset that she was not breast-feeding her. She talked knowledgeably about Harriet's 'failure to thrive' and how this had changed when solid food was introduced into her diet at 4 months.

For the first few weeks of Harriet's life Grace had been low in mood, describing a sense of failure because she had not had a natural birth. She had experienced intense anxiety about Harriet's survival. She had also not been able to breastfeed her which had been a source of some disappointment to her, particularly as her best friend, who had recently given birth, had described the sense of fulfilment that she had derived through successfully breastfeeding her son. Grace had not been breastfed herself and had found her own mother unsympathetic to her difficulties in feeding Harriet.

Despite her acknowledgement of the anxiety and disappointment surrounding Harriet's birth Grace was adamant that her relationship with her baby was good and that Harriet was a 'good baby' who rarely cried. This was contradicted by her husband who described his difficulty in functioning at work because of the baby's frequent waking and prolonged crying fits, particularly when she was aged around 8 weeks and he had taken on a challenging project at work. He was an insurance broker and had recently been promoted to a senior position at his firm. He reported that although Grace had 'not been herself' for the first three months of Harriet's life she had 'taken to motherhood' and been 'brilliant with her' ever since. At 10 months Harriet had just begun to crawl; Grace described how she had no conception of danger and would put wire flexes into her mouth. She appeared somewhat nervous about the increased mobility of her child and the sense that she might not be able to prevent Harriet from coming to harm.

As medical examination progressed it became evident both that the fractures were non-accidental in origin, and that the child had suffered multiple injuries over the past few weeks, as revealed through the X-rays. Although the rash around the eyes was not fully explicable it was possible that the infant had developed this as the result of strangulation attempts. This would also explain her reported breathing difficulties, which had not been observed on medical examination, nor had an organic basis which could be identified. The unanimous medical opinion of four different paediatric specialists was that the injuries were perpetrated by an adult and were non-accidental. The breathing difficulties could not clearly be diagnosed or explained and there was some suggestion that either the symptoms had been fabricated altogether or that the difficulties were the result of strangulation attempts by one of Harriet's adult carers. The balance of probability pointed to the mother as the likely perpetrator; the father was away at the time that Harriet had been brought to the surgery with the bruising to the eyes and reported breathing problems. The child psychiatrist, the paediatrician and I were aware that in cases of MSBP the perpetrator is almost always the mother. We considered it important to bear this hypothesis in mind. Although a police surgeon examined Harriet and considered the injuries to be non-accidental, the police did not consider there to be sufficient evidence for charges to be made against either Grace or her husband for assault or cruelty.

I assessed Grace in order to determine the extent of the

long-standing psychological difficulties alluded to by the psychiatrist who had examined her, and to evaluate risk factors in her parenting capacity. She presented as an articulate, attractive and intelligent woman who spoke in a soft, flat voice as she described her unresolved worries about the health of her child and her sense of confusion about how she could have come to sustain serious injuries. She stated that Harriet must have twisted her arm while rolling over in her cot, and that the other injuries could have been sustained when she caught her leg in the cot bar. She was aware that these explanations had been considered improbable and were inconsistent with the medical evidence but did not appear to be troubled about this discrepancy, repeating that she had never harmed the child. There was a bruise to Harriet's face which appeared to be a cut, scratch or abrasion. The police surgeon had suggested that this could have been caused by either a hard smack on the face or a gag which had been tied around the baby's mouth and had cut into her skin. Grace rejected these explanations and maintained that any facial bruises had been caused by Harriet banging her head into the cot bars accidentally. She stated that she herself had pointed the bruises out to the examining physician because of her concern.

Although her self-reported behaviour suggested that she was vigilant and concerned about the health and welfare of her daughter, she had only limited recognition of the serious worries about her own psychological vulnerabilities and wholly denied the possibility, as expressed by medical experts, that she had perpetrated the injuries herself. She appeared very calm and distant and did not seem to have engaged fully with the professionals involved, including myself. She was pleasant and co-operative but described her apprehension and unhappiness about undergoing a psychological assessment. Although she seemed candid in her description of the tensions within her marital relationship and her sense of abandonment when her husband left for business trips, there was no acknowledgement that she required help herself in order to cope with her feelings of inadequacy and distress. When I offered a referral for psychological counselling she rejected this suggestion outright, saying that she had no difficulties other than her worries about her ill child, who she felt was not receiving appropriate medical attention. She repeatedly asked for explanations regarding the organic cause of Harriet's breathing difficulties. Grace frequently flushed during the interviews and she conveyed an impression of being an injured party, who herself felt assaulted by the intrusive nature of the care proceedings assessments.

Grace had experienced great difficulty in separating from her own parents, having been a clingy child who had found it hard to socialise with her own peer group. It seemed to be that profound difficulties arising from separation were reactivated in her relationship with her daughter. Grace had left home at 16 to live with her first boyfriend, Mick, whom she had later married. Her descriptions of herself and her daughter suggested that she saw Harriet as being very like herself, and had an inadequate sense of differentiation from her. The enforced separation when Harriet was only 2 days old and needed to be placed under lights to treat her jaundice, the failure to breastfeed and the removal of the baby from her womb under Caesarean section were all events which appeared highly disturbing to Grace, who had viewed her baby as an extension of herself rather than a separate and ultimately autonomous individual. She had been pleased after all to have a girl, whom she described as 'just like me'. The early separations and difficulty in breastfeeding were distressing experiences for her, which she acknowledged, but she was unable to see any relevance in terms of the immediate consequences for her relationship with Harriet, or to discuss the features in her own background which had affected the development of her sense of identity.

Grace indicated that there had been strict physical punishment in her own childhood but felt that she wanted to 'put it behind her' and focus on the future. Her own mother had been a strict woman who had brought all five of the children up on her own, as the father had left the family when the youngest child was 8 months old. Grace described herself as having been a sickly child who had received little attention at home except during her periods of acute illness when she would enjoy the comfort and care of her usually busy and preoccupied mother. She described these occasions as the times when she felt most cared for and loved, and said that she had sometimes even exaggerated her symptoms in order to prolong her special status in the sick role. Investigation of her medical history revealed that her own mother had presented her to hospital on at least six occasions during her childhood, requesting urgent medical investigation for acute stomach pains and, on one occasion, breathing difficulties. Despite repeated investigation no medical explanation or diagnoses for Grace's conditions had been forthcoming.

The professionals had doubts about how to establish the cause of the injuries and considered the option of covert video surveillance in order to determine whether Grace was harming Harriet directly. It was decided not to pursue this option at the present time but to bear it in mind for the future, in the event that Harriet remained in Grace's care and received further injury. The child psychiatrist, the paediatrician and I remained of the opinion that Grace had harmed Harriet.

Throughout the duration of care proceedings, Grace and Mick had continued to deny responsibility for the injuries to Harriet who was placed with a paternal aunt under a full care order. She was, however, eventually returned to her parents' care, despite serious concerns expressed by the medical experts and myself. The social worker and guardian *ad litem* in the case did not consider Grace to pose a risk to her daughter and felt that rehabilitation was the most desirable option, fulfilling certain conditions specified in the Children's Act in that Harriet would be cared for by her natural parents. The care plan prepared by the local authority outlined conditions to be met by the parents to ensure Harriet's safety: these included attendance at a marital guidance clinic, regular meetings with the social worker, Harriet to attend a local authority nursery full time, and attendance at regular reviews at the nursery in which their parenting skills could be assessed. Mick had also changed jobs to enable him to be at home more and help Grace with the child-care.

One year after the care proceedings case had been closed Mick reported to his GP that he had, on one occasion before Harriet's removal from the household, seen Grace place her hands around Harriet's neck in what appeared to be a strangulation attempt but he had screamed at her to stop and she had. He had not disclosed this at the time because he had not wanted to prevent his beloved daughter from returning home, but had internally vowed to supervise the situation closely, and had felt guilty about his deception. He had presented to his GP with insomnia and it became clear that his anxiety about the significance of what he had witnessed played an important part in his sleep disturbance. Although the GP alerted the social services about this disclosure and requested a re-examination of Grace, the case was not reopened as Harriet did not present with evidence of any further injuries or difficulties. Grace denied that this incident had occurred and thought that Mick had been under stress, which resulted in his imagination playing tricks on him. This appeared to be an attempt to undermine him, but his statement, though less eloquent than hers, rang true in the light of the suspicions of the child-care professionals about her culpability.

It was most unfortunate that Grace had escaped formal recognition of her dangerous and distressing condition. The diagnosis of MSBP would not have shifted her status from that of perpetrator of abuse to that of victim through a psychological sleight of hand. If anything, the diagnosis would have underlined the extent of her disturbance and potential dangerousness. It was, however, possible that the involvement of the local authority, and the care order placed on Harriet, even in the absence of a formal diagnosis of Grace, would help her to resist the temptation to fabricate illness in her child, and that more support and vigilance offered by Mick helped to increase Harriet's safety in the home.

DISCUSSION

Despite the clear parallels between Grace's childhood experience of emotional deprivation and the significance of being ill for her, and what appeared to be her fabrication of symptoms and the production of injuries in her own daughter, with whom she strongly identified, these links were not consciously accessible to her. She acted out her psychological difficulties, with little capacity to verbalise her distress, and had only limited understanding of the physical and emotional needs of her daughter. She appeared to be presenting her daughter at the surgery to elicit the help and attention of the medical professionals, which seemed to mirror the only form of concerned parenting that she had experienced in her own childhood. Her method of coping with and defending against psychological distress was to split off her good and bad feelings; this was clearly reflected in her dual role as aggressor towards her child and apparent protector of her, the caring mother who brought her to the attention of the emergency services. The attention on her child satisfied a need in her to be cared for and responded to. It was possible that this frustrated and confined woman, whose husband placed harsh restrictions on her freedom, enjoyed the involvement with the team of medical experts, who would consult her about the etiology and manifestation of the symptoms. In this setting she could be important and involved.

Grace's flight from the possibility of treatment and consistent denial of her involvement in the creation and fabrication of Harriet's injuries reflected the difficulty of engaging her in psychological work which directly addressed her own problems. It appeared that she relied on an indirect means of getting help for herself and could not articulate her concerns in her own voice. It was possible that she could not actually distinguish her infant's needs from her own because of her distorted perception of herself and her baby, and that she so identified with the helpless and damaged child that she could not recognise the cruelty of her actions or the extent of culpability in endangering Harriet's life. Her behaviour was undoubtedly dangerous and violent but she was not diagnosed formally with MSBP. She had powerfully projected her internal splitting into the team of child-care professionals, who were polarised into those who saw Grace as a danger, and those who viewed her as a competent mother, victimised by the over-protectiveness of the local authority. Eventually the guardian *ad litem* and the health visitor, who championed the parents, convinced the social worker to draw up a care plan that would result in rehabilitation of Harriet to her parents' care. The parents readily accepted this care plan. I strongly opposed this plan but was, at least, able to refer the family to the child and family psychologist who agreed to see them; the child psychiatrist had refused to see them until there was an admission of culpability for the injuries.

Clinical interview had suggested that Grace had convinced herself that she had not actually produced Harriet's symptoms through physical injury and through fabrication of symptoms which were never seen by others, as though the power of her need to create this situation also produced a form of dissociation in her. In this emotionally distanced state she seemed to believe that her child was genuinely ill and that she was the concerned and vigilant mother requesting help; the knowledge of her own role in producing symptoms could be denied, allowing her to engage in the drama that she had created. Grace did not seem aware of the pretence and fantasy of this scenario and had fully entered into the drama. At some level she must have been aware of the lie upon which the medical crisis rested but her powers of dissociation were such that she could keep this knowledge at bay. Grace's difficulty in linking her past and present behaviour, and her denial of her own role in creating illness in her child, appeared to have different psychological origins. As previously suggested, it appeared to reflect a profound dissociation and capacity to split off the aggressive part of herself. It was also possible that her current role as protective parent, despite the murderousness that she had directed towards the infant, mirrored her own experience of being deceived and mistreated by her own mother whose care had been inconsistent but who had essentially acted the part of the caring mother when Grace was ill, perhaps genuinely believing herself to be one. Grace had herself also been subject to a deeply confusing experience of apparent care but actual neglect, within the context of being presented for care at medical settings. Grace may have perceived her mother's vigilance towards her when ill to be a kind of lie, in that the concern was only short-lived and directed towards overt injury. Concern for her emotional development and abuse was clearly lacking in Grace's own childhood and in the care provided by her own mother. It was not clear whether Grace's own mother had actively induced symptoms in her or had simply exaggerated her symptoms, possibly using her to express her own somatisation disorder. It was clear that she had been emotionally distant from Grace except when Grace was ill, when she would rally to her bedside and act out the part of a fully devoted mother.

Relevance of this case to MSBP in general

Close consideration of features of Grace's background and psychological functioning can help to provide a general understanding of the development of MSBP. Her own experience of physical abuse in the form of harsh chastisement in childhood, her failure to develop a sense of her own separate identity, and her impoverished relationship with her mother were important factors in the development of her capacity to understand and relate to her own daughter as a separate entity. Research which identifies the importance of attachment difficulties for later personality disorders highlights the centrality of early bonding and the development of essential psychological capacities, such as a sense of self (Fonagy and Target, 1995). The intergenerational transmission of such difficulties has also been well described in relation to early disorders of attachment. Jones et al. (2000) also identify attachment disturbances between parent and child as one of the key factors in the development of what they term MSBP abuse, citing other factors including illness or illness behaviour in the fabricator's childhood, somatisation in her adolescence, capacity for dissociation, personality disorders, self-harm, somatisation to self, foetal MSBP abuse and postnatal depression as other important aspects of the development of this disorder.

Grace was split off from the part of herself that could function as a caring and protective mother and seemed to have projected this caring and thinking part of herself into others, specifically into the parental figures of the medical professionals. Having distanced herself from this good object she then had to gain access to it, which she achieved through generating and fabricating physical ailments in her child, with whom she strongly identified. She could then present her child and herself to the medical services and would alternately identify with the injured and deprived baby, whose needs must be taken seriously, and with the competent adults who could diagnose and treat these injuries. Although part of her wanted to be like the adults who could meet the needs of the child, another part of her wanted to be distant from them, to retain secret knowledge that made their efforts ridiculous. Her hostility was born out of unmet dependency needs.

There was an element of aggression in what appeared to be Grace's deceit in relation to the injuries. Meadow (1977) and Adshead (1997) describe the thrill which MSBP mothers derive from tricking the professionals. Grace's motivations appeared more complex and ambivalent than this; she appeared to have convinced herself that there was an organic cause of Harriet's illness. Her psychological manoeuvres, as she operated both as vigilant semi-professional and as destructive saboteur, seemed to occur at an unconscious level and to meet profound psychic needs, involving a great deal of self- and other deception. The elements of splitting, dissociation, somatisation, lack of differentiation between herself and her child, and failure to distinguish between fantasy and reality were all evident in Grace's complex presentation. Her intelligence, motivated by her underlying disturbance, enabled her to engineer situations in which she could appear as saviour, although, in fact, she was the perpetrator of injury. At an unconscious level Grace was requesting recognition of the reality of her own despair, deprivation and capacity for violence. A psychodynamic formulation of Grace's behaviour would highlight her unconscious request to be caught and 'found out', to escape from the compulsive cycle of her perverse behaviour.

Clinical response: denial of female violence

The response of the professionals included the splitting of the experts into those who considered the mother to be a risk to her daughter and those who refused to accept or recognise the extent of her violence. Grace's apparent competence and the commonly held belief in the natural tendency of women to be caring mothers, with protective maternal instincts, were two crucial factors which prevented the truth from being seen in this case. That an articulate, attractive and apparently co-operative woman could also be someone who systematically abused her child was too threatening and unfamiliar a notion to be easily understood and accepted. Only the medical and psychological professionals who had seen the mother for a limited number of assessment sessions could hold this possibility in mind, while those who had more direct and long-term contact with the mother became much more fixed in their views about which one or other of these aspects of the same woman was her 'true self'. It became impossible for those involved with Grace to retain a sense of her ambivalence towards her daughter, and her powerful internal conflict. She seemed to polarise the professionals, reflecting the split in the good and bad aspects of herself. Her inability to integrate splits in her personality was reflected in the professionals' failure to have a balanced view of her.

There was no real possibility of an integrated team view of her, at least initially, because Grace's intrapsychic split was dramatically mirrored in the attitudes and beliefs of the professionals involved in the case. Despite the overwhelming medical evidence stating that the injuries were likely to have been non-accidental and perpetrated by the mother and the opinion that she had fabricated some of the baby's symptoms, particularly in relation to breathing difficulties, the local authority was determined to rehabilitate the child to her parents' care. Neither the father nor the mother admitted any responsibility for the injuries and both remained adamant that Grace was an exceptionally competent mother. My recommendation was that rehabilitation should begin only once an acceptable explanation for the injuries and alleged breathing difficulties had been forthcoming: this was ignored.

The clear voice of the psychological and medical experts was silenced, evoking the image of the gagged baby whose cries were unheard because she was not even allowed the freedom to cry. This gagging of the medical professionals in the face of apparent maternal competence reflected both the seductive and convincing power of this dissociated, split-off and disturbed mother and a profound denial by other involved professionals of female violence in general, particularly in an articulate and attractive young woman, 'a good mother'.

In understanding how to detect and treat mothers who may have MSBP it is important to be aware of the intense countertransference responses which such women evoke in those involved in the case. There is a powerful dynamic in operation in which the professionals may be silenced so that all potentially vigilant carers become like the helpless child whose cries will not be responded to. In this sense the professionals become impotent and negligent. In this dangerous and difficult-to-treat syndrome, the mother is able to rid herself of the experience of being let down and lied to by setting up a situation where her infant (part of herself) is brought for help but where the true source of danger is disguised and the apparent protector is actually the persecutor. Those who might actually be able to help, the medical professionals, are sabotaged in their attempts and so share the experience of being useless, humiliated and impotent. This powerfully illustrates the psychic defence of projective identification.

The single source of hope in this disturbing and confusing syndrome is that through the presentation of the damaged infant at the surgery the mothers are effectively bringing into the public domain the evidence of private abuse and betrayal which often characterises their own backgrounds. They are alerting professionals that they are in danger of continuing this pattern by re-enacting it. In this sense MSBP creates a situation in which an individual adult's distress and abuse is made public through the presentation of an apparently ill or damaged child for medical attention. The use of a child's body as a medium of communication is clearly perverse.

Maternal perversion: failure of differentiation

In the case described it was significant that the onset of the injuries coincided with Harriet's increased mobility, expressing in concrete terms her increasing independence from her mother. Grace's difficulty in differentiating between herself and her child, and in finding separation very threatening and potentially unmanageable, became particularly intense as her baby began to crawl. Abusive mothers characteristically experience serious difficulties in separation and individuation, both in terms of their own relationships with their mothers and with their daughters. Grace found it intolerable that her infant could now, physically at least, move away from her. The earlier experiences of unexpected separation from Harriet, and disrupted bonding with her, may have been painfully evoked by this development. Indeed, the act of injuring the child directly, or fabricating symptoms of her illness, which appeared to be the case in terms of the inexplicable breathing difficulties, may have been Grace's attempt to assert her authority over her child and make a bid for her body. It expressed hostility towards her daughter's physical and emotional separateness and an attempt to merge the boundaries between herself and her child, whom she considered, narcissistically, to be an extension of herself.

When the female child is targeted in cases of MSBP there is a clear illustration of the underlying psychological process of identification between mother and child, and a failure to recognise and negotiate the fact of separation and differentiation. The calling-in of the third party, the medical professionals, to protect the child may be an unconscious recognition of the need for intervention and a symbolic attempt to enlist the help and protection of the absent father. Despite the danger and despair evident in the expression of MSBP it nonetheless represents a solution, though maladaptive and destructive, to a problem: the mother does not know how to relate to or protect her infant from her own murderous fantasies about her. This formulation does not deny the mother's capacity for violence against her child, who, like herself, is viewed as the appropriate target for injury and revenge, and one of the only provinces of power and control for her. Nonetheless, there may be a profound ambivalence in the enactment of these murderous fantasies and an unconscious request for containment, understanding and control. The element of secrecy takes its excitement and power from the fear of discovery as well as the unconscious desire for such discovery, and the possibility of recognition and understanding. This may be masked even to the abusive mother herself, who, when confronted with reality, may deny her role in creating and fabricating symptoms in her child. Her massive self-deception may protect her from recognising the violence of her own actions.

MSBP AND FALSE ALLEGATIONS OF SEXUAL ABUSE

Barker and Howell (1994) accept the classifications of what Rand (1989) called 'classical MSBP', related to apparent medical and physical complaints in children, and apply the categories to cases where mothers make false allegations of sexual abuse of their children.These sexual abuse allegations are fabricated either when the mother was convinced that it occurred or when she actually induced physical symptoms in the child. The diagnosis would not be considered applicable when there were clear cases of secondary gain or conscious manipulation involved in making such allegations, i.e. divorce and custody battles. In cases where women falsely allege sexual abuse of their children in what appears to be genuine and conscious belief, it is clear that the dynamic motivations parallel those found in mothers with 'classical MSBP', i.e. inadequate separation from the child so that an almost delusional identification occurs, vicarious enjoyment of entering the care-giving situation, failure of parental empathy or possible personality or factitious disorders in the mother which contribute to her bizarre and apparently inexplicable treatment of her child. Again, the high prevalence of female perpetrators in MSBP may suggest that it is 'a women's disorder tied to their expression of power and negative emotion within their social roles' (Barker and Howell, 1994: 500). Barker and Howell describe MSBP in cases of false allegations of childhood sexual abuse as 'contemporary type MSBP' and acknowledge that, although uncommon, it is a disorder that demands attention because of its potential harm to children. The authors describe the presence of 'classical MSBP' symptoms in the mother as the best predictor of this disorder and stress the need for physical protection of the child to be provided should there be evidence for this diagnosis.

In the light of this expansion of the notion of MSBP, the degree of emotional abuse which either 'classical' or 'contemporary type MSBP' inflict on a child should not be underestimated.The association between Munchausen's syndrome and MSBP indicates the intergenerational transmission of the disorder and the mother's concrete identification both with her own body and with that of her child – both are instruments of power and control. The mother is staging a profound deception against the medical and legal professionals, her child or children, and ultimately against a rational and truth-seeking part of herself. There are potentially many victims in any manifestation of MSBP and there is intrapsychic as well as interpersonal damage.

CRITERIA FOR DISTINGUISHING MSBP

The differential diagnosis

A central difficulty for professionals involved in child protection cases or working with suspected perpetrators of physical injury towards children is the complicated clinical picture which MSBP presents, and the complexity of making the diagnosis, as it relates not only to the etiology of the symptoms sustained by the child, but also to the psychiatric status of the mother. The diagnosis in relation to the nature of the child's injuries must be made in accordance with the medical evidence available following examination of the child but this, in cases of MSBP, will have been heavily distorted by the mother, who has usually presented the child for examination.

Consideration of the clinical presentation of the mother may require the involvement of professionals skilled in the evaluation of psychological difficulties in adults. The medical evidence may subtly shift from attention to the abuse suffered by the child to the psychological 'illness' suffered by the mother, which may reflect a tendency to pathologise and excuse female violence and to view maternal abuse as a product of illness rather than as aggression.

There are many difficulties inherent in making a diagnosis of MSBP, and the need for corroborative and independent evidence is of paramount importance. At a practical level the diagnosis of MSBP is notoriously difficult to make and the risk of false diagnosis and overlooking a 'genuine' or organic illness in the child is great; there is an additional problem in that the secrecy of the maternal abuse means that covert techniques may need to be used to uncover it, which generates ethical as well as technical difficulties for practitioners.

Morley (1995) argues that the diagnostic criteria suggested by Meadow are non-specific and may therefore lead to false diagnoses of MSBP as well as detracting medical attention from the nature of the injuries sustained by the child or children. He notes that for each diagnostic criteria or 'pointer' there are situations in which the presence of such a factor does not necessarily point to MSBP and can lead to unnecessary suspicion in relation to concerned and/or anxious parents who may appear to 'fabricate' symptoms when they are actually *exaggerating* certain aspects of their child's physical presentation, either because of their genuine ignorance of medical matters or their high level of anxiety in relation to their child's health.

Some of the indicators that the presenting symptoms may be fabricated are similarly non-specific, and hence open to misinterpretation. The factors which have been identified as signs of fabrication include the following: inconsistent histories taken from different observers; symptoms and signs that are unusual or bizarre and inconsistent with known pathophysiology; observations and investigations inconsistent with parental reports or the condition of the child; treatments which are ineffective or poorly tolerated; symptoms or signs which begin only in the presence of one parent or carer. These indicators are not conclusive evidence of fabrication. It is clear that the interpretation of inconsistency in medical histories depends on the perspective of the doctor taking the history as well as on how the history was obtained, i.e. what questions were asked and which areas were highlighted. The determination of 'unusual signs or symptoms' also depends, in part, on the judgement of the doctor as well as on the observational accuracy of the parent or carer. Similarly, there may be a benign explanation for the fact that symptoms began in the presence of one parent or carer, in that many concerned mothers are with their ill child all the time (Morley, 1995).

Morley's caution in relation to practical concerns about the MSBP diagnosis highlights the need for medical professionals to focus on the child's injuries and illness rather than the mother's mental state and to bear in mind the likelihood that *most* mothers who bring children to the surgery when they believe them to be ill are acting out of ordinary concern and appealing in a trusting way to a medical authority. It is nonetheless significant that in a small minority of cases of presentations of ill children the illnesses will either have been fabricated or actually induced by a parent, and in the vast majority of cases this parent is the child's mother. It is essential that those involved in child protection are able to acknowledge this possibility and bear it in mind when considering cases of childhood illness that appear to defy medical explanation, despite the apparent concern and dedication of the mothers. Education about the presentation of mothers with MSBP and the dynamics that they can create within staff teams could help in accurate detection of this potentially lethal disorder.

IMPLICATIONS OF THE MSBP DIAGNOSIS

The usefulness of the diagnosis of MSBP has been questioned and its validity challenged (Morley, 1995). A central concern is that the diagnosis of MSBP gives no indication about what happened to the child. Instead of the nature of the abuse being elaborated upon, i.e. suffocation, poisoning, putting blood in the urine, false reporting of fits or other difficulties, the mother's state of mind becomes the central focus of investigation. The abuser becomes identified as a patient who is 'suffering from MSBP' rather than a perpetrator of particular physical and emotional abuse on a child, who is the real victim. This subtle reframing of the situation facilitates the process described by Busfield (1996) in which the 'madness' of women locates them outside the realm of aggression and delinquency, shifting the emphasis in sentencing from punishment to treatment. The term *MSBP abuse* is helpful in emphasising the destructive aspects of MSBP for child victims, rather than simply identifying the parents as patients.

A full understanding of the perverse and destructive dynamics inherent in MSBP may lead to enforced separation of mother and child, which, although apparently cruel, may actually be essential in ensuring the child's physical and psychic survival. At one level the mother, aware of her own limitations, may symbolically be asking for the care of the child to be taken from her, to protect the child from her own murderous impulses.

Meadow poignantly describes a case in which a mother had given her child toxic doses of salt, resulting in the death of the child. A necropsy revealed mild gastric erosions indicating chemical ingestion. The mother learned of the results of this investigation, wrote to the doctors, thanked them for their care and then attempted suicide (Meadow, 1977). The link between her homicidal and suicidal urges was explicit. She had first made murderous attacks on her child and then turned this rage on to herself, attempting suicide. The confusion in the mother's mind between herself and her child is clear in the sequence of events. An alternative explanation for her behaviour would be that the mother had not really intended that the child should die, but hoped that she would stay alive, allowing the deceptive game to continue. When the child died the pretence could not continue and the psychic functions that it had served for the mother were removed; at this point she became seriously depressed, finding her own life unbearable. The death of the child may also have forced her to confront the reality of her own aggressive impulses. The subsequent guilt might have triggered her desire to kill herself in an act of remorse, coupled with grief. It is also possible that the mother became suicidal because she was 'discovered', i.e. her poisoning of her child was revealed in the postmortem. This case illustrates the strong link between suicidal and homicidal urges in MSBP mothers generally, who have an inadequate sense of differentiation from their children, expressed through their abuse of their own and their children's bodies.

MANAGEMENT OF MSBP ABUSE

The diagnosis of this disorder should alert the physician to contact the appropriate agencies so that child protection measures can be put in place. These may include the removal of the child from the parent's home and possible long-term provision for care, psychiatric assessment of and treatment for the child, and consolidation of the child's medical care with one medical centre, which should be fully aware of the history of the medical presentation. The somatising mother may 'doctor shop' until medical intervention is obtained for the child, and the fact that this disorder is often associated with fatal maltreatment must be borne in mind by the relevant agencies; it is for this reason that attempts should be made to confine the child's medical care to one agency or centre, which is fully aware of the nature of the maternal disturbance and the possible implications for the child of her disorder. The practical problems of detection, treatment and prognosis of MSBP are addressed in the recently published text, *Munchausen Syndrome by Proxy Abuse* (edited by M. Eminson and R.J. Postlethwaite), a comprehensive guide, which goes into considerable detail in these areas. The legal and therapeutic aspects of these cases are dealt with sensitively and clearly, outlining those issues most relevant to practitioners and clinicians attempting to engage victims and perpetrators of MSBP. This important text outlines the developmental pathways leading to MSBP abuse.

TREATMENT CONSIDERATIONS AND PROGNOSIS FOR MSBP

Is there any point in recommending psychological treatment for someone diagnosed with MSBP in the face of denial of responsibility for injuries? If treatment is considered should it be individual, family-based or treatment of the couple? What theoretical perspective is most effective in the treatment of MSBP? Can a mother with MSBP be helped to relate to her daughter as a separate entity? These are crucial questions for child protection specialists to address.

One of the most important factors in the accurate and early detection of MSBP is the recognition by professionals that maternal violence exists and that it can occur even where there is apparent maternal competence. In conducting accurate risk assessment it is essential that involved professionals gather as much information as possible in order to generate a comprehensive understanding of the factors which led to the mother abusing her child in a particular way. This task may be more difficult in cases of MSBP in that some women will never admit that they have deliberately produced or fabricated symptoms in their children; hence the justification for the use of covert video surveillance techniques (Cordess, 1998). It is important that professionals retain an objective view about the probable cause of the injuries and do not allow sentimental and idealised views of motherhood to affect their judgement and allow a child to continue to be at serious risk.

Some child-care experts argue that rehabilitation of a child to the home in which abuse has occurred can only be instituted in cases where acceptable explanations for non-accidental injuries have been given (Weiner, 1998). Other experts argue that only through engaging the family in treatment can denial be challenged and shifted and that to disrupt the bonds between a child and her family is to do harm to the entire family. Denial has been recognised as a major obstacle to therapeutic change in families where abuse has occurred. Trowell (1997) suggests that if greater levels of confidentiality existed in relation to child abuse, the problem of denial could be reduced and more families successfully engaged in treatment; such therapeutic alliance could potentially reduce the risk of re-abuse and enable families to stay together. This risk assessment can be undertaken when the child has been removed from the abusive situation, according to procedures determined by a child protection conference, which would be convened to bring together the relevant professional groups required to conduct such an evaluation, and ultimately construct a child-care plan in which risk of future harm was minimised. Berg and Jones (1999) were able to follow up a small number of families in which MSBP abuse had occurred. Ten of the thirteen families for whom treatment had been possible were reunited following the child and family intervention. They found that

> overall, the children had done well in terms of their development, growth and psychological adjustment . . . Berg and Jones (1999) cautiously conclude that family reunification is feasible for a subgroup of cases of MSBP abuse, but only where there can be long-term follow-up involving continuing health monitoring, social casework, and psychological treatment.
>
> (Jones *et al.*, 2000:293)

Whether or not treatment and rehabilitation are indicated in the face of consistent denial of abuse is not a issue about which a general policy has been formulated. Individual factors in the case, including the nature of the abuse inflicted, and the demonstrated level of co-operation by the parents, appear to be the key elements in determining outcomes for abused children. In cases of maternal abuse the threshold for removing children from their mother's care has been shown to be higher than in cases where a male has been the perpetrator of abuse. The role of the mother as nurturing and caring appears to be so entrenched in social perceptions and expectations that it persists even in the face of stark and alarming evidence that she can be deceptive, violent and dangerous to her own offspring.

Livingstone (1987) describes the problems in treating abusing parents if they have somatisation disorder and therefore require regular supervision and management by a primary care physician and notes that individuals who have MSBP, with or without somatisation disorder, are likely to be resistant to psychotherapy. Important factors to consider when determining treatment include the duration and medical severity of the abuse, 'whether acknowledged or denied by the parent, and the extent to which features of sociopathy are present' (Livingstone, 1987:214). He argues that a psychodynamic formulation of the basis of the abuse is also potentially helpful; such possible formulations as cited in the literature include respite from parenting responsibilities, vicarious receipt of caregiving, and 'symbolic re-creation of a previous loss'. It is clear in such cases that the mother's sense of identity may be fragile, and the boundaries between her and her child blurred. Livingstone notes: 'In any case, the first priority in treatment should be protection of the child' (1987:214). A psychodynamic treatment of the mother should be aimed at addressing the aggressive and deprived child within; facilitating recognition of this neglected and destructive aspect may help her to develop the ego strength to function in a maternal capacity and gain a sense of her child as a separate entity.

PSYCHOTHERAPY WITH MSBP MOTHERS

The work of the Cassell Hospital, a therapeutic community in Richmond, Surrey, provides a unique opportunity to engage violent and sexually abusive families in psychotherapy over an extended period of time, and to assess the capacity of these families to care for children and respond to treatment. Coombe (1995) describes successful treatment of a mother with MSBP to the point where her child remained in her care following discharge from the Cassell Hospital. Kennedy describes the history of the work at the Cassell Hospital with mothers with postnatal depression in the 1950s and the development of treatment of families in which mothers display MSBP, stating:

> At times, the children were seen as objects to be used by the others for mere comfort for themselves. The mothers who completed the treatment programme revealed powerful and primitive aggressive fantasies, centred around both their own bodies and their children, possibly related to their own childhood experiences of being abused. At times they were close to collapse and disintegration, and needed considerable amounts of help and support of the kind which seems able to be provided only in an in-patient setting . . . Treatment was prolonged in two of these [three cases] requiring nearly two years before the families were considered safe enough to return to their communities . . . Crucial to change was the capacity of the parents, particularly the mothers, both to face their own destructive feelings and to experience feelings of dependency, towards both staff and other people, without collapsing.

(Kennedy, 1997:126)

Forensic psychotherapy, as well as the individual and family therapy approaches used at the Cassell Hospital, offers a framework for understanding MSBP and a treatment approach for the mother, to help her recognise her underlying difficulties.

CONCLUSION

Psychological understanding of maternal motivation should be comprehensive and recognise aggressive impulses in mothers towards their own children. It has been objected that such an understanding may actually be abused to distort the truth, to exonerate the abuser by minimising her aggression and portraying her as a victim. This accusation rests, to some extent, on the false dichotomy in which victims and abusers are seen as mutually exclusive. This objection does, however, raise an important issue about the possibility that an over-emphasis on a mother's or carer's psychological vulnerability can shift attention away from her aggression and potential dangerousness, presenting a false picture. A psychological model which emphasises the link between aggression and victimisation will make these connections explicit and explain how it is that damaged and depressed women can pose a risk to children, moving from victim to victimiser. This model may well meet with resistance, in part because of the strength of idealisations of motherhood.

The denial of female violence is evident in the ready acceptance of psychological disturbance in women to the point where their culpability and aggression are overlooked. In the case of MSBP this can be seen in the professionals' shift of emphasis from careful identification of the types of abuse suffered by the child-victim to the state of mind of the mother who has engineered the situation. It is essential to bear in mind that the mother is a perpetrator of abuse who, because of her own psychological disturbance or unmet needs, has either fabricated the symptoms or perpetrated injuries to induce illness according to her own internal script. Attempts should be made to uncover the nature of this internal narrative in order to protect the child and help the mother, if there is to be a possibility of the child remaining in her mother's care. In order for child protection to occur it is essential to recognise the possibility of female abuse. As Welldon notes, 'it has been extremely difficult for society to acknowledge that women can sexually or otherwise abuse their children, and this has left children unprotected' (1996:177); this denial and 'conspiracy of silence' also spreads to professionals.

There is a dramatic element to the MSBP scenario in which the mother becomes a highly significant and valued person on the ward, where her concerns and the health of her child are taken very seriously. The ward becomes the theatre where her own unresolved emotional dramas are played out and her child, in this situation, becomes a means to an end and an extension of herself. This reflects Welldon's notion of female perversion in relation to children where the child becomes the narcissistic extension of the self and the whole body is used in the perversion. In this sense MSBP has strong parallels with self-harm, in which psychic conflicts are literally embodied and fought out on the flesh. In MSBP the child's body is used as the mother's own, and her violence is directed against herself as well as her child. Her thinking is concrete and just as she somatises her own psychological pain she also projects this on to her child, either in fantasy (fabricating symptoms) or through physical violence, overstepping the body barrier and actually inducing illness in her child.

In order to understand this and other forms of child abuse it is necessary to consider and elaborate the symbolic function of these acts and the meaning of this performance for the mother. The communicative function of maternal physical abuse should not be overlooked and can sometimes be elucidated by reflecting on the institutional response to suspected abuse. The mother's psychic conflicts may be mirrored in the divisions within the team, who may fail to recognise opposing aspects of her personality. When the possibility of abuse cannot even be entertained by child protection specialists and other professionals, a dangerous situation may be allowed to continue. It may only be the existence of video evidence which can bring to light this perverse and dangerous form of abuse; I suggest that the invasion of privacy produced by the use of covert surveillance is a lesser evil than the possibility of potentially fatal maltreatment of a child. The denial of this danger is a frightening consequence of false beliefs about the impossibility of female violence.

Chapter 3

Maternal physical abuse

A young single mother holds her screaming child in her arms; sensing her own distress, she realises that there is no one to hold her, to make her feel better. Her baby has unwittingly become the source of her old pain, once again revived. She needs to stop the pain. This pain is her child screaming but she can no longer feel it to be her child: this mother is back in the nightmare of her own childhood. The baby has become her tormentor, the one who hurts, whose screaming needs make the young woman feel she is bad and useless. She can no longer see her baby, for it has become the 'monster' she once was, that had to be controlled, to be beaten into shape. *She becomes her own mother, her own terrifying parent with whom she has identified, as so many victims do.* In her raging pain this woman smashes the baby's head until the crying stops. In the silence that follows, a mother may discover herself to be a murderer . . . The child she wanted to love seems dead. At this point her mind comes to the rescue. She 'forgets'. She 'splits off' the memory of her past and the memory of what she has just done to her little girl, a child she probably wants to love and protect. It may be that this time, and possibly the next, her child survives her destructive assaults.

(De Zuleta, 1993:4–5, added emphasis)

To deny female violence is to deny female agency. In the passage cited above, De Zuleta describes how the reactivation of traumatic memories can lead to violence towards an infant, and how dissociation, as a psychological defence against pain, can protect the violent mother from full understanding or recognition of her actions. This passage illustrates the nature of reactivated pain and demonstrates how mothers who were themselves neglected re-enact destructive patterns with their own children. The context in which this occurs is one in which the mother is young and single, by which I understand De Zuleta to be referring to a social environment of isolation, and possible economic hardship. Although I do not specifically explore social factors in the genesis of physical abuse of children, in which the intervening variable is maternal depression, I consider that the social environment plays a significant role in contributing to the sense of despair and abandonment which can lead to maternal physical abuse of children. There is a wealth of significant literature and empirical research related to social factors in the development of depression (Brown and Harris, 1978; Brown et al., 1996; Harris and Brown, 1996) and the intergenerational transmission of neglect, which also emphasises the interaction between early experiences of disturbed attachment experiences and later vulnerability to depression (Bifulco and Moran, 1998; Harris and Bifulco, 1991). My emphasis in this chapter is not, however, on the social context of maternal depression and physical abuse of children, but on the inner world of the mother who abuses: I explore the dynamics of maternal physical abuse. Clearly emotional abuse and neglect of children may be interwoven with physical abuse. I focus my discussion on actual acts of violence, on the premiss that such violence itself reflects an emotionally unavailable and abusive relationship with the child, in which it becomes the receptacle of unwanted feelings.

In chapters 1 and 2 I explored the nature of maternal sexual abuse and Munchausen's syndrome by proxy. In this chapter I focus on the expression of violence through direct physical abuse, caused by shaking, hitting, punching, kicking, twisting, beating with weapons or other instruments, or burning. The physical abuse of children by their mothers may bring their private violence into the public arena, particularly when social services' involvement generates the introduction of legal proceedings. Physical abuse often remains hidden from view, occurring in the privacy of the home. As in the case of sexual abuse the victims may be too frightened or ashamed to let anyone know about the abuse. They may also have come to accept physical abuse and cruelty as normal, or believe that they deserve to be treated violently. The nature of physical abuse can vary greatly from woman to woman and can range from sadistic violence to a unique loss of control. The violence may reflect systematic physical chastisement for misbehaviour or an uncharacteristic explosion of anger and frustration which is born out of depression, social isolation and a sense of complete helplessness. In this chapter I provide a case example of maternal violence against an infant by an isolated and depressed young mother, echoing De Zuleta's description of maternal violence.

Maternal physical abuse may reflect the collusion of a dependent woman with an abusive partner, who insists on the parental right, and even duty, to administer severe physical punishment to a child. She may mete out this chastisement in order to placate her violent partner even if she does not herself agree with the use of harsh punishment. It may occur in conjunction with occasions when she fails to protect her children from physical abuse by her partner out of fear of the consequences of challenging him, or because of her difficulty in recognising the emotional and physical consequences of such abuse. Such passivity can result in children suffering serious neglect and cruelty and may reflect the mother's own state of helplessness and intimidation, within the context of domestic violence in the relationship.

In some cases the mother has herself experienced serious physical and/or emotional abuse in childhood and finds it difficult to comfort her child or provide containment for its demands and rages. This difficulty may be rooted in memories and experiences to which the mother does not have conscious access. The passage introducing this chapter describes how the mother's identification with the inconsolable infant reactivates her own intolerable experiences in childhood, producing violence as an attempt to annihilate the source of reactivated pain; after she lashes out the mother's 'mind comes to the rescue', in that the psychic defence of dissociation protects her against 'the memory of her past and the memory of what she has just done to her little girl, a child she probably wants to love and protect'. The irrevocable link between the mother and her child, and the failure of psychic differentiation between them, play a major role in the genesis of maternal violence against children, as does the identification of the mother with the 'terrifying parent' whom she has become. In this powerful passage De Zuleta describes some of the most important dynamics in and conditions of maternal physical abuse, which I will further illustrate and explore.

Kennedy (1997) distinguishes between three major and overlapping categories of female abuser:

> the 'active abuser', who is the main instigator and perpetrator; the 'complicit abuser', or 'inciter', who takes part in the attack but does not instigate it directly, and instead incites the partner to abuse; and the 'denier', who does not want to believe that their partner has abused their child or children. The denier, as with the others, may also be intimidated by the partner. But with the really difficult cases, intimidation is often fairly mutual . . . But, in the end, it is likely that these distinctions do not have that much explanatory value; furthermore, they might also give a false impression that being an active abuser is somehow much worse than, say, giving your child to

someone else to abuse. There is not much to choose in terms of horror between different ways of torturing a child.

(Kennedy, 1997:109–10)

Reviews of the perpetrators of abuse conducted in the United States have found that mothers or 'mother substitutes' were found to be responsible for 47.6 per cent of the physical abuse cases studied while 39.2 per cent of the incidents involved fathers or father substitutes (Gil, 1970). This is consistent with more recent research which found females to be more likely to use physical violence against children than males (Gelles, 1980). Other studies have found that there is approximately a 50/50 split between mothers and fathers as perpetrators of physical abuse of children, e.g. Anderson *et al.*, 1983. Ninety per cent of abuse incidents take place in the child's own home (Garbarino, 1976).

The most interesting finding of these studies is not that women assault children more than men do, but that when women are violent, the aims or targets of their violence are far more likely to be members of their family, including their children. That is, women are far less likely to be violent than men in general, and when they are violent they target their own bodies and those of their children. It is a shocking statistic that so much violence is directed at children by the people into whose care they are entrusted. This fact must challenge the myth of the all-nurturing, protective mother.

Physical injuries to children are often detected by general practitioners or paediatricians who are asked their opinion about whether such injuries could have occurred by accident. The existence of injuries deemed non-accidental is an important indicator of physical abuse of a child and a medical practitioner who has detected such injuries has a statutory duty to inform social services. Clinicians who are informed that child abuse is occurring have a similar responsibility. The local authority will then convene a case conference to determine whether the child should be placed on the At Risk Register, to be reviewed and monitored.

The 1989 Children Act sets out the various statutes and orders available to Courts, outlining the criteria for determining whether a child has suffered, or is at risk of suffering, significant harm in its parent's care to the extent that the local authority can institute care proceedings. For a comprehensive, clear and highly informative account of the 1989 Children Act, the interested reader is referred to Allen's excellent 1996 book, *Making Sense of the Children Act*. I will briefly summarise the main points of the Act, particularly in relation to the involvement of the forensic or child psychologist in such cases.

Determining whether a child has suffered significant harm is the decision of the Courts, who may consider expert evidence in making this decision. Section 31 in Part IV of the Act defines 'harm' to mean ill-treatment or the impairment of physical or mental health or development. Harm may relate to physical, emotional or sexual abuse, and impairment of development covers any area of neglect, including poor nutrition, hygiene or emotional care (Herbert, 1996). The Act does not, however, define what counts as 'significant' harm and mental health professionals may be asked to clarify this issue. In cases where there is concern about the possibility that a child may be suffering significant harm or impairment of development, care proceedings by the local authority may be initiated, and the case will then come before the Courts. A court, either at magistrate's level of family proceedings, County Court or a Family Division of the High Court, will decide whether or not to accept the local authority's application. This application may be supported or challenged by expert evidence from psychiatrists and psychologists who have assessed either the parents, the children, or both. Mental health professionals as well as medical practitioners are often asked to act as expert witnesses and testify in court on the basis of the written reports they have provided, addressing the questions of whether parents pose risk to their children, and whether the children can be considered to have suffered significant harm.

The Court will ultimately decide whether the application by the local authority is acceptable, that is, whether the criteria for granting a care or supervision order have been met. Section 1(1) of The Children Act 1989 states that 'when a court determines any question with respect to the upbringing of a child . . . the child's welfare shall be the court's paramount consideration'. There are different levels of care orders which can be granted by the Courts: the most stringent is the full care order, in which parental responsibility is held by the local authority. There are some cases where the child is rehabilitated to the parents under a care order; in these cases the local authority and the parents share parental responsibility, although ultimately the local authority can dictate placement of the child. In cases where the criteria for the granting of a care order have not been met, a supervision order may be granted. Under a supervision order the child continues to be monitored and seen by a social worker, but parental responsibility is not undertaken by the local authority. This is a less interventionist order, and it has been suggested that this order does not, in practice, have anything like the protective capacity of a care order, although it may have the benefit of facilitating co-operation between parents and the local authority (Allen, 1996). Before final hearings occur children can be placed on interim care orders or interim supervision orders and, at times of emergency, can be removed from their parents under an emergency protection order.

In the context of this complex legal system, forensic and child clinical psychologists and psychiatrists are often asked to act as independent experts, offering clinical opinions and recommendations to the Court. This is clearly not a simple task, and one which may be taxing emotionally as well as intellectually. The expert is sometimes asked to assess the parents' suitability for treatment and this question, posed in the context of care proceedings, carries an urgency which may interfere with the usual clinical considerations regarding suitability for psychotherapeutic intervention. Parents may attend these interviews with the expectation that the nature of this expert opinion will shape the decisions regarding their children's future, and, indeed, the 'expert' may also feel that he or she has been placed in this omniscient position, to help make decisions which may feel cruel and punitive. The ultimate fate of the child entering the care system is uncertain, and this places enormous pressure on the mental health professionals to assess the degree of risk the child faces at home as carefully and accurately as possible, in the awareness that separation from loved, if abusive or negligent parents, will almost always be traumatic. Parents may agree to treatment in order to facilitate rehabilitation of their children. Therapists offering treatment may be requested to address progress in reports prepared for Court proceedings, illustrating the powerful tension between confidentiality and duty to protect children, which such work creates. There is also a powerful coercive element when parents agree to engage in treatment in the context of child-care proceedings. This will inevitably play some role in the transference and the progress of therapy.

This brief description of the legal system of child-care proceedings cases illustrates how intellectually complex and emotionally loaded the task of producing assessments for the Court can be. Forensic psychotherapists may find themselves being drawn into being asked to act as advocates for or adversaries of parents, and struggling to retain their professional neutrality. Omnipotent rescue fantasies, of saving either abused children or victimised parents may interfere with the objective and independent clinical judgements which are required and desperately needed.

In any psychological assessment of parents for the Court, the psychologist is reminded that the paramount consideration of the Court is the welfare of the child, which itself creates a somewhat adversarial situation, in which one is asked to consider the client in relation to someone else and focus on the notion of risk to others. The fact that there is always a third party to be considered, as well as evaluation of the client's own needs and difficulties, creates a certain tension in the interview, as does the limited nature of confidentiality when preparing a report for the Court.

The mother, who has either perpetrated serious non-accidental injuries on a child, or has not been able to protect the child from injuries perpetrated by her violent partner, may be assessed separately from her partner. The central issues which the psychologist or other mental health professional is asked to address generally include the risk posed to the child or children of remaining in the care of this mother, given the history of non-accidental injuries, her psychological characteristics, suitability and motivation for psychological treatment, and the possible effects of separation on the children. The essential questions are the mother's ability to protect her child, her understanding of the child's needs for safety and welfare, her own level of impulse control, her capacity to place the child's needs above her own, and her insight into the need for change.

The intersection between the private domain of female power and the public arena of legal intervention and control can be seen clearly in those cases in which the future of a family, and the continuation of contact between mother and child, are decided by the Courts. The emotional significance for mothers of being considered unfit to care for children, and the psychological damage to children who are allowed to stay in the custody of abusive mothers compared to the emotional effects of separation from them, are sensitive and complex areas which will also be explored. The backdrop to this discussion is the pervasive myth of the idealised mother against whom all others are to be compared (Motz, 1997). It should be noted, however, that a large number of child abuse cases will never be dealt with through the Courts, and that many abusing parents will never be detected. The self-report of our clients testifies to the fact of severe physical and emotional abuse going undetected in the lives of many, some of whom have gone on to repeat these patterns with their own children.

MATERNAL DEPRESSION AND PHYSICAL ABUSE OF CHILDREN

The link between depression in women and physical abuse of children has been elucidated by Mills (1997) and Cox (1988) who report that nearly half of inner-city, under-resourced mothers in the United Kingdom, at home with young children, are suffering with clinical depression. Mills suggests that the women who have experienced depressed or rejecting mothers in their childhoods may have substituted an idealised internal mother. Their desire to have a child of their own may reflect a wish to please their internal objects, with the consequence that 'the child they produce is of course nothing like the ideal child whom they would like to offer to their internal mothers as a gift and thus is often rejected' (Mills, 1997:186).

This rejection may take the form of physical aggression towards the child. Mills describes the work of Shanti, an all-female psychotherapy centre in which such depressed and abusing mothers can receive brief psychodynamic psychotherapy; she argues that by offering women the safety of an all-female environment women can escape from the experience of powerlessness and alienation which pervades the 'phallocentric discourses of their everyday world, where they exist without much access to economic independence, with only limited outlets for their creative talents and with little experience of an unmenaced physical autonomy' (Mills, 1997:187) This form of psychotherapy was found to have lasting benefits in terms of the women's psychological well-being two years after therapy ended (Reader, 1993).

Clearly, there are many factors and motivations which produce female violence towards children, some of which are also found in male child abuse and some of which reflect the particularly intense relationship between mother and child, and the limited spheres of influence and control available to many women. A crucial factor is the link between the demands of the babies and children and the reactivation for the woman of her own experiences of abuse and neglect, echoing the sentiments expressed by De Zuleta in the opening passage of this chapter:

> Whenever they are put into the position of being a mother, having to look after a dependent child, particularly when there is the possibility of feeling vulnerable, they blank off their maternal feelings. To be a mother, for these women means having to identify with their own neglectful mother, the one who allowed abuse to happen.
>
> (Kennedy, 1997:111)

Women who have alcohol or substance abuse problems may become physically abusive or neglectful to their children when they are disinhibited by these substances and lose control of their behaviour; others may use their children to express sadistic impulses or to provide themselves with a sense of mastery and control. Mills argues that women who have themselves been subject to deprivation in childhood find it very difficult to provide their children with clear boundaries, to say 'no', because of a profound identification with the child who is refused or deprived of something. The children who have never had limits set for them may become out of control and disturbed and the mothers, who have effectively relinquished the adult role of boundary-setting, will only take back the authority at the moment where the behaviour becomes too unmanageable and they respond through violence. There is no internalised voice of parental authority for the mothers themselves. They alternate between identifying with the deprived children and overindulging them and then, suddenly, 'flipping' and administering harsh physical punishment.

Violence may occur in conjunction with emotional and sexual abuse, cruelty and neglect. For women who have themselves been abused physically, their own violence towards children may reflect the psychological process of identification with the aggressor, in which the mother gives to the child the experience that she herself suffered as helpless victim. She turns her passive role of victim into the active one in which she is in control, as the aggressor. The following case study illustrates how a physical assault on a child can be an echo of earlier experiences for a mother, expressing her need for help for herself, and her need to discharge her anger. There is an important sense in which the mother's assault on her child reflects the reactivation of her own memories of abuse and an intensification of her feelings of helplessness and murderous rage towards her own internalised mother, whom she had idealised. The birth of her own child shatters this idealisation: 'Back come emotions in memory, feelings and specific images, many of which do not accord with the idyllic and satisfying treatment that was fantasised as part of a life-long defence against disillusion and object loss' (Mills, 1997:178).

Case illustration: Melissa: Distress and isolation in a physically abusing mother

I first came into contact with Melissa when her solicitor requested a Court report evaluating her capacity to care for her 18-month-old son, Ethan, for care proceedings, in the light of her history of physically abusing him. I agreed to undertake the assessment. There were also concerns about her ability to mother her second child, with whom she was seven months pregnant at the time of the assessment. She was in a new relationship, her previous relationship with Ethan's father, Clifford, having broken down following the intervention of the local authority and her disclosure of his violence towards her.

Melissa was late for her first appointment, and seemed a shy, softly spoken and nervous young woman. She was delicate and attractive, with a fragile and youthful appearance: she seemed slight and doll-like although she was heavily pregnant. She was accompanied at the initial assessment interview by her new boyfriend, Joshua. At first she appeared to find it difficult to communicate and was somewhat reticent and unforthcoming; she nodded when her boyfriend spoke, as though she were mute. This indicated to me how hard it was for her to have a voice, or express her own needs, a hypothesis which was later supported by analysis of her offence.

Despite her initial reticence and shyness Melissa grew increasingly confident and articulate as the assessment period progressed. She expressed some insight into her difficulties concerning assertiveness and communication when seen on her own at the second interview. She was open and descriptive in her account of the non-accidental injuries of Ethan, the nature of her relationship with Clifford and her history of non-compliance with social workers.

She was living with her partner Joshua, whose child she was expecting. The two had met initially when they were 17, Joshua had moved to Spain for two years and had recently returned to live with Melissa. Neither Melissa nor Joshua was employed at the time of the assessment, but he was hoping to start his own business eventually and Melissa said that she would be pleased to obtain part-time work of the kind she had held before, working in a factory. Joshua presented as a competent, realistic and assertive man who was fully aware of the complications facing the couple in their application to be reconsidered as potential carers for Ethan.

Melissa was the only child of parents who had separated when she was approximately 2 years old. When she was 10 her mother told her that her father had sexually abused her when she was a baby and that he had served several prison sentences for sexual offences against two other children. She could not recollect anything about her father, had no memories of the abuse and had only been told by her mother that it had taken place, but had not felt able to discuss it further with her. She had been aware that her father was in custody for much of her childhood and knew that her mother did not want her to make contact with him. He had not attempted to contact her at any point.

Her mother remarried a 39-year-old plumber when Melissa was 8 and both she and Melissa were physically abused by him. He was an alcoholic who became violent when inebriated, and often accused Melissa of 'winding him up' and trying to 'get in the way' of his relationship with her mother. When she was 12 years old Melissa had been sexually assaulted by two local boys and feared that she had become pregnant. Her early experience of sexual abuse appeared to have left her vulnerable to repeat victimisation and she blamed herself for failure to protect herself during this encounter. She had been out on her own later than the other girls she occasionally socialised with and had agreed to go to the park with two older adolescent boys who had subsequently raped her. She had not told her mother about this experience until she became afraid that she was pregnant, because of her feeling that she had somehow deserved this assault. She described feeling powerless in the face of male aggression and becoming almost entirely mute during the sexual assault. She had not actually been pregnant.

She first became known to social services at age 15 when her name was placed on the At Risk Register for physical abuse of which her stepfather was the perpetrator. She believed that her mother had been too intimidated by her stepfather to protect her adequately, and stated that it was only following her mother's relatively recent separation from her husband that they had been able to build a satisfactory relationship with each other. Melissa's mother had herself suffered from periods of depression and had few sources of social or family support; the few friends she had once had were estranged from her because of her husband's possessiveness and jealousy. At the time of assessment Melissa had regular contact with her mother, whom she described as considerate and supportive and against whom she expressed no anger.

Much of Melissa's time in secondary school was marred by bullying at the hands of other schoolgirls. She described herself as 'very shy' and 'backwards socially' and reported that other girls would call her names and physically assault her. She had enjoyed the academic side of school but had received little encouragement at home and had eventually left school after receiving five GCSEs. She would have liked to stay on at school but left because her stepfather had insisted that she earn money: her mother had not intervened.

Melissa then worked on a Youth Training Scheme as a nursery assistant which she said she 'loved'. She recalled the sense of comfort derived from being in a safe environment, filled with toys. Later she had worked in a factory where she found the routine of work and the companionship of the others rewarding. Her first serious relationship had been with Clifford who was six years older than her and whom she described as violent, intimidating and a heavy user of alcohol. She had met him shortly after finishing her placement on the Youth Training Scheme and had agreed to go out with him mainly out of a sense of loneliness, and because he initially appeared to be caring and protective. He soon discouraged her from continuing with her training as a nursery nurse, to which she subsequently agreed. She gradually began to perceive him as domineering and frightening. She described them as having frequent arguments about his drinking and his use of their shared income for buying alcohol. Six months into the relationship, Melissa, who had moved in with Clifford, became pregnant with Ethan. This pregnancy was unplanned and Melissa felt isolated, helpless and unsupported. At that time she had little contact with her mother and her stepfather, who had encouraged her to move in with Clifford. She had no close friends from school.

Following Ethan's birth, Melissa became increasingly isolated and distressed, finding it difficult to manage the conflicting demands of her small baby and her partner, who had become violent to her during the course of her pregnancy. She felt that she had no means of communicating her distress or exerting any influence over Clifford who would often leave her with the baby for hours at a time without letting her know where he was going. On several occasions he stayed out all night, which Melissa found frightening and upsetting as she had become anxious about being alone with Ethan, whose needs she found difficult to fathom. She would frequently question Clifford about where he had been and was regularly assaulted by him in response to what he perceived as 'interfering'. She did not report these assaults to the police, believing that she had provoked this treatment and also out of fear that without Clifford she would be on her own with sole responsibility for a child; she considered this a frightening and unmanageable prospect.

Social services first became involved after Melissa shook Ethan hard when he was 8 weeks old and suffering from colic. Clifford had reported this shaking incident to the health visitor who, in turn, informed social services. Following this, there was a second occasion in which Melissa presented Ethan, aged 15 weeks, at the Accident and Emergency Department of her local hospital saying she was worried about her child's welfare, showing the medical personnel that he appeared to have a fractured arm which she later stated had most likely been caused by Clifford's rough handling of him. She also reported that she had herself been assaulted by Clifford, to whom she had attributed Ethan's injuries. Ethan was then removed from the home and placed with foster carers at the request of Melissa, who disclosed that she herself had also repeatedly hit him on the side of the head with his plastic milk bottle in complete frustration and despair. She later confessed that she had actually broken Ethan's arm by twisting it as hard as she could. An interim care order was granted in relation to Ethan as neither Melissa nor Clifford was considered to be a suitable carer for him at the time; he went into foster care. The couple remained together for several months following Ethan's removal until Clifford decided to leave Melissa and started an affair with someone else, saying that he found her depression 'too much of a downer'.

After Clifford left, Melissa asked to be considered as a carer for Ethan and undertook a residential assessment with him. They both flourished within this environment and Ethan was eventually returned to her care, only to be removed again when it became known that Clifford was visiting the family and Melissa was again subject to violence. At this point the environment was considered unsafe for Ethan because of Melissa's vulnerability to violence and her unreliability in terms of reporting contact with Clifford.

Although Melissa had confessed to causing the injuries, it was still thought likely by social workers that she might be covering up for Clifford's violence and she was repeatedly questioned along these lines. She later regretted her decision to have Ethan accommodated and attended contact visits reliably and continued to assert her desire to have her son returned to her care. After she and Clifford separated, he attended contact visits only sporadically. It seemed that, at some level, she had been aware of her potential and actual danger to the infant and had taken the only responsible action that she could have in her situation, by relinquishing custody.

Her relationship with Joshua appeared quite different in kind. The couple had been together for one year before Melissa became pregnant again; this pregnancy was also unplanned but the consequences of the birth and the financial implications had been thought through carefully and discussed. There was no violence in the relationship and Joshua had no history of drug or alcohol dependence. The couple felt persecuted by Melissa's former partner and unsure as to why they were no longer being assessed as potential carers for Ethan. Melissa had been silent in the case conference when asked about whether she would like to continue the assessment. She later disclosed that this silence resulted from her long-standing difficulty in speaking when she felt intimidated. She was aware that this was misinterpreted as hostility or lack of co-operation and hoped to have help so that she would no longer 'clam up'. She was adamant that she wanted the assessment to continue.

Melissa had asked to have Ethan accommodated in care at a point in her life when she felt heavily criticised by social services and abused by her partner. Her request may also have expressed her ambivalence towards her child, and her recognition of the potential danger of these feelings. She appeared to have made this decision out of a sudden fear about the extent of her own rage and uncontrollable feelings of frustration. She felt that she had not known how to keep him safe and had lost faith in her own degree of self-control and maternal competence. This appeared to have been triggered, in part, by relatively trivial criticisms of her child-care which the health visitor had made, in relation to warming the milk bottles and sterilisation techniques for the bottles. Her request for help could be understood as responsible and protective action which had, unfortunately, not been recognised as such, but seen as confirmation of her inability to cope.

Melissa's degree of vulnerability to perceived bullying made it likely that she would magnify any criticism or suggestion that she was incompetent, and then become overwhelmed with feelings of worthlessness and helplessness as a result. She also, at some level, recognised how overwhelming her anger towards the baby was, and how it resonated for her with her own unmet needs for protection and care. She found his crying intolerable when on her own with him.

It was striking that when she herself felt contained, when she was in a residential assessment unit, or when Ethan was placed with foster carers who treated Melissa like another of their charges, she could interact well with Ethan. The Mother and Baby Unit had been positive about her capacities, saying 'overall two-way bonding between mother and child was observed' and 'it was evident from the beginning that she found caring for Ethan very enjoyable and used advice and guidance well'. Melissa was reported to have gained confidence, 'her own personality' and an understanding of Ethan's needs. At this point social services were seriously considering rehabilitation of Ethan to Melissa's care but this plan was suspended as a result of information coming to light about a reconciliation between Melissa and Clifford, calling into question her reliability and her capacity to place the needs of her child above her need to be in a relationship.

That this reconciliation followed a successful assessment by the Mother and Baby Unit appeared to make little sense to social services, who had perceived Melissa to be a vulnerable woman in need of protection and assistance. They considered that her decision to resume a relationship with an abusive partner, about whom concerns were still held in relation to his role in the physical abuse of Ethan, reflected impulsiveness and lack of understanding of the needs of her child. Social workers were also concerned by what appeared to be Melissa's wilful deceptiveness regarding her relationship with Clifford; for example, she denied that she had maintained contact with him while at the Mother and Baby Unit, which he later contradicted. She appeared to have been confused about the permanence of her relationship with Clifford and reported to social services that she had fully separated from him, and wanted protection from him. Social workers began to view her as deceitful, selfish and manipulative, rather than an innocent victim who could be helped by them. It appeared that this sense of having been deceived left the professionals involved with a residual anger at Melissa and confirmed fears about her as an incompetent mother, in stark contradiction to her evaluation at the residential unit.

My recommendations to the Court were that a care order should be granted in relation to the unborn child, with Melissa to retain custody in accordance with local authority objectives and contractual arrangements; and that she was to be reassessed by social services in relation to her acting as primary carer for Ethan following a period of work with the psychology outpatient services. The outcome of the Court case was that Ethan would remain in long-term foster care under a full care order and would eventually be placed for adoption. The new baby would be placed on a care order at birth and progress closely monitored, with the possibility that a permanent long-term placement would be found for him, should there be sufficient grounds for removal from the parents' care. Despite this disappointing decision for Melissa in relation to Ethan, I was informed by the guardian *ad litem* that she had been pleased by my report, which identified some positive features of her personality and parenting and was sympathetic to her difficulties.

I referred her to the local Department of Clinical Psychology. Although she initially attended the appointments offered to her, she found it physically very difficult to attend in late pregnancy and decided that she did not want to continue treatment after the first four sessions. She described the sessions as helpful and said that she would be re-referring herself to the Department following the birth of her child. The female psychologist who had offered her therapy interpreted Melissa's withdrawal from treatment as a reflection, in part, of how painful it was for her to address issues of self-esteem relating to her own experience of abuse; avoidance of confronting distressing aspects of her past appeared to Melissa to be the safest option available to her.

It seemed that Melissa had again found it easier to enact her distress than to address it verbally, because of the intensity of her traumatic experiences. She was too frightened to engage in thera- peutic work and also felt suspicious about the degree to which social services might be involved in the psychological work, feeling that she was being coerced into undertaking painful and intrusive treatment. It was clear that the referral had arisen out of her assessment in relation to the care proceedings and there was therefore a coercive element to the referral. It was evident that the process of making explicit her memories of traumatic experiences would be a very threatening task, which Melissa did not feel ready to take on. In a sense, she found her silence comforting, and did not want to give it up. I hoped that she would, one day, feel ready to confront her inner demons, and defuse their destructiveness.

DISCUSSION

Given Melissa's history of traumatic abuse, her difficulty in self-expression and her reliance on dissociation as a protective mechanism are precisely the kinds of psychological difficulty that one would expect to find. The degree of learned helplessness, that is perceived difficulty in effecting change in her environment and asserting herself, seemed clearly to express the impact of her traumatisation, both in childhood and in her recent violent relationship. There appeared to be no recognition that women who have been victims of domestic violence often find it hard to leave the situation and have little confidence in their own abilities or that independent living is a threatening prospect, which is attempted unsuccessfully, before the women are coerced back into the abusive partnership.

I understood Melissa's act of inflicting injuries on her son and bringing him to hospital to reflect the extent of her sense of distress, victimisation and helplessness. I imagined that these feelings were rooted in early experience but reactivated in her violent relationship and also by the experience of motherhood itself, which powerfully reawakened memories of her own neglect and helplessness. Melissa expressed regret and remorse about the injuries which she had inflicted on her son, describing them as reactions to extreme stress. The fact that she brought Ethan to the hospital suggested that she was aware of his need for medical attention and wanted witnesses to the damage which she had inflicted on him. At another level her behaviour could be understood as her inability to request help in her own right, because of her lack of self-confidence and repeated abuse, and her attempt to highlight the situation through the presentation of her son's injuries. This was her way of letting the caring agencies know that there was a domestic situation in which neither she nor her child was safe. Rather than request help in her own voice, Melissa attended the Accident and Emergency Department with Ethan, stating that he had been injured by his father, but later confessing that she had inflicted injuries herself, in despair. This indicated her sense that she would not be listened to if she asked for help for herself.

Her communication difficulties reflected the depths of her sense of inadequacy and her fears of not being understood. It appeared that she could gain confidence sufficiently to develop her capacity to articulate her unhappiness and sense of isolation only very gradually, and after working through the impact of her own sense of abandonment and victimisation in childhood. There were some hopeful signs that she could be helped to develop her parenting; when she felt safe and protected herself, for example, she had demonstrated a capacity to protect Ethan and care for him within the supportive environment of the Mother and Baby Unit.

Melissa had deeply ambivalent feelings towards Ethan and her relationship with him had strong echoes of the experience of her own mother as an unreliable object, who could not maintain a safe environment. This relates to her degree of disturbed attachment, and her own sense of maternal deprivation, which appeared to have affected her sense of herself, leaving her with a high level of emotional dependency on others, and an inability to tolerate intense states in herself or others. She appeared to have not internalised a containing and reliable maternal object, who could manage her rage and distress. These difficulties were exacerbated and reactivated when she was faced with the task of coping, unsupported, with her helpless and demanding infant. I felt that this could best be addressed through ongoing psychological work which in fact Melissa had herself requested. This work could eventually help her to gain confidence and assertiveness and work through the traumatic experiences of her earlier life. She struck me as a frightened young woman, profoundly lacking in confidence, whose own experiences of victimisation had interfered with her capacity to care for her son. The description of physical abuse which introduced this chapter fitted Melissa well: De Zuleta (1993) writes of victims of childhood abuse who become parents themselves:

> They want to be really good parents. But for some, these childhood terrors and torments have not been allowed to disappear. Though apparently forgotten, the experiences of their parents' cruelty or indifference have been 'internalised' in the form of mental representations which will persist in their minds, albeit in an unconscious state. It is often in the midst of their own children's screams and tears that those traumatic experiences are reactivated, even if they continue to remain unconscious.
>
> (De Zuleta, 1993:4)

General considerations which emerge from this case illustration include Melissa's identification with the aggressor as her psychic defence against overwhelming feelings of vulnerability, her history of victimisation, and her transition from being a child on the At Risk Register to a young mother who placed her own child at risk. The symbolic significance of social services' 'care' to Melissa, who had not received adequate protection during her own childhood, could not be underestimated in this case, as she felt persecuted by her social workers, and condemned to fail in the assessments that they conducted. Likewise, the information which was available to the social services department about Melissa's background already placed her in the category of women who might pose a risk to their own children; this was based on maternal neglect in her background and a history of sexual and physical abuse. In this context it became very difficult for either professional or parent to approach the child protection problems with a wholly objective perspective and they, inevitably, became polarised. Melissa had surrendered her own role as a mother to the local authority, perhaps requesting unconsciously that her son would be protected from the abuse that she had suffered, and which she had not been able to work through. It may therefore have reflected her unconscious fear of re-enacting this abuse through physical or sexual violence towards her baby. She had already found herself using physical methods of expressing frustration and anger with the baby, and this had clearly frightened her.

It appeared that the perception of Melissa as a victim of domestic violence was at odds with the discovery that she had lashed out at her child. It seemed hard for the professionals to recognise that, unacceptable as it was, Melissa's aggression towards Ethan was one of her only ways of communicating her own sense of desperation and isolation. When she was seen as colluding with her violent partner (rather than being wholly intimidated by him) and betraying the trust of the local authority, she was treated as a 'hopeless case', incapable of change, and she felt cast out. She then lost the chance to show that she had developed parenting skills and protectiveness. Sympathy for her as victim seemed to turn into anger at her for remaining involved with her violent partner, failing in her maternal duties, and expressing her aggressive feelings. Although she had, by her own admission, directed violence towards her son, she had taken full responsibility for this, expressing remorse and making use of the support subsequently offered to her. She seemed to have lost the trust of social workers involved in protecting her child, who viewed her as 'dangerous' rather than being 'in danger' herself.

Implications for practitioners involved in child-care cases

Melissa was both victim and abuser, which created a tension for those working with her. This dual status, as perpetrator and victim, is common in forensic work and clinicians must attempt to address both aspects of their patients: the temptation is to address one or other aspect, because to try to acknowledge both is far more confusing and complex, for patients and therapists alike. The difficulty of this dual status is particularly pronounced when women who are already known to social services because of abuse in their own childhoods become mothers themselves, sometimes with violent partners. These women may feel that they have suddenly lost the protection and support that they needed and craved for themselves, as abused children, and are now treated as abusers, or as unfit and unprotective mothers. Although the dynamics in the relationship between social workers and the mother are not necessarily conscious to the participants, it is striking how often the same battles appear to be played out, and the possibility of collaboration becomes unlikely. There can sometimes be a strong sense of mutual suspicion and hopelessness about the future for the child. While both parties accept that the welfare of the child is paramount, they may not be able to agree on how best to proceed. The mother may feel that everything she has that is good is being taken from her; the social worker that the mother's needs make it impossible for her to parent her child effectively. This is related to the complexity of, and difficulty for adults in, overcoming abuse and neglect experienced in childhood in order to cope with the demands and needs of their own children, and the need for child-care agencies to work out strategies to 'parent the parents', i.e. to empower parents who were themselves abused or neglected and enable them to parent their own children.

The highly emotive nature of child-care proceedings cases also seems to reflect how the vulnerability of children 'in care', with no certainty about their future, evokes painful, sometimes unbearable, feelings for all those involved in the proceedings. The trauma that these children experience seems to be projected into the whole network of individuals involved and may reactivate tremendous anxieties and painful memories for the parents and professionals alike. For children who have been abused and then become parents themselves, the loss of their own children can reactivate a tremendous sense of deprivation and injustice, leading to anger and great difficulty in engaging with the child protection team. These feelings must be recognised and respected before an allegiance can be forged.

In my reports to the Courts I attempt to point out the dangers of mothers and social workers becoming polarised. I consider it important to emphasise the positive aspects of the maternal functioning, as well as areas of difficulty, and to highlight the possibility of offering psychological therapy to break the intergenerational cycle of abuse and neglect. I also attempt to provide the Courts with an understanding of how aggression may arise in the context of otherwise good mothering, at times of acute stress or crisis. It is possible to recommend that a mother who has become violent to her child is offered therapy, to help her to understand and manage her anger, if she is motivated to do so, and the depression, isolation and traumatisation which may underlie it.

Mothers need to be empowered to address their own experiences of abuse in childhood and to learn to protect themselves before they can protect their own children, or manage their own feelings of deprivation and anger. It is also important that a woman whose children are subject to care proceedings, and who is faced with the possibility of losing them, has the experience of being understood and supported. If she loses her children in care proceedings she will face profound and ongoing grief, for which she may need help. This can be suggested and discussed with her solicitor and a referral can be made to the appropriate agency. Likewise, referrals can be made to child and family psychiatry and psychology services to help mothers in need to understand and manage their children's behaviour and develop some understanding of how to set boundaries for them through parenting groups (Redfern, 1999).

It is essential to raise awareness of how unconscious expectations of female behaviour affect professionals' judgements about maternal competence. The capacity to understand the complexity of maternal behaviour, rather than simply reacting with horror when women display aggression, can help decisions about the child's best interests to be made fairly. Women who display aggression towards others, particularly their children, may be perceived to be extraordinarily unmaternal creatures, rather than people who are likely to have been treated with violence themselves, who require help and understanding in order to care adequately for their children. Support and treatment are often in the best interests of the child and may prevent a painful separation or break-up of the family.

The difficulty for women in leaving a violent partner should also not be underestimated by child protection agencies: the fact that women may stay in, or even return to, violent situations is not evidence that they have put their own needs above those of their children. They may be considering their children's needs when making this decision, or when finding it impossible to do otherwise than to stay. The degree of pressure placed on women to leave violent partners or risk losing their children through care proceedings does not take into account the emotional and practical difficulty such a move may involve, or necessarily provide alternative means of support. This forced choice may encourage women to lie, as Melissa did, about the extent of involvement with a partner; this deception will then be used as evidence of the unreliability of the mother and her 'failure to protect' herself or her children. In order for mothers to be enabled to bring up their children safely, they must be recognised as complex subjects, capable of mixed feelings and loyalty. They need to be sure that they will receive practical and emotional support if they attempt to leave the relationship and establish an independent lifestyle. In the context of social and religious pressures on women to 'make the most' of their relationships and the prejudice against single mothers, it is unsurprising that leaving a violent partner may be fraught with difficulty and ambivalence (see chapter 7).

CONCLUSION

For some women whose children are subject to care proceedings the experience reawakens memories of their own childhood, and their own placement into local authority care. Aside from the painful reactivation of memories of parental cruelty or neglect, these women may also have been sexually, physically or emotionally abused while in care, by foster parents or residential staff in children's homes. This raises particular difficulties for these women and makes the process of undertaking care proceedings even more poignant and painful. As young children or adolescents these mothers tried to understand and cope with their own removal from their parents' care and being placed in strange and uncertain fostering or institutional settings. As they grew up they would have been unlikely to have received psychological help in coping with their new situations and may only have come to the attention of the psychological or psychiatric services once they became pregnant. As mothers these women become identified as potential abusers rather than victims of abuse and feel stigmatised by their own history of being in local authority care. They may be ambivalent about becoming a mother and may sometimes even feel relieved when their own potential to repeat abusive parenting is recognised.

These women often express the feeling that social services have been involved with them for their entire lives, that they have no experience of being part of a normal family either as children or parents. If the women were abused but had no protection from social services in their childhood they may feel deprived and envious, asking why their children are receiving the care and attention which they missed out on. They may strongly identify with the child at risk and hope that they, too, will receive help and protection from the professionals involved. This hope can be a stepping stone in engaging the women in therapeutic work. Efforts made to 'parent' these women may include fostering the mother and child together, encouraging them to attend local authority-run family centres and nurseries where basic child management skills can be taught, and engaging them in 'parenting groups' at child and family psychiatry clinics, and organisations like NUPIN. Recognition of the dual status of these women, as survivors and as perpetrators of abuse, requires a sensitive understanding of the intergenerational transmission of abuse and how to prevent it.

At the present time women seem to be doubly punished, first by the greater likelihood that they will be victims of male violence in the home than men are victims of female violence, and second by being vilified if they cannot easily leave the situation of violence and oppression in which they find themselves. The difficulty of this task indicates that the circumstances of mothers faced with long-term or permanent separation from their children should be given close consideration and all avenues explored before the mothers are deemed 'unfit' to parent.

The existence of cases of serious sexual, physical and emotional abuse of children in local authority care is a tragic indication that simply removing vulnerable children, from environments in which there are known risks, to situations where risks are unknown does not guarantee their safety and welfare. Likewise, the tragedy of children being killed within their own homes and by members of their families, in cases where they were known to the statutory agencies, raises crucial questions about the need to acknowledge the existence of serious violence within families. Failure to take protective action can lead to fatal child abuse and the subsequent blaming of child protection agencies and families, as Reder and his colleagues have explored in their analysis of thirty-five major inquiries into cases of deaths of children within their families (Reder *et al.*, 1993). Clearly, mothers as well as fathers have a capacity for potentially fatal violence against their own children, which may be enacted at times of intense psychic stress. When possible, psychotherapeutic support should be attempted to help the mothers manage their frightening feelings of destructiveness, rage and desperation. Being allowed to articulate these unacceptable impulses, and encouraged to trace their origin, can be a powerful relief for these mothers and an essential first step in enabling them to separate their own experience of neglect, abandonment and violence in relation to their parents from their current relationship with their own children. The overwhelming identification which these mothers may have with their vulnerable and demanding children, and the consequent reactivation of uncontrollable anger, can potentially be thought about and managed through therapy, whether individual or group, rather than simply, and destructively, enacted.

This therapeutic work may be essential in some cases, and can significantly affect whether or not mothers repeat patterns of their own abuse with their children, in order to 'convert childhood trauma into adult triumph' and project into their children their own unresolved feelings of neediness, vulnerability and rage. Therapy, whether psychodynamic or short-term and supportive, can provide such women with the space to think about their behaviour and their children's needs, and to identify aspects of their own histories that might make apparently trivial parenting tasks very difficult and painful to manage. Therapy can help these women to recover from the traumatic consequences of their own abusive experiences in childhood and enable them to begin to manage their own feelings and memories, which will, in turn, allow them to manage their children's needs for containment and protection. The opportunity to reflect on the experience of mothering, as well as on the experience of having been mothered, is the starting point of a necessary psychic separation between mother and child; that is, that the mothers can gain a real sense of their children as existing in their own right, rather than as mirror images of themselves or receptacles of their own needs and desires.

Chapter 4

Infanticide

Violating those taboos held most sacred, infanticide is an offence which bewilders and appals both the general public and professionals. In this crime the attributes conventionally assigned to motherhood are grotesquely distorted. The twin taboos of child killing and female violence are dramatically and irrevocably interwoven in this offence. The public imagination feeds on tales of infanticide, devouring the details with disbelief and fascination. According to the recorded crime statistics it is a very rare crime: in 1997 there were only three convictions for the crime of infanticide, and over the previous ten-year period the greatest number of convictions for this crime was in 1988, when eight women were found guilty of infanticide, of whom seven received a probation order (HMSO, 1998). Infanticide is a crime which can only be committed by women, as the law does not recognise paternal killing of a child under the age of 1 as an instance of infanticide.

Women who kill their own children may be afforded some sympathy if it is clear that they have themselves suffered through their behaviour, but less so if there is an element of revenge or retribution. Women who kill other people's children are generally perceived to be wholly evil. The case of Myra Hindley illustrates the extent to which women who kill children violate notions about the natural maternal role of women:

> The new demons of crimes against children still act in character as biological women, but they have disqualified themselves from the rank of mother, and from the category of woman altogether. A woman like Myra Hindley is seen to embody a violent sexuality that is more appropriate to the male than the female.
>
> (Warner, 1998:3)

Analysis of criminal statistics suggests that most cases of maternal killing are dealt with under the Infanticide Act and that the perpetrators usually have their charges dropped from murder to manslaughter on grounds of diminished responsibility (Bluglass, 1990). While a proportion of such crimes are committed by women suffering from severe mental illness, a substantial proportion are committed by women who have not received psychiatric diagnoses and who have different, distinct psychological motivations. Indeed, a proportion of the cases of maternal infanticide are the result of negligence or child battering, as discussed in the previous chapter, where the maternal intention was not that of killing.

In this chapter I address the questions of how women who kill children can be classified and their actions understood, as well as the treatment of these offenders. The model of understanding female violence described in previous chapters can also be used to provide an analysis of how women come to kill their own babies. According to this model, first proposed by Welldon in 1988:

> the main difference between a male and a female perverse action lies in the aim. Whereas in men the act is aimed at an outside part-object, in women it is usually against themselves, either against their own bodies or against objects which they see as their own creations; that is, their babies. In both cases, bodies and babies are treated as part-objects.
>
> (Welldon, 1994:477)

PERVERSIONS OF MOTHERHOOD

'Odd though it may sound, motherhood provides an excellent vehicle for some women to exercise perverse and perverting attitudes towards their offspring, and to retaliate against their own mothers' (Welldon, 1992: 63). Where she might turn the force of destructive rage on herself, she instead turns that murderous impulse towards her narcissistic extension, her child. The function of child killing thus mirrors, in fantasy, the function of a suicide. By killing off the bad part of herself, as projected into the child, the mother has relieved herself, temporarily, of the unacceptable aspects of herself which she has not integrated. She has powerfully identified with the helplessness of the child, and has found her own inability to provide for the needs of the infant intolerable. The identification is so painful and so unbearable that the situation cannot be allowed to continue.

This child murder is therefore a self-murder in a situation where a mother's identity is perceived to be fatally threatened by the child. The inability to tolerate dependence in the child and the memory of her own inability to have her needs met by her mother generate a life or death struggle between mother and child. The infant's needs are perceived as life-threatening attacks which must be defended against. In the case of ongoing child abuse the object is kept alive to be tortured, in the case of murder it has literally been killed off. This may be the result of continuous abuse or the consequence of a one-off, unpredictable attack, where the mother's intention was not murder. An example of the latter would be the death of a baby following an incident of violent shaking, when the mother's intention was to silence temporarily the screaming infant rather than to kill it.

THE NATURE OF FEMALE HOMICIDE

Female homicide is mainly directed towards family members; about 80 per cent of victims of female homicide are family members; 40–45 per cent kill their children and approximately one-third kill their spouse or lover (D'Orban, 1990). According to a study of homicidal parents by Bourget and Bradford (1990) the sex distribution was as follows: male, 30.8 per cent and female, 69.2 per cent in a sample of thirteen homicidal parents and in forty-eight cases of non-parental homicides, 81.3 per cent were male and 18.7 per cent female. These data, albeit based on a small sample, suggest that women are more likely to be homicidal parents while men are more likely to be perpetrators of extrafamilial murder. The rates of female homicide are much lower than those of male homicide: in 1997 eight women were convicted of murder, compared to 153 men; eight women were convicted of section 2 manslaughter, compared to thirty-two men; and nineteen women were convicted of other manslaughter, compared to 120 men (HMSO, 1998).

CAUSES OF INFANTICIDE: THE BIOLOGICAL ARGUMENT

The notion of biological causes of female madness is perhaps most clearly demonstrated in the theoretical approaches to understanding infanticide. Both psychodynamic and psychiatric models emphasise the 'disorders of mind' brought about by childbirth and the resulting chaos and irrationality that ensue. According to the biological model the mother is a vestige into which uncontrollable hormonal forces flow, compelling her to act upon them. There is a tradition of considering that the suppression of the menses gives rise to acts of uncontrollable violence, for which the woman has no responsibility.

Neonaticide is linked with hysterical denial of the pregnancy in immature young girls. It has also been linked with postpartum psychosis, which is suggested as being connected to pineal gland activity (Sandyk, 1992). This is one possible biological explanation for the 'disturbance of mind' required for the charge of infanticide to be levied. Sandyk concedes that the pathophysiology of postpartum depression and psychosis is poorly understood but suggests that the substantial hormonal fluctuations play a significant role. While some evidence exists for the association between the decline in progesterone plasma levels and postpartum depression (Dalton, 1971), other studies could not find a correlation between post-partum depression and levels of luteinising hormone, oestrogen or progesterone (Nott et al., 1976). Recent studies failed to demonstrate associations between postpartum psychosis and thyroid function tests in thirty women hospitalised for postpartum depression (Stewart et al., 1988). Sandyk claims that drastic changes in pineal melatonin secretion during the postpartum period have been observed and concludes that since there is an association between pineal melatonin function and psychotic behaviour, alterations in the activity of the pineal gland are causally related to the genesis of postpartum psychosis. One implication for this hypothesis is that melatonin secretion should be increased in therapeutic management of postpartum psychosis. This would include such measures as exposure to bright light or the administration of oral melatonin.

While this reductive biological model may have intuitive appeal, there is insubstantial evidence for the causal association between falling melatonin levels and the onset of postpartum depression and psychosis. Even if these two factors are correlated one cannot conclude that one *causes* the other. Consideration of the relation of postpartum depression to homicidal urges does not demand the existence of a psychosis. It has been well documented that non-psychotic depression may give rise to both suicidal and homicidal urges (Campbell and Hale, 1991).

In the following case illustration, I describe the motivations and treatment of a mentally ill mother who was convicted of infanticide.The links between her suicidal and homicidal urges are evident and it could be suggested that her killing of her 11-month-old son was a symbolic act of suicide. I describe this mother's own experiences in childhood and her treatment within the medium secure unit, in which she evoked powerful responses from staff and patients. Close analysis of this tragic case makes it possible to highlight dynamic processes involved in the killing of an infant, and how these illustrate the phenomenon of female violence.

Case illustration: Dawn, a 28-year-old mother convicted of infanticide

Dawn was 28 years old when she was admitted to a regional secure unit following her conviction for infanticide of her 11-month-old son, Gabriel. He had been taken from her care almost from the moment of his birth following Dawn's frequent admissions to psychiatric hospital for depression since the time of her separation from her husband, when she was four months pregnant and on previous occasions. Dawn had a long history of psychiatric admissions for severe depression and suicide attempts, but had not previously been charged with a violent offence. She had suffocated and strangled Gabriel after making a special request to spend the night with him at his foster parents, after a contact visit which was supposed to have lasted only three hours. She had called the police on the evening of the offence and informed them of her intention to kill Gabriel, saying that she felt certain she would go through with it unless they could find her, but she had telephoned from a pay phone, without leaving her name or any other information about her whereabouts.

I saw Dawn for a short period of focused psychotherapy during her time as an inpatient at a regional secure unit. This therapy ended after six months because Dawn felt that she no longer wished to see me. She had been referred by the consultant psychiatrist, who had serious concerns about whether an understanding of her offence had been achieved in the 18 months since she had been admitted to the unit.

Dawn was the only child of a mother who had been diagnosed with psychotic depression, and who had spent long periods in Dawn's childhood in a psychiatric hospital. She had never known her father. Dawn had been in numerous children's homes throughout her childhood and had vivid memories of waiting anxiously for her mother to visit and reclaim her. In two of these children's homes she had been sexually abused by other residents and in one of these homes a member of staff had also abused her.

Dawn had planned the offence on the day it occurred and had worked out how she would get to spend time with Gabriel on his own. Prior to this visit she had only short periods of unsupervised access to him, but had established a good relationship with the foster parent whom she saw as maternal and warm towards her. The foster mother was later to say that she had been persuaded to allow Dawn the contact with Gabriel because of her insistence that she had missed him terribly over the past three weeks and would find it so comforting to sleep in bed with him. The foster mother had pitied her, she said, and had found the image of Dawn returning late at night to a lonely bedsit unbearable. She had, it seemed, become confused about whose needs to protect, and had inadvertently placed Gabriel in mortal danger out of sympathy for Dawn. This response to Dawn's pathos, which blinkered the foster mother to her violence, was one which characterised Dawn's relationships, particularly with mother figures.

An important fact of which the foster mother had been unaware was that Dawn's estranged husband, Gabriel's father, had recently petitioned Dawn for a divorce. Dawn described herself as having felt 'devastated' and had been furious with him; she reported that the overwhelming sense she had of rejection and abandonment made her feel that she would lose her mind. She felt that this played a central role in the killing and had been aware at some level that she was in terrible danger of doing something awful to get rid of this feeling. She saw Gabriel as intricately connected to his father, and to herself, and became convinced that he should not be allowed to live. She felt that her own life had been destroyed by her husband leaving her, Gabriel being taken into care, and, finally, being asked to give her husband a divorce. She could not clearly recall the logic of her decision that she would kill Gabriel unless the police could find her and provide her with the requisite help, and did not have any sense of what an impossible mission she had given them, asking for help, threatening to kill an infant, but not providing them with her name or address. When help was not forthcoming she carried through her plan, killing her sleeping son as he lay next to her. She had then informed the foster mother of Gabriel's death, and the police were called. She was reported to be calm and dispassionate during the police interview.

The focus of my work with Dawn was on the offence but she found this very difficult to address. She presented as child-like and dissociated, speaking in the quiet and polite tones of a well-brought-up little girl, which was in stark contrast with the violence of her offence. Her voice had an unreal, other-worldly quality, and, her breathy high-pitched tones, almost whispers, were suggestive of strangulation. She spoke so softly that one strained to hear her and leaned forward to her. This seemed to be an unconscious attempt on her part to bring her carers closer to her, and she appeared to crave some form of physical proximity and contact.

Dawn had always felt that she was different, that she didn't belong. This had been reinforced through her early childhood and adolescence. Through her early years of abuse and traumatisation at a strict children's home, in which she was further taunted because of her peculiar, whispering, speech, Dawn said that she had learned to stifle her anger, for fear of being 'told off'. The cheerful and compliant 'false self personality' (Winnicott, 1964) that she had developed in infancy, to enliven her emotionally withdrawn mother, covered up her feelings of sadness and despair which lay dormant, ready to emerge in a moment of absolute rage and despair. Her pregnancy with Gabriel had been fraught with difficulty for her, and she had found it impossible to visualise the baby inside her as he grew. She suffered similar fears to those of Kate, of being invaded by an alien (this was described in chapter 1).

Dawn had found it very difficult to separate herself from her own mother psychologically, and could not conceive of herself as capable of mothering. Although she was able to relate the facts of the offence, she could not convey the emotional flavour of the event, or portray her son with any sense that he had a separate identity to her. She seemed to have little capacity for symbolic thinking, illustrating the phenomenon described by Fonagy (1991), Fonagy et al. (1993), Fonagy and Target (1995) as 'a failure to mentalise'. 'Both self harm and mindless assaults on others may reflect indadequate capacity to mentalise' (Fonagy and Target, 1995). They trace the development of this failure to a stage in self-development when the child would be looking for a representation or mirror of her own mental states in her mother or other primary caregiver. When this does not occur, possibly because of the mother's depression or inability, the child fails to build up a picture of her own, and hence other people's, mental states. This failure in the development of symbolic thought relates to reliance on the violent act as 'an attempt to obliterate intolerable psychic experience' (Perelberg, 1999:5). Dawn could not bear to think about the pain of abandonment;

she seemed to have converted this mental despair into bodily action, through a murderous assault on her son, a representative of herself.

Her strong identification with Gabriel also seemed to be reflected in her voice, which echoed the voice of the strangled or suffocated infant whose mother did not allow her to develop a separate existence. Her violent strangulation of Gabriel seemed essentially a concrete re-enactment of Dawn's own infantile experience: she had been emotionally and psychologically, although not literally, strangled. Her inability to speak clearly, loudly or with any force, coupled with the few occasions of dramatic violence in which she set fire to her room, revealed the essentially split nature of her personality. She was unable to allow her aggression to be expressed in her 'ordinary' persona and in the interactions of daily life, even to the extent that she repressed any suggestion of anger in her speaking voice. She was aware of the peculiar effect that her little girl's voice had on others and of the anger that it evoked in staff, who thought she was pretending and 'manipulative'. In some ways she invited this punitive attitude from them and her behaviour was often provocative. She appeared to be emotionally detached from her offence, presenting herself as a victim of violence and rejection rather than as an aggressor herself.

At the moment of the killing Dawn had become enraged by her own abandonment, by her husband, son, and at a deeper level, her own mother. In fantasy she became the abandoned infant whose depressed mother had neglected and rejected her. She powerfully projected these feelings on to Gabriel, who became the embodiment of the unwanted, demanding and completely helpless child. She also saw him as absolutely hers, and felt that if she couldn't have him then neither could anyone else. She was later able to recollect this thought precisely and dispassionately during the course of therapy. Although she had been diagnosed as psychotic, Dawn had features of borderline personality disorder. Welldon (1992) suggests that in cases of murderous mothers the ultimate object of revenge is their own abandoning mother, as identified in themselves and then in their extensions, their babies. At the moment of the killing Dawn could be considered psychotic in the psychodynamic sense, of operating at a primitive level of functioning rather than in the strictly psychiatric sense, in which particular symptomatology needs to be demonstrated. Dawn had never reported the experience of clearly psychotic symptoms that could have merited a psychiatric diagnosis of psychosis.

For women like Dawn, violence is an aspect of their personality which has not been integrated. When it does surface it functions as a highly effective communicative strategy, although it is not one which has been consciously chosen. One motivation for Dawn in killing her child was her anger about being denied help from the emergency services. She had requested such help for herself prior to the offence, phoning the police to report that if she were not apprehended she would kill her son. Unfortunately, she could not be located in time to avert the killing. She created a situation in which she became the indirect victim of the failure by the police to take effective protective action in time, transforming herself from active killer to the passive victim who is deprived of the requisite help, which further fuelled her murderousness. At one level, however, her telephone call to the police, which placed significant responsibility on to them for potentially saving Gabriel's life, was a highly sadistic act, which placed the police in the role of incompetent witnesses to a murder, which she had led them to believe could have been prevented.

The offence seemed to function on many levels for Dawn; first, through the temporary annihilation of the hated aspects of herself; second, through the fantasised revenge on her mother and actual revenge on her husband; and third, to draw her own alienation and despair to the attention of the paternalistic psychiatric and custodial services. It also communicated to the world her symbolic ownership and control of Gabriel. Her request for containment and a 'place of safety' was expressed through the infanticide, and tragically it was only through this act that her needs for psychiatric treatment were met. She did not feel able to ask for help in her own strangled voice and needed to gain some sense of power through her own capacity for destruction. In the past she had used threats about her own suicidal intentions to gain entry to the psychiatric services.

DISCUSSION

The value of risk assessment

There is great clinical and therapeutic value in a thorough assessment which includes a full account of the index offence. Major considerations are the diagnosis of the offender, the prognosis for therapeutic response, the risk to the offender themselves, the risk to the public and the likelihood of re-offence. The latter can only be determined by reference to a comprehensive assessment and a careful, precise formulation of the offence. In Dawn's case her status as a restricted patient under section 37/41 of the Mental Health Act, her offence, and her intense dependence on institutions made it highly unlikely that she would ever be granted custody of a child in the future, even if she were to become pregnant and give birth again. The risk of re-offence was therefore low.

A thorough assessment, identifying key factors in the index offence, was necessary to inform the clinical management of Dawn's care and reduce the risk of violence and self-harm. In Dawn's case a significant trigger for her offence was her perception of abandonment. At points in her stay in the regional secure unit, where she felt similarly abandoned, she retaliated against the organisation as a whole, and against particular, significant individuals. An example of this occurred when her psychiatrist failed to keep two appointments with her. Dawn was heavily dependent on him and felt rejected by this. On the second occasion she vented her rage against him by attacking her own room, which she set alight. Through this act of arson Dawn was clearly endangering the lives of nursing staff and residents.

By identifying the threat of abandonment as a significant trigger for Dawn's past violence, the analogue situation of abandonment or perceived rejection on the ward could also be identified as a time when the risk of violence would increase. The link between the consultant and other significant, abandoning figures in Dawn's life, such as her mother and her estranged husband, was relevant to anticipating that disappointment in her psychiatric treatment could reawaken earlier feelings of murderous anger. Those most significant to Dawn were most at risk of provoking her anger as she invested them with fantastic power. Such figures were inevitably going to disappoint Dawn, confirming her fears about herself which centred around being rejected and hurt by seductive but unreliable people. It was possible that I too became such an object for Dawn, and she ultimately chose to leave me rather than risk being abandoned by me.

Dawn set fire to her room after we had agreed to end after four more sessions. She had started the fire by burning a diary in which she had written about the offence, an entry which she had said that she wanted to read to me in the following session. It was possible that the horror of her offence would be reawakened if she were to continue in the work with me, and disclose details of the killing. She seemed to feel that everything she had ever had that was good had been lost and I wondered if she felt that if she were to discuss Gabriel with me, she would lose her memory of him, and her sense that he was hers alone. There was a self-protective aspect to Dawn's resistance to engaging in psychotherapeutic work, in that to do so would be to take the risk of becoming overwhelmed by feelings of grief, despair and guilt.

At times she expressed nihilistic feelings which included a sense of suicidal despair. In one sense her homicide was, symbolically, a suicide. She remained at risk of self-harm and often endangered her health and safety, wandering around the grounds with little clothing on, becoming a target for sexually predatory male patients and setting fire to her own room when she was in it. This expressed both her homicidal and suicidal feelings: through her act of arson she was placing herself and others at grave risk. It appeared significant that she burned her own belongings, including her diary, in which she had recounted the offence, illustrating the unbearable nature of the crime that she had committed and her desire to obliterate all evidence of it, both psychologically and physically.

The consultant psychiatrist, the medical officer responsible for her, was pessimistic about Dawn's capacity to survive outside a secure setting and she remains an inpatient, with no real prospect of rehabilitation into the community because there was no evidence to date of therapeutic change or the beginnings of insight into her difficulties. She never expressed a sense of remorse for her offence to me, or spoke of Gabriel as a real child, with a separate existence; he had served as a receptacle for her murderous projections, and she had annihilated him in a similar way to her assaults on my capacity to think. It was almost as though she couldn't bear to have any hope, and had to destroy anything that could be hopeful. She seemed disengaged and vacant, adopting the part of an obedient, timid little girl in a way that starkly contrasted with the violence of her behaviour. It was this eerie contrast that made sessions with her particularly uneasy and disconcerting, overshadowed as they were with the implicit threat of her violence.

Transference and countertransference issues

In the context of Dawn's capacity for violence, which surfaced with catastrophic intensity and disastrous consequences, it was essential for all members of the multidisciplinary team to have clear and fixed boundaries and to communicate a clear and consistent message to Dawn. This would minimise the possibility of generating disappointment and retaliatory attacks. The quality of deprivation inherent in her presentation and interactions with staff generated strong maternal and protective feelings. Some members of the team were tempted to try to make up for the lack of care she received in early life. Dawn had been seen weekly for approximately three years by an occupational therapist who had undertaken a counselling course. While ostensibly working with her supportively, the occupational therapist was, in fact, heavily drawn into colluding with Dawn's fantasies about an idealised relationship with an omnipotent mother. She took her for long walks and gave her Christmas presents, displaying compassion and humanity but little awareness of Dawn's need for clear boundaries and roles. While these countertransference feelings were understandable reflections of the degree of Dawn's traumatisation, the occupational therapist had not used her feelings to inform her work but had acted on them without reflection. Her behaviour only set up false hope in Dawn and led to confusion about the nature of their relationship. Breaking professional boundaries and acting as a surrogate mother meant that the occupational therapist was doomed to fail and disappoint Dawn, who was not after all her daughter, and who could not ultimately be brought home and cherished.

An illustration of the depths of Dawn's neediness, and the strong responses that she evoked in professionals, was provided by her primary nurse whom I saw for supervision. She reported that she brought Dawn winter clothes to stop her from wandering around the hospital grounds in winter wearing only a thin dress and jumper. No other patient had elicited this response from the nurse who then found herself 'targeted' by Dawn for individual attention and asked many intrusive and personal questions, particularly about whether she had children. There was a point when Dawn became very angry and threatening towards this nurse, out of frustration that the relationship did not progress. Because the boundaries had already been broken through the special act of dressing Dawn, acting out the maternal transference, the nurse found herself 'targeted' and her own boundaries challenged. She found this very distressing, particularly because of the feelings of guilt and helplessness that Dawn awakened in her. This was especially difficult because of her particular responsibility for Dawn's ward-based programme. Eventually this nurse was able to use supervision to discuss the degree of her over-involvement with Dawn and to re-establish clear limits. She salvaged the relationship before the confusion overwhelmed either her or Dawn. Eventually Dawn's anger towards her subsided; although she wanted the attention of a special relationship it also appeared to be reassuring to her to have clear limits re-established. She was also able to recognise that her curiosity about the nurse's personal life was something that she had to manage and control.

Other staff found Dawn's crime so unbearable that they avoided working with her. This was particularly true of staff who had just given birth or who had difficulty in conceiving. The feelings evoked by women who have killed their babies in such staff need close supervision before therapeutic work can be undertaken. If unchecked, staff may adopt a punitive approach to these clients, which is a destructive form of over-involvement to be guarded against.

Women with borderline personality disorder may project their unwanted impulses and internal conflicts on to those around them: staff groups may mirror their psychic splitting. In Dawn's case some staff members wanted to mother and nurture her, in response to her deprivation and childlike dependence, while others wanted to punish and humiliate her, in response to the aggressive, narcissistic aspect of her personality. Very few felt indifferent to her or were able to adopt a stance of 'therapeutic neutrality'. It was for this reason that individual psychotherapy needed to be undertaken by someone who was not directly involved in her daily care. Those supportive aspects of individual nursing care, involving individual meetings, required close supervision to prevent boundary confusion. Dawn's despair and anger were powerfully projected, making it difficult for professionals to think about her care and respond effectively to her needs. Her psychic disorganisation made it impossible for her to think about her mental states, and also attacked the thinking of those around her, who, like Dawn herself, found themselves acting rather than reflecting. The power of the anxieties that she projected seemed to create this compulsion to act, and this action seemed to be a manic defence against actually understanding and thinking about her early and recent experiences of trauma, abuse and loss. This compulsion to act was mirrored in the offence itself, which seemed to be an attempt to annihilate a source of unbearable pain and longing.

Although I had attempted to forge a therapeutic alliance with her, Dawn found the perceived focus of work with me, on the offence,

bereavement, guilt and her future, unbearable to think about. She avoided
real engagement in the work and constantly attempted to draw me into a
more friendly discussion in which I would share information about my
own life with her. Her resistance to working therapeutically was evident
and, given the degree of trauma which she had experienced and the horror
of her offence, understandable. In the end, very little work was actually
achieved but she had, at least, had an experience of boundaried and clear
meetings with me. It was possible that by killing me off as a therapist
symbolically, preventing us from addressing significant areas of her life,
she would protect me from the murderous feelings towards me that would
emerge if she were actually to engage in work with me and allow herself
to become dependent on me. The depths of her murderous rage made it
feel unsafe to her to become involved with another person, and she
seemed desperate to retain a polite but distant relationship with me, and
one in which her status as an infanticidal patient in a regional secure unit
was wholly denied.

Infants as 'poison containers'

In his powerful and illuminating work, deMause (1990) argues that child
assault has been prevalent throughout different societies and throughout
history. He is committed to ending this destructive and cruel practice and
analyses its roots in unfulfilled psychological needs of the perpetrators
for love and protection, related to their own early experiences. His
perspective is that of psychohistory, 'the science of historical motivation'
which combines the approaches of psychodynamic psychotherapy and
the social sciences. DeMause states:

> The history of humanity is founded upon child assault. All families
> once practiced infanticide. All states trace their origin to child
> sacrifice. All religions began with the mutilation and murder of
> children. All nations sanction the killing, maiming and starving
> of children in wars and depressions. Child assault is, in fact,
> humanity's most powerful and successful historical group-fantasy.
> Using children as scapegoats to relieve personal internal conflict has
> proved an extremely effective way to maintain our collective
> psychological homeostasis.
>
> (deMause, 1990:1–2)

Infanticide, he argues, is universal and is found more in humans (in
relation to their offspring) than in any other species.

With great insight, deMause describes the psychodynamic processes involved in infanticide, in terms of treating children as receptacles of unacceptable impulses, 'poison containers', who can then be manipulated, tortured or killed:

> The main psychological mechanism that operates in infanticide is the same as is present in all cases of child assault – physical, sexual, or psychological. It involves using the child as what I have termed a 'poison container', a receptacle into which one can project disowned parts of one's psyche, so that one can manipulate and control these feelings in another body without danger to one's self.
>
> (deMause, 1990:4)

Dawn's killing of Gabriel reflects this psychic process. In the cases of women who kill their children there is a conflict between the desire to have children and the fear of motherhood, which may reflect a complex relationship between them and their own mothers, in which feelings of rivalry, envy, anger and deprivation may be evident. The mother who cannot bear to hear her infant scream may be rejecting, or assaulting, it because she wanted the baby to contain *her* despair, and feels unable to perform that maternal function herself. Again, this may relate to abuse, neglect and trauma in her own experiences in childhood, which dramatically interfere with her own relationship with her children (Bifulco and Moran, 1998). DeMause (1990) suggests that infanticidal mothers have had highly inadequate child-rearing experiences and have harsh, punitive superegos that demand punishment of their strongest wishes, including their wish to be a mother.

LEGAL ISSUES

Is infanticide a special case?

The classification of infanticide is contingent upon the mental state and intentions of the mother at the time of the child's death. An important question to consider is whether there are good conceptual and/or ethical grounds for the existence of a separate crime called infanticide, which refers to maternal killing of an infant who is less than 1 year old. The separate recording and classification of this crime has significant implications for the legal disposal of offenders and is premised on a particular, biological understanding of maternal 'disorders of mind'. Does this clarify this complex and tragic crime or is it an unnecessary and inaccurate notion?

Sentencing practice

In the United Kingdom but not in the United States the law has special provisions for the crime of infanticide. It is punishable like manslaughter which gives judges complete discretion over the sentence. Since 1976 the outcome for the charge of infanticide has always been a hospital order, probation order, conditional or absolute discharge (Bluglass, 1990). If murder, and not infanticide, is charged the woman may be allowed to plead guilty to infanticide, thereby avoiding a trial or medical evidence. This has the clear advantage of allowing the mother, who is already in a highly distressed state, to avoid the trauma of a public criminal trial.

A historical approach

The Infanticide Act has written into it the notion of instability of mind owing to childbirth and, if '*the presence of disturbance of mind*' at the time of the killing can be demonstrated, the mother will often receive a lighter sentence than she would if the infanticide plea were disallowed, or if, for instance, she had not succeeded in killing her child and was charged with grievous bodily harm or attempted murder. Under the 1803 Act the prosecution had to establish that the child had been born alive, with 'a separate existence'. The Offences Against the Person Act 1803 reformed the statute of 1623 and established infanticide as a crime, no different from murder. The mother was presumed innocent unless proved guilty; if a murder charge failed the jury could return a verdict of 'concealment of birth', with a maximum penalty of two years' imprisonment. Trials for concealment increased threefold between the 1830s and the 1860s.

The Offences Against the Person Act 1828 made it clear that the separate-existence rule did not apply to cases of concealment of birth (of a child born stillborn, for instance). The Offences Against the Person Act 1861 allowed the prosecution to bring an independent charge of concealment of birth and provided that this could be an alternative to a murder charge. Judges were unhappy with the law as they had to pass the death sentence on convicted women, knowing that, because of an increasingly sympathetic attitude to mothers, the sentence would not be carried out. Because of the harshness of the penalty, judges were increasingly reluctant to convict. The Infanticide Act of 1922 reduced the offence of child murder to manslaughter: 'where a woman caused the death of her newly born child by any wilful act or omission but at the time of the act or omission she had not fully recovered from the effect of giving birth to such child, by reason thereof the balance of her mind was disturbed' (cited by Bluglass, 1990:524).

The Infanticide Act 1938

The Infanticide Act was the result of a Bill introduced by a doctor and clarified anomalies in the 1922 Act but widened the psychological and physiological reasons for reducing the offence of child killing from murder to one of infanticide; Section 1(1) of the Infanticide Act states that a woman who has wilfully caused the death of her child under the age of 12 months will be punished as if she were guilty, not of murder, but of manslaughter if 'at the time of the act or omission the balance of her mind was disturbed by reason of her not having fully recovered from the effect of giving birth to the child, or by reason of the effect of lactation consequent upon the birth of the child'. This Act required only that there be a disturbance in the balance of mind at the time of the killing.

It has been argued that the courts are generally sympathetic to this group of offenders and, in practice, the degree of disturbance acceptable to the Court seems much less than would have been required if the defence had been one of diminished responsibility (Faulk, 1988). The sentences given are usually a probation order with or without psychiatric supervision. Infanticide applies only in the case of a mother killing her child as, presumably, the father could never be considered to be subjected to the hormonal imbalances produced by pregnancy and childbirth.

Critique of the Infanticide Act

The notion of female hysteria is woven into the fabric of the Infanticide Act. Women who have given birth are considered to be likely candidates for 'disturbance of mind' and, indeed, the supposed 'effects of lactation' are presumed to contribute to this mental disorder, in which state killing is justifiable. Far from considering the decision by a young woman, facing social censure, isolation and emotional upheaval for at least the next fifteen years of her life, to kill her child to be a rational, if highly unethical, decision, it is more palatable to justify this behaviour on the grounds of mental instability. The task of proving that her decision arose from disturbance of mind owing to raging hormones, to which she was victim, appeared to be relatively easy, given the preconceptions of the judges and the general public at the time the Act was framed. It would be hard to imagine a case where a neonaticide was not committed in the context of considerable despair. The social reality of shame, isolation and hardship should not be equated with the biological condition of postnatal instability. It is relatively easy to make a case for infanticide:

> this offence is ubiquitous in that the law requires only an association in time between the existence of a 'disturbance of mind' and the death of the child. There is no requirement for a causal connection. It is this that allows courts and experts considerable flexibility in each case.
>
> (Bluglass, 1990:527)

Despite suggestions that judges and public sentiment are sympathetic to women who kill their children, I would argue, on the contrary, that the presuppositions implicit in the Infanticide Act relate to deep-seated fears of women's procreative capacities. The fear of menstrual women and the mystique of childbirth are taboos which have held tremendous influence cross-culturally for centuries. Evidence from folklore and anthropology suggests that these taboos have shaped behaviour and attitudes towards women for centuries and led to their segregation. The implication is that woman is wholly ruled by biological forces.

Lotte Motz (1997) disputes the Jungian notion of 'The Great Mother' who was universally revered and respected, arguing instead that

> when we regard the beliefs of modern hunting and herding peoples of northern Eurasia we note that their attitude toward the 'mystery of the fertile womb' is far from reverent. The climate of emotion is, in these regions, so deeply affected by a fear of women's biological functions, menstruation, pregnancy and parturition that numerous rules and prohibitions were created to counteract the potential danger.
>
> (Motz, 1997:6)

These prohibitions included various rules regarding the demarcation of special 'women's places' in which the unclean women, menstruating, pregnant or following childbirth, are confined. Indeed, modern religions retain vestiges of these beliefs concerning the unclean nature of menstruating women, as is evident in the Orthodox Jewish tradition of the *mikvah*, in which women must immerse themselves in a pool of water, under strict supervision of a female attendant, after child birth and several days after the cessation of a menstrual period.

The tradition of fearing women and the mysterious biological forces which supposedly govern them is evident in the creation of the Infanticide

Act. Though apparently sympathetic to women, it actually deprives them of moral agency and feeds into the notion of woman as intrinsically hysterical and untrustworthy, literally a product of the unpredictable and terrifying womb which she houses. The scientific premises of the Act, with its inclusion of 'the effects of lactation' as a factor which contributes to mental derangement, are themselves open to dispute on scientific grounds. The supposed correlation between premenstrual syndrome and criminality in general is used to support the notion of hormonal causes of criminality. This form of argument is analogous to the biological reductionism evident in claims that rapists are governed by uncontrollable biological urges which must be satisfied. In both cases a simplistic but intuitively appealing model of deviance is proposed which portrays the offender as a victim of his or her own biology. In the case of rape, the psychological literature concerning motivations for rape indicates that while biological predisposition may be one factor in contributing to sexual offence, it is by no means a sufficient, or even necessary, cause of sexual offending. It has been documented that rapists often do not have full erections and it is widely accepted that the offence is far more connected with aggression, with the sexualised expression of dominance and control, often in people who feel humiliated and powerless, than with sexual arousal *per se* (Craissati, 1998). Sex offenders may themselves request hormonal treatment of their sexual drives but this can be interpreted as a form of denial of their own responsibility for their offending.

Similarly, the woman who commits a crime as serious as killing while distressed following childbirth cannot simply be assumed to be a hapless and passive subject of her hormones; she also displays a complex, and even rational, set of motivations and considerations within a particular social context. While her hormonal changes may have contributed to her behaviour and can be presented as a mitigating factor in consideration of her offence, to assign them the degree of primacy outlined in the Infanticide Act is to caricature and objectify the female offender and deny her agency. It also minimises the role of cultural and social pressures which may have tremendous influence on the decisions of young mothers faced with unwanted babies. In some cultures neonaticide of girl babies is not uncommon because of the open disregard for the value of female as opposed to male life, yet this practice could hardly be attributed simply to hormonal imbalances.

Infanticide is a tragic act of violence, which can result from a tremendous fear of social stigma, feelings of total helplessness in relation to an unplanned baby, or a range of complex psychological factors, which result in an almost psychotic panic, in which killing seems the only solution, particularly when the baby is newborn and has not yet been recognised by the mother as a separate human being, The threat of social stigma, coupled with profound psychic threat, may contribute to the mother's desperation to be free of the baby. In dynamic terms, infanticide can be seen as an expression of suicidal feelings on to an aspect of the self, the baby, who becomes a 'poison container' which must ultimately be destroyed.

Case illustration: Marina, a 22-year-old charged with concealment

Marina, a 22-year-old woman, the second daughter of a middle-class professional family, was brought to the attention of the forensic services following her arrest for concealment and suspicion of murder of a newborn infant. She was held in custody where her presentation and index offence were of concern to the prison doctor. She appeared to be in a state of shock and was at considerable risk from the other inmates because of the nature of her suspected crime. Psychological reports were requested in order to assist the Court in understanding how this apparently stable, middle-class woman had come to be charged with this shocking crime. She strenuously denied killing the baby and her solicitors were convinced that there was insufficient evidence to prosecute her for the charge of infanticide. The Crown Prosecution Service eventually dropped this charge and Marina pleaded guilty to the lesser charge of concealment. Marina had no previous convictions and was not known to the psychiatric services. Although her affect was flat and she seemed disorientated, she did not display signs of suicidal depression and had no symptoms of psychosis. Her manner and her behaviour appeared incongruous to the prison officers who tended to her on the hospital wing and who expected her to appear more mentally unwell and distraught than she seemed to be. She seemed, more than anything, to be vacant, to be devoid of emotion or life.

I visited Marina in the hospital wing of the women's prison where she had been placed on remand. She was dressed in casual, clean clothes but her self-care was otherwise poor and she seemed to have little awareness of her physical condition. Her hair was unwashed and her nails were badly bitten. She presented as a well-spoken, articulate and gentle woman who appeared emotionally detached from her situation. She described a sense of observing herself in the interview, and had difficulty in recalling the precise sequence of events surrounding the birth of her daughter. Marina seemed to be unaware of the severity of her situation and showed no signs of remorse related to the crime for which she had initially been investigated. She repeatedly said that she thought there had been a mistake and that, as far as she knew, she had neither intended to kill nor killed an infant.

Marina was polite and pleasant throughout my assessment of her but retained a detached and subdued manner throughout. Although she appeared to understand the purpose of the interviews at an intellectual level, she did not appear to engage emotionally. She described an uneventful childhood, with good relations with her parents, her elder sister, aged 25, and a younger brother, aged 19. Both mother and father had treated her with affection and concern and she had been raised a strict Catholic, with strong views about right and wrong. Her innocent and sheltered upbringing had been shattered when several years prior to this pregnancy, at age 17, she had been raped by a man with whom she was vaguely acquainted. She had become pregnant as a result of the rape and had a termination subsequently despite her beliefs that this would, in other circumstances, have been an unacceptable choice.

Marina had reported this rape to the police and her assailant had pleaded guilty to the lesser charge of indecent assault. He had been sentenced to three years' imprisonment, of which he served one and a half. She had not given evidence against him as he had pleaded guilty to the lesser charge. Although she had felt disappointed that he was not convicted for rape she had been greatly relieved that she had not been required to give evidence in Court. The crime had been publicised in the local papers and Marina had become the subject of much attention, which she had hated, feeling that her private trauma was being used in a sensational and public way. She had, however, continued with her studies, obtaining three A Levels and had gone on to university, where she received an honours degree in French and German. Her present boyfriend had been a fellow student at university and she had not told him about the rape, saying she had 'pushed the memories away', feeling that the entire experience belonged to someone else. Although she had friends from school she had not talked to them about the rape and had also fielded her parents' concerned and angry questions about it. She had known her assailant from her voluntary job where she worked in a shelter for homeless youths with drug and alcohol problems, and she had befriended him. He had accused her of 'leading him on'. She had felt too ashamed to discuss the rape with anyone, including her family.

Marina acknowledged that she must have been pregnant and given birth but said that the reality of 'what had happened' was only just beginning to dawn on her. She tended to speak of herself in the passive voice, which indicated how disconnected she had felt during and after the pregnancy and the birth of the baby. She was adamant that she had been unaware that she was pregnant, until she actually gave birth, noticing only that she had gained weight and suffered from tiredness and dramatic mood swings over the past year. She recalled that she had felt particularly exhausted on one afternoon a few weeks ago and that she had taken herself to bed. She had then begun to experience intense stomach pains and feelings of queasiness. She had attributed this to possible food poisoning and gone to the bathroom where she thought she might be sick. After two hours of lying and kneeling on the bathroom floor and attempting to throw up, the pains had intensified and the time between pains had shortened considerably. She had the desire to contract her vaginal muscles and push; she later recognised that she had been experiencing labour pains.

She had delivered the baby herself, alone in her flat, and described a sense of total disbelief and horror, as she had not had any awareness of being pregnant. She could not remember how the baby had been delivered or how the cord had been cut. She had noticed the sex of the baby and said she knew that the tiny thing was a girl, although it had seemed more like a strange creature than an actual child. The details of what happened next were vague but a picture emerged of Marina attempting to wash the blood and vernix off the baby and then becoming more frightened and distressed as she tried to get the baby to breathe. She claimed that the baby had never taken a breath, had been essentially stillborn and completely lifeless. When pressed on this point she became very quiet and still, looking around the room in a distracted and vacant way and then back at me, repeating that she was convinced that she had not given birth to a live child.

Following its delivery Marina had tried to wrap the baby in a blanket, she said, hoping that by keeping it warm she could create life in her. She had no sense of wanting to revive the baby because as far as she could remember it had never been alive. She placed the baby in her wardrobe, still wrapped in the blanket, and checked it periodically over the next four hours. It was, at this point, quite cold and stiff, still wet from her attempts to wash it. She described a growing realisation that she could not trust anyone with the news of what had occurred and a desire to push all the traumatic events out of her mind, to get the baby out of her sight altogether. She had decided to place the baby in the attic, in a shoe box and still wrapped in a blanket. She waited until she herself had stopped shivering and bleeding, which had been happening on and off since the baby had been born. She then put the shoe box, with the baby inside, into one of the suitcases which were stored in the attic. She said that at this point she was not aware of the illegality of her actions or had any idea that she should have contacted the emergency services. She described herself as 'out of it'.

Three days later she had still been physically weak, bleeding and exhausted, and her parents, who had come to visit her, noticed how pale and unresponsive she seemed. They became increasingly worried about her but she did not reveal any of the details about the previous three days. Her mother decided to come and stay overnight to keep an eye on her at the weekend, which was now six days after the birth of the baby. She noticed that Marina frequently went up to the attic, saying that she had to check on something, and eventually she followed her. Marina seemed to be talking to herself or to something inside a suitcase, and appeared to be totally preoccupied. Her mother confronted her about this, asking to look at the contents of the suitcase herself, to which Marina fiercely objected, becoming quite insistent that she should be left alone. Her mother demanded to see what was inside the suitcase and eventually Marina allowed her to see inside, where she discovered the tiny body of an infant.

According to her mother's witness statement, Marina had not seemed to be fully aware of the infant's condition, and had talked about making sure that the baby was still warm, and checking that the blanket was still securely wrapped around it. The mother, in a state of considerable distress, took her daughter and the baby, still in the suitcase, to the police station. Marina, in contrast, remained calm and composed throughout the police interview and was arrested on suspicion of murder and taken to the hospital wing of a women's prison. She was reported by the prison officers there to have remained calm, detached and even cheerful at times, as though she had not accepted or understood the seriousness of her situation. She did not show remorse for her act of concealment, or seem to grieve for the baby, who might still have been alive had she not acted with such impulsivity and desperation. It never became clear whether, in her panic, she might have suffocated and killed a living baby. Her psychic defences, including her powerful dissociation, had enabled her to split off and forget aspects of the awful events. She had lost all sense of agency.

Outcome

Marina received a two-year probation order for her conviction for concealment and a condition to attend for psychological treatment. She continued to maintain that she had not committed infanticide, although as her therapy progressed she acknowledged the degree to which she remained confused over the events immediately following the delivery of the baby, whom she named Laura Jane. She also began to relate the details of the rape and to describe her sense of being passive, powerless and invaded. This seemed mirror her experience of pregnancy, which she had therefore found painful to acknowledge, even to herself. In therapy she was able to make some sense of the experiences which she had undergone and to address the trauma of her rape. She never accepted her possible culpability for the death of her baby and remained horrified by the memory of its birth.

DISCUSSION

Hysterical denial of pregnancy

In understanding the psychological process involved in what appeared to be Marina's hysterical denial of her pregnancy certain factors are highly significant. The first of these is the role played by the traumatic rape and the attendant shame, distress, physical and emotional turmoil. Hysterical denial of pregnancy is generally associated with the first pregnancy in an immature woman (Green and Manohar, 1990).

A model of post-traumatic stress disorder could also be applied to Marina's situation. It is possible to understand that the various elements of her denial of pregnancy and experience of dissociation during the birth and shortly after delivery reflected psychic defences against reactivated trauma: she appeared to be in a state of considerable shock and disbelief. Her sense of emotional detachment and almost robotic actions as she attempted both to preserve the dead baby's life through wrapping it in blankets and to conceal and hide the fact of its birth through excessive secrecy are also indicative of a distress so profound that she lost all sense of reality.

According to a post-traumatic stress model the original rape and abortion would be seen as the initial trauma, which had been reawakened by the second pregnancy. One of the symptoms of post-traumatic stress disorder is dissociation, emotional numbness, shock and a sense of anxiety about situations reminiscent of the traumatic one. In interview Marina reported that she had experienced frequent flashbacks to the rape, that she had felt generally anxious around men, and that she had found sexual relations very unpleasant and frightening, although she had allowed her current boyfriend to have intercourse with her. She had been aware that they had not used contraceptive protection but had never considered the possibility that she would become pregnant; again this reflected her level of denial.

An important aspect of her behaviour was the desire to keep this baby in a concrete sense, that is, to hide and keep the baby, in secret, all to herself. She had been deprived of the opportunity to grieve for her earlier loss, through termination, or to process the traumatic events which she had experienced at the time of the rape. It seemed that her complicated, mixed and very painful feelings were buried until the birth of her child. It is possible that her awareness of the later pregnancy was heavily repressed by the traumatic associations of violation and invasion, in that pregnancy and childbirth can evoke very painful memories in women who have been sexually abused (Pines, 1993). It appeared that not until labour had begun in full had she allowed herself recognition of what was happening to her, which she experienced as an assault on her body and mind. It would not be surprising if she played a role in the baby's death, although her perception that the baby was stillborn may still have been a genuine one. Her apparent dissociation and emotional numbness were so powerful that her immediate actions directly following the birth were probably lost to her memory.

Marina's psychological disturbance was clearly evident in her attempt to preserve the baby, to keep it warm, safe and hidden: she was clearly unable to recognise the fact of the baby's death. It also suggests that some part of her was functioning maternally, in that she treated her baby as a loved, though lost, object. The checking on the baby, dead in the attic, can be seen as a tragic expression of what Winnicott describes as 'primary maternal preoccupation' where the mother is almost wholly focused on the needs of the infant and constantly checks on it, remaining in a psychic unit with the newborn. Marina's behaviour during pregnancy and after delivering the baby reveals her loss of any rational connection with the world, and an attempt to control and keep at bay the intense feelings of grief and anger which threatened to overwhelm her. She had, in one sense, become so alienated and passive during a violent sexual assault that pregnancy, with its powerful evocation of this, became impossible to think about. Her unconscious defence against intolerable feelings of shame, guilt and violation was to switch off and operate wholly through denial and dissociation. Additionally, the shame of the public recognition that she and her boyfriend had engaged in sexual intercourse appeared to play a significant part in her inability to acknowledge her pregnancy.

A related case of hysterical denial of pregnancy and neonaticide is described by Green and Manohar (1990) who describe the case of a young woman who killed her newborn baby by drowning her in the lavatory bowl in which she was born. The mother and her dead infant were later discovered by her boyfriend and police investigations brought a charge of second degree murder, later reduced to infanticide. Following her admission to hospital the mother maintained her denial of any memory of being diagnosed as pregnant, despite a positive pregnancy test conducted at four months following her presentation at her general practitioner's consulting rooms for non-specific malaise. Confirmation of the pregnancy had also involved an ultrasound examination. The young mother had repressed all memories of these events and maintained that she had had no idea that she was pregnant and had not realised that she was in labour until the baby was born and she had collapsed in shock. There was no evidence of psychosis or of an intention to kill. The authors link the patient's initial denial of memory of pregnancy diagnosis with her childhood memory of deceiving her parents and argue that the denial has an hysterical etiology. The features of the case illustrate many of the characteristics of neonaticide as described by Resnick (1970), including the patient being an immature girl giving birth to an illegitimate child and feeling oppressed by strong parental influences. The manner of the infant's birth and death by drowning in the lavatory bowl is also a common feature of neonaticide.

THEORETICAL APPROACHES

Maternal filicide and depression

There is strong evidence to suggest that depression is the diagnosis most often associated with filicide, although it must be remembered that the occurrence of child murder following childbirth is still much rarer than the occurrence of severe depression in puerperal women (Brockington, 1996). The most common type of crime found in depressed assailants (West, 1965) was maternal homicide of small children. The data on filicide are, however, somewhat contradictory in relation to incidence of child murder in general (Bourget and Bradford, 1987). For example, some authors, such as Gibson (1975), reported that 81 per cent of murdered children in England and Wales under age 16 were killed by their parents while Jason (1983) found that parental homicide is only a minority of the cases of child homicide and constitutes 29 per cent for all victims over age 3. The studies of Jason (1983) and Bourget and Bradford (1990) provided support for the research findings of previous literature in identifying the greater incidence of maternal rather than paternal perpetrators in cases of filicide, indicating that a higher proportion of these crimes are committed by mothers. In some cases of homicide of children the act is followed by suicide; the role of major affective disorder is clearly significant in these crimes. West (1965) found that this pattern occurs in more than 50 per cent of the murders committed by women. The suicide attempts are often serious and successful.

Herjanic *et al.* (1977) reported that female offenders suffering from affective disorders were charged with more serious crimes than schizophrenics or those with a personality disorder. This indicates the potential dangerousness of depressed sufferers with their tendency towards self-harm and nihilistic outlook on life. Although Bourget and Bradford (1987) suggest the possibility of a genetic predisposition for homicide, in individuals who may be at higher risk of developing major affective disorders, they emphasise the multi-faceted aspects of the crime, and the significance of psychosocial factors in the etiology of severe depression.

Major depression with psychotic features is the most common diagnosis in maternal offenders. Since the most critical period has been described as the first six months of life, this corresponds with the risk of maternal postpartum psychoses and depression. Another significant diagnostic category associated with filicide is schizophrenia.

Altruistic filicide is often associated with an underlying depressive illness and is characterised by the desire to kill the child 'to relieve real or imagined suffering' (Bourget and Bradford, 1987: 224). Extended suicide-homicide is significantly associated with altruistic motives. Psychological identification with a child may contribute to the conversion of suicide to filicide. Sullivan (1924) suggests that child murder in psychotic mothers is primarily an expression of suicidal tendencies. West (1965) concludes that murder-suicide in the course of depressive illness occurs at periods when the suicidal risk is at its greatest.

Bourget and Bradford (1990) add further support to the research pointing to parental filicide as being predominantly a female activity. In their study 69.2 per cent of the perpetrators were females. They note that in accidental filicide such as a fatal battered child syndrome the homicidal intent is lacking; in such cases the abusive parents are under intense and unusual stress at the time that the battering occurs, have been abused in childhood, and the victims are likely to be young and unwanted. They identified accidental filicide as occurring twice as often as pathological filicide which might be psychotically driven and have altruistic motives; it is likely that psychosocial factors play an important role in such cases.

In contrast, in their later study Bourget and Bradford (1990) found that a diagnosis of borderline personality was slightly more prevalent than diagnoses of major depression in mothers who kill accidentally, i.e. through fatal battering or neglect. This suggests that the link between hormonal imbalance postpartum, depression and killing may be weaker than previously assumed. They attribute this somewhat unexpected finding to the high proportion of 'battered child syndrome' cases in their sample, noting the similarity between battering parents and borderline personality disorder patients in terms of background characteristics. The authors highlight the significance of psychosocial stressors in filicide offences. Exposure to a variety of psychosocial stressors appeared to have been a major factor in most cases of filicide. Sixty-one and a half per cent of cases in their study had experienced severe psychosocial stress prior to committing the filicide. Possible stressors included financial hardship, moving house and relationship breakdown.

CLASSIFICATIONS OF FILICIDE

Parental killing can be roughly divided into two types:

1 Neonaticide – the killing of a newborn child within the first few hours of life.
2 Filicide – the killing of a child who is more than 1 day old. Infanticide refers to the killing by a mother of an infant who is less than 12 months old. Research has attempted to identify the types of child killing according to various classificatory systems, one of which is based on parental motive (Resnick, 1969, 1970) while another is based on the source of the impulse to kill (Scott, 1973).

Scott further classifies the following categories of parents who kill, based on their motivations during the killing:

1 Parents who kill an unwanted child.
2 Mercy killing.
3 Aggression attributable to gross mental pathology.
4 Stimulus arising outside the victim (displacement of anger, avoidance of censure, loss of status or loss of love object).
5 Stimulus arising from the victim (the battering parent who responds to the perceived provocation of an infant who will not stop crying).

D'Orban (1979) added a sixth category to this list:

6 Neonaticide, as defined by Resnick (1970), in view of its special characteristics and medico-legal interest from the point of view of the Infanticide Act.

Yet another classificatory system is provided by D'Orban, who studied women who killed their children and divided them into the following groups:

1 Battering mothers (36 subjects). In these cases the killing occurred as a sudden impulsive act characterised by loss of temper; immediate stimulus to aggression arose from the victim.

2   Mentally ill mothers (24 subjects). These mothers were severely mentally disturbed at the time of the killing and had been diagnosed with either psychotic illnesses, reactive depressions associated with suicide attempts, or personality disorders with depressive symptoms of sufficient severity to require hospital admission.

3   Neonaticides (11 subjects). These mothers attempted to kill their children within twenty-four hours of giving birth.

4   Retaliating women (9 subjects). For these mothers aggression towards the spouse was displaced on to the child, fitting the pattern of 'the Medea situation' described by Stern (1948). This category would correspond to Scott's categorisation of retaliatory killings and Resnick's 'spouse revenge filicides'.

5   Unwanted children (8 subjects). Women killed unwanted children by passive neglect or active aggression.

6   Mercy killing (1 subject). A genuine degree of caring for the victim and absence of secondary gain for the mother. This could arise, for example, in the case of a terminally ill child.

The notion of *stimuli arising outside the victim* refers to the kinds of major disturbances in psychological functioning found in mentally ill women and other mothers suffering depressive reactions as a result of real or perceived changes in their relationships, situation or status. Such women, who may not be considered to be severely disturbed prior to pregnancy and childbirth, are likely to have felt highly ambivalent about the pregnancy and the consequent changes in personal appearance. As outlined in the previous three chapters, Dinora Pines (1993) discusses with great sensitivity and poignancy the psychological conflicts that pregnancy and childbirth may awaken, and how unconscious conflicts can be dramatically reawakened during this time.

Perhaps the most difficult group of women for Courts and professionals to understand and empathise with are those who can be classified as *spouse revenge filicides*. Resnick (1969) and D'Orban (1979) describe these 'retaliating women' as a highly unstable and disturbed group with a high combined score on measures of stress. They were characterised by severe personality disorders, aggressive or impulsive behaviour, and suicide attempts leading to previous psychiatric hospital admission. They had chaotic and hostile marital relationships and were considered to have used their children to manipulate their spouses. Bluglass (1990) found them to have immature, child-like and histrionic personalities which, when followed up for extended periods following the initial acute episode, would often be misdiagnosed as psychotic. This appears consistent with a diagnosis of personality disorder rather than depression.

Neonaticide appears to have the most accessible social explanation, as it occurred with greater frequency in earlier times when contraception was primitive, social conditions such as overcrowding common, and women easily exploited. Many unwanted babies were produced and disposed of. Bluglass claims:

> Such deaths still occur from time to time, often to young, immature, dull mothers who are often ignorant and naive. In a number of cases the mother has denied the reality of her pregnancy, or frankly claims that she was totally unaware of it, in convincing terms. The babies are sometimes born in hotel rooms and death is by drowning in the toilet. Others are strangled, suffocated, or other methods are used.
>
> (Bluglass, 1990:527)

The most common reason (80 per cent, Faulk, 1988) for neonaticide is psychosocial in that the mothers want to be rid of the baby immediately after its birth; 'The majority of the offenders are young women who have become pregnant and wish to get rid of the unwanted child because of shame or fear' (Faulk, 1988:253).

The other cases of filicide, a small minority, have been classified as follows (Resnick 1970):

1 An acute psychosis with delusional motivation.
2 Altruistic killing.
3 Child battering.

Resnick (1970) states that filicide is committed twice as frequently by mothers as by fathers and that when the mother is responsible she is *frequently assessed as mentally disturbed*. He discusses acutely psychotic women with delusional motivation and women who kill their deformed or damaged babies altruistically.

Infanticide, filicide and psychosis

In addition to maternal mental state there are features of the killing which contribute to an understanding of the motivation for it: these include the specific circumstances and method of the killing, the presence or absence of others involved in the death, and the history of child-care prior to the offence. In cases where a woman is actively psychotic when she kills, there may be the presence of delusions in which the child must be killed to ensure its salvation or for other reasons of special significance to the mentally ill mother. An omnipotent enemy may be imagined, who can only be defeated through the death of the child. These psychotic beliefs may, in part, be considered to be projections of the mother's own murderous impulses towards her children, and her fear of being out of control and dangerous. In her confusion she may feel compelled to act on her false belief that she must kill her child to save it and may have no insight into her own degree of psychic stress. Her homicidal act is often followed by her suicide, or a suicide attempt.

One of the most distressing aspects of working with the mentally ill mother who has killed is that when the florid symptoms of psychosis abate the full impact of the bereavement will surface, coupled with tremendous guilt once insight has occurred. Although the psychotic features may persist, any insight can leave the mentally ill killer overwhelmed by her grief and tortured by guilt. In a sense, the psychotic delusions that she had killed to save her child were self-protective. Once her mental illness abates, and the psychotic beliefs lose their intensity, she may long to make reparation for her action, even wishing to become pregnant again to replace the loss of the child. When women have killed in the context of a psychotic delusion about their child being subject to danger, the return of mental health can be a torment, as it brings with it the realisation that the killing was not necessary: the combined weight of bereavement and responsibility for causing the death of a child may seem unbearable to these women, who may seek to kill themselves once they are mentally well enough to understand what they have done. The task of therapy is not only to help them to come to terms with their grief, and manage the traumatic experiences related to their offences, but to help them to cope with their overwhelming guilt feelings and sense of absolute loss. The fear of becoming ill again, and of losing the distinction between fantasy and reality, may be profound.

Elimination of an unwanted child

Women whose social and psychological circumstances may make the prospect of caring for a child untenable, to the extent that the existence of the child cannot be tolerated, can be further subdivided into those mothers who kill their children violently and those whose children die as the result of neglect. This may be referred to as the act/neglect distinction. It is important to recognise that neglect itself contains aggression. It would be useful to distinguish between levels of awareness of the consequences of actions; the woman who deliberately starves her child or deprives him or her of comfort may in fact be more consistently aggressive and abusive than the woman who unthinkingly lashes out at her child in a moment of loss of control. In Bluglass's (1990) review the mothers in the 'neglect' category were younger than those in the second group and historically accounted for large numbers of child deaths, through neglect or starvation and denial of the pregnancy. Denial of the pregnancy, despite weight gain and amenorrhoea, was a common feature. In such mothers no psychiatric diagnosis is usually found or 'there is evidence of abnormal personality with neurotic features and an early personal history of family discord and maltreatment. Neglect of the child may reflect the mother's own pathology, for example death by malnutrition in a child whose mother suffers from anorexia nervosa' (Bluglass, 1990:525). The mother's lethal over-identification with the infant in these cases is evident.

CRITIQUE OF CLASSIFICATORY SYSTEMS

The classifications presented fail to mention those mothers who were themselves subject to physical violence at the hands of partners and were unable to protect children adequately; they may have been subsequently charged with killing their child, or being an accomplice to this crime. The classificatory schemes outlined tend to emphasise individual psychopathology at the expense of understanding the social context, or the degree to which the woman could have been acting out of fear of a violent partner, or in the context of being heavily influenced by a man. There is little emphasis on the tremendous cultural pressures which may contribute to the woman's actions, and her sense of isolation and despair in relation to caring for an infant. Although Bourget and Bradford (1900) highlight the role of psychosocial stressors in filicide offences they do not incorporate this into their system of classification.

The notion of altruistic killing reflects a certain *naïveté* in its assumption that the killing could occur without an aggressive or narcissistic component. The term altruistic is used to describe motivation to prevent distress and suffering, but this avoids the issue of the impact of the existence of disability on the mother, and the particular threats to her identity that a disabled child poses for a narcissistically driven mother. Indeed, Resnick (1970) describes such 'altruistic' killings as delusional on occasion, and sees them as sometimes part of an extended suicide. It appears that such an 'altruistic' killing always reflects a significant element of suicidal motivation, in terms both of an 'elimination fantasy' (Campbell and Hale, 1991) and of the mother's narcissistic identification with her damaged baby. The notion of elimination of unacceptable parts of the self through murder (or suicide) is congruent with the idea of children as poison containers.

The finding of a strong association between depression and maternal killing has been used to highlight the role of individual psychopathology decontextualised from the social factors which lead to and exacerbate depression, leaving depressed mothers socially isolated and without practical support. It could be argued that the intervening variable of major affective disorder is genetically loaded but that its expression in a violent or non-violent form is multiply determined. There is a powerful link between homicidal and suicidal urges. Depression is the precipitant which can lead to the enactment of either or both impulses. The assessment of depression plays an important role in determining the risk that a woman poses in terms of harm to herself or others. This evaluation should take into account her social circumstances. The quality of social, practical, emotional and psychological support available to a depressed mother is crucial in risk assessment. If the mother requires psychiatric treatment of depression, early recognition of this will reduce the risk that she poses to herself and her baby.

CONCLUSION

The lack of data about the best treatment for depressed mothers and the most useful settings for assessment has hindered the development of informed practice. Although there are specialist settings for mentally ill mothers and babies to be kept together while the mother is treated and observed, there is a paucity of data comparing these units with others where mother and baby are separated. Kumar *et al.* (1994) note the difficulty of making informed decisions in the light of the absence of comparative data. Kumar and Hipwell (1996) have developed a clinical rating scale, the Bethlem Mother–Infant Interaction Scale, designed to assess mother–infant interaction within the clinical setting in an attempt to evaluate the degree of risk which a mother may pose to her infant. It remains to be seen whether such a scale will have predictive validity in enabling clinicians to evaluate a mother's capacities to provide safe parenting for her child. Oates (1994) describes the practice of inpatient psychiatric treatment for mothers and babies, such as that offered at the Queen's Medical Centre, Nottingham. Such specialist treatment is not, however, usually available for women who are already mentally ill, or known to the psychiatric services when they give birth. The relative lack of treatment for mentally ill mothers and their babies may reflect a social resistance to acknowledging the fact of maternal violence. This denial results in a failure to provide appropriate facilities.

There is profound resistance to acknowledging maternal violence. The tragic cases of infanticide and other maternal killings tend to be viewed as evidence of biological disturbances of mind, as reflected in the Infanticide Act. It is essential to recognise the possibility of female violence, and its manifestation in violence against children. Analysis of the dynamics of female violence and repeated abusive patterns of mothering is crucial. Empirical evidence for the intergenerational transmission of abusive patterns of parenting is vitally important and has contributed to our understanding of the impact of early experience on parenting and the need for interventions, such as individual psychotherapy and parenting groups, to help to break the cycle of child abuse. Clearly, social conditions which contribute to maternal depression, parental discord and stress will impact adversely on child-rearing, and in a society where young single mothers are treated with contempt and hostility one could expect the offence of infanticide to continue to occur, as an act of desperation.

There is no need to rely on biological causes of mental instability in cases of infanticide; rational and psychological reasons exist. Cases where psychiatric disturbance leads to mothers killing their children can be dealt with under the Homicide Act and a plea of manslaughter on the grounds of diminished responsibility can be made. The Infanticide Act appears to be unnecessary and predicated on a dangerous model of female instability.

Part II

Violence against the self

Chapter 5

Deliberate self-harm

INTRODUCTION

'Deliberate self-harm is a symptom of internal distress, which has both a private and a public message' (Adshead, 1997:111). Like other manifestations of female violence, self-harm is viewed with horror and incomprehension by many and its origins and purpose are ignored. I consider it to reflect the typically female expression of anger, which is to turn it against the self. While men tend to cope with anger by directing it outward, viewing themselves as the victims of injustice in a harsh and punitive world, women often blame themselves, and take responsibility for wrong done to them. When memories of abuse or feelings of anger threaten to overwhelm them, and destroy their conciliatory stance in relation to aggressors, they turn the anger inwards, and, rather than damaging the other person, inflict injury on themselves. For self-harmers the scars caused by cutting symbolise their psychic pain to the outside world. Self-harm makes public this private pain and expresses that which cannot be thought about. The action of self-harm replaces and prevents thinking.

In this chapter I discuss two central models for understanding deliberate self-harm, the psychodynamic and the psychiatric, and consider treatment approaches from the perspectives of psychodynamic psychotherapy, feminist theory and dialectical behavioural therapy. I provide a critique of the psychiatric model of self-harm which stresses its link with borderline personality disorder. In my extended case illustration I explore the various functions which deliberate self-harm can serve.

Self-harm occurs in the general population, in individuals who have no contact with psychiatric or psychology services. The clients whom I see may have difficulties which are on the extreme end of the continuum but their underlying experiences and mode of expression relate to female experience in general, and female violence in particular. To pathologise these women is to ignore the existence of female violence and its manifestation in aggression against the self.

Self-injury is not necessarily a suicide attempt or simply manipulative behaviour. It is a complex set of behaviours, with different meanings in different contexts. Its significance for a particular individual can be gleaned only through sensitive analysis. Any attempt at treatment of this behaviour must be based on a thorough and sophisticated understanding of the thoughts and desires which gave rise to it, and its psychological functions. Understanding the reasons why a woman self-harms is the first stage in enabling her to find other, less violent, ways to articulate her distress and alleviate her pain.

DEFINING THE PARAMETERS OF DELIBERATE SELF-HARM

The term 'self-harm' has sometimes been used to include apparent suicide attempts but it has been argued that there is a distinction between lethally motivated suicide attempts and what has been termed the self-harm syndrome (Pattison and Kahan, 1983). The latter is marked by late onset in adolescence, multiple episodes over many years and harm which is directly inflicted upon the body (Sabo et al., 1995). Suicidal motivation is not a feature of deliberate self-harm as defined by Pattison and Kahan. This contrasts with the model of self-harm described by Campbell and Hale (1991) who identify unconscious suicidal motivations in self-harm, including a fantasy of 'elimination', in which bad bits of the self can be evacuated through attacks on the body.

In their study of deliberate self-harm in women in Ashworth Hospital, Liverpool, a special hospital for patients considered to require both maximum security and psychiatric care, Liebling and Chipchase (1993) found that the most frequent types of self-harming behaviour were cutting, attempted suicide and self-strangulation. They used a broad definition of self-harm which included suicide and suicide attempts, endorsing the notion that self-harm expresses a suicidal fantasy.

The term 'deliberate self-harm' in the specific sense is generally confined to cutting, strangulation, head-banging, burning and insertion into the body of sharp or painful objects. Although burning and/or cutting oneself may appear to be highly unusual and bizarre activities, they are not, in fact, uncommon in certain populations, such as among adolescent girls who have been sexually abused. These acts of violence, while directed against the self, also have indirect victims, such as parents and medical professionals who witness these acts of self-mutilation and the scars which are produced. The failure to protect the young woman from her own destructiveness may induce strong guilt feelings in these carers when they are faced with these indelible images of distress.

Deliberate self-harm is a powerful bodily enactment of psychic pain which women demonstrate much more frequently than men. In the United Kingdom one in seven women prisoners will self-harm and self-mutilate, while the comparable figure for male prisoners is one in thirty-three (Lloyd, 1995:178). The gender difference in self-harming rates may reflect social conditioning, which requires women not to express anger, and to value their appearance and social acceptability above all else. Attacking themselves is not only one of the legitimate channels allowed women to express their anger, it is also a defiant protest against the idealised, sentimentalised image of them which others hold. It is an attempt to use the body to point to an underlying, psychic damage, and, as such, is eloquent. It reflects the way that women communicate their experiences and assert control over their private spheres of influence, their own bodies. It can also be understood as an attack on the body of the mother, as symbolised by the woman's own body.

Women typically locate their sense of identity in their bodies, which is itself a reflection of the tremendous cultural emphasis placed on women's bodies, and their reproductive capacities. They express anger, contempt and shame through injuring their bodies, using the concrete experience of pain to symbolise psychological anguish.

DELIBERATE SELF-HARM AND THE MODEL OF FEMALE PERVERSION

Self-injury has a compulsive aspect that parallels the strength of a perversion: self-harming temporarily affords a fantastic, but short-lived, sense of release from depression. The model of perversion described by Welldon (1992) can be applied to self-injury, which she views as a typically female act of violence in which the crime is committed against the body. In female perversion it is the woman's whole body which is the instrument of sexualised aggression whereas in the male it is the phallus. Although there are cases of female flashers, this is a much rarer perversion than self-harm, which involves the whole body, not just the genitals. The aggressive impulse is turned inwards on to their own bodies for self-harmers. This may have a sexual component, creating a release from tension similar to that achieved through orgasm. For Welldon, the origin of this self-harm is the woman's early object relations, that is, her experience of being mothered in infancy:

> During adolescence, if she hates her mother's sexual body and is unable to identify with her and her body, the adolescent girl will use her hand to attack her own body in a compulsive way by, for example, cutting her arms or wrists . . . In doing such harm to their bodies they are expressing tremendous dissatisfaction, not only with themselves but also with their mothers, who provided them with the bodies they are now fighting.
>
> (Welldon, 1992:40)

In their study of the link between self-mutilation, anorexia, and dysmenorrhea in obsessive compulsive disorder, Yaryura-Tobias *et al.* (1995) define self-mutilation as 'a volitional act to harm one's own body without intention to cause death' and argue that there are four distinct populations in which self-mutilation is found: in mental retardation and other organic conditions, in psychoses, in personality disorders, particularly borderline personality disorders, and in inmates. The latter appear to be responding to their incarceration. The authors state that 'these acts were compulsive, ritualistic, usually painless, and capable of relieving tension' and noted that the frightening content of the obsessions which led to self-mutilation often involved the fear of harming others' (Yaryura-Tobias *et al.*, 1995:35). This finding highlights the profound link between homicidal and suicidal actions, i.e. aggression directed towards others and towards the self. Self-harm may be a 'safe' alternative to murderous assaults on others. It is possible that the 'fear of harming others' actually disguises a wish to harm others, a desire to enact revenge which is suppressed.

THE FUNCTIONS OF DELIBERATE SELF-HARM

The function, as well as the definition, of self-harm has been variously identified. The reasons why women self-harm include depression, to regain control, and to reduce feelings of anxiety and tension (Sellars and Liebling, 1988; Burrow, 1992; Cookson, 1977). The communicative function of self-harm is central: women harm themselves primarily to express their distress and anger, in the hope that others will respond to this communication. They manage the intense internal pain which they feel by directing it on to themselves, and externalising it in an attack on the self. For these women self-harm serves two central psychological functions: to temporarily alleviate mental pain, and to channel their anger. The desire to self-harm can be so powerful that it can mirror a compulsion, an overriding urge to act, which takes precedence over other considerations and desires. It is overwhelming and once it has occurred in thought there is a tremendous pressure to act. The avoidance of painful thinking, through its behavioural enactment, is one of the central functions of deliberate self-harm.

Self-harm often coexists with other difficulties. Williams's (1989) study of self-injurious behaviour of women in the community associated self-injury with social anxiety and found that women who self-injured were unhappy with their bodies and themselves and felt that their lives were out of control. Self-injury appeared to offer them a means of obtaining control, however temporary.

A PSYCHODYNAMIC MODEL OF SELF-HARM

Self-harm and early trauma: attacks on thinking

Adshead stresses that 'a psychodynamic formulation needs to complement a psychiatric diagnosis and behavioural description of deliberate self-harm' rather than presenting a mutually exclusive alternative (Adshead, 1997:111). Self-harm can be understood as a cruel attack on the body which represents an attempt to kill off the self (Campbell and Hale, 1991). These assaults are the expressions of previous traumatic experiences which are expressed through and on the body; the scars left by self-mutilation are literally the embodiment of the traumas which they reflect. Adshead (1997) argues that a central reason for the expression of these traumas through violence on the body is the attack on thinking that the traumatic experience produces, with the result that the experience is somatised, that is, expressed through the body. It is as if a memory of terrible overwhelming pain is imprinted on the body through its own actions. The self-mutilating woman may not be able to process the experience at a symbolic or intellectual level because of the tremendous power of the traumatic experience, or because she has been traumatised at an early developmental stage. The trauma can safely be enacted through her own body, which is symbolically linked to her mother's body. Campbell and Hale (1991) suggest that the suicidal fantasy expresses a symbolic attack on the mother's body.

The link between childhood sexual abuse and deliberate self-harm

The experience of childhood sexual abuse or incest can contribute to the emergence of suicidal behaviour, as expressed through self-harm. Campbell and Hale (1991) emphasise the aggression inherent in self-harm and the underlying fantasies which motivate such behaviour, seen as a type of acting out, in which the action serves as

> the substitute for remembering a traumatic childhood experience, and unconsciously aims to reverse that early trauma. The patient is spared the painful memory of the trauma, and via [his] action masters in the present the early experience he originally suffered passively . . . the internal drama passes directly from unconscious impulse to action, short-cutting both conscious thought and feeling.
>
> (Campbell and Hale, 1991:280)

Self-harm occurs as the result of an 'elimination fantasy' in which the body is experienced as a potential destroyer which threatens to kill the self. For an incest survivor the guilt of having enacted Oedipal fantasies will be profound, generating a perceived need for punishment. The difficulty of integrating 'bad' desires within the self is evident in the need to split off these impulses and then, having located them in the split-off body, attempt to kill them off.

For an abuse survivor, the split-off body is the object upon which is projected her murderous impulses in order for her 'real' self to survive; that is, the violence is fundamentally self-preservative. She is attempting to eliminate the 'bad' self which had sexual relations with her father or other adults. During the experience of being sexually abused, the child or adolescent might find it protective for the body to be split off to preserve some sense of a good object; that is, the mind could float above the violence which being inflicted on her body, and thus survive. The sense of her body as a source of badness will be particularly intense for an abuse victim whose adjustment to her sexually maturing body, with its confusing and overwhelming infantile wishes, was grossly disturbed by paternal abuse. Her conception of her body as 'other' and as a receptacle for violent impulses makes it possible for the survivor of sexual abuse to inflict violence against her body; her sense of guilt for the sexual abuse, and the false belief that she may have invited the abuse, may also contribute to a need for punishment, which will be self-inflicted.

In their psychoanalytic discussion of depersonalisation and self-mutilation, Miller and Bashkin (1974) write of a patient that 'he preserved in the flesh, in a dramatic and conspicuous manner, the history of events he could not integrate into the fabric of his personality' (Miller and Bashkin, 1974:647). This description powerfully evokes the experience of women who have been sexually, physically or emotionally abused in childhood and who express their traumatisation through their bodies. There is also a sense in which the events, which could not be talked about in childhood, were preserved through their inscription in the flesh. The difficulty in integrating or assimilating these early experiences is revealed through the literal splitting-off of the anger and focusing it on to the body. Deliberate self-harm may be an attempt to preserve the good bits of the self, which were not corrupted by abuse, and which are located in the mind or 'soul' of the survivor, by identifying the damage clearly in the body, and, in a sense, confining it to that realm.

The common association between deliberate self-injury and a history of childhood sexual abuse has been widely documented; some studies have found that over 50 per cent of patients who displayed deliberate self-harm had been sexually abused by one of their primary caretakers (Briere and Zaidi, 1989; van der Kolk *et al.*, 1991). Both phenomena coexist in very disturbed women as well as in women who do not suffer from major psychiatric disorders. The diagnosis of borderline personality disorder is itself associated with serious sexual and emotional abuse in childhood and may reflect the extent to which very distressing and traumatic experience interferes with personality development. The personality organisation which results may be one in which early or primitive psychic defences are heavily relied upon and the world is perceived to be a frightening place, which indeed it has been for these abused women. The defences of splitting and projective identification are used to ward off feelings of unhappiness which threaten to overwhelm and engulf them. Self-harm can be seen as one type of projection and one manifestation of profound difficulty in managing anger and unhappiness. Because these women have not had the experience of a parent who is able to contain these feelings, they have not internalised this containing capacity, and they strive instead to get rid of these feelings by enacting them.

Therapy can demonstrate that apparently intolerable psychic pain can be borne and thought about, that memories and feelings of despair do not necessarily require urgent action. The therapist can offer the woman an experience of containment, and can show her that she can bear to think about her history. The link between sexual abuse, in which essential boundaries and taboos have been violated, and the pain of self-injury is evident in the way that the self-mutilator violates the boundary between thought and action, internal and external, psychological and physical pain, in an apparent attempt to locate and circumscribe the damage. The taboos of not cutting one's own flesh or piercing oneself internally are also broken and the scars on the body can be considered to be symbolic 'battle scars'. Self-injury demonstrates the historical damage which has been done and bears witness to crimes which have already been committed against the body; as Miller and Bashkin describe in their account of a man who could not experience his life as continuous, and who had no sense of stable and enduring personal identity 'F's self-inflicted wounds with all their visibleness became for him constant and concrete reminders that he, in fact, had lived and suffered in time' (Miller and Bashkin, 1974:647).

Once self-harm has occurred and the body barrier has been broken it is increasingly easy to enact violence against the self. Because self-harm offers only short-lived relief there is a compulsion to repeat the action whenever anxiety reaches unacceptable levels. The function of therapy will be to articulate these thoughts, reducing the need for splitting off good and bad feelings and acting out. Women who have suffered rejection, abandonment or neglect by their mother may express anger and disappointment through vicious attacks on their own bodies, and through direct assault on their sexual organs. Women who insert objects into their vagina that cut or harm may symbolically be attacking their mother's body. The self-harming woman 'internalised the source of her original trauma, and acts sadistically towards her own body' (Adshead, 1997:41). They may also be attacking their own identity as mothers or potential mothers and and symbolising the dangers inherent in sexual relations. To attack the body in this way may still have a self-preservative function in that the bad part of the self, the body, specifically the genitals, can be damaged in order that the rest of the self can survive; the danger is located in a particular place and then annihilated.

Self-harm as primitive defence mechanism: splitting

An important component in the development of self-injurious behaviour is the primitive defence mechanism of splitting, in which good and bad aspects of an experience are kept separate in order to protect the person against unbearable feelings of loss or anxiety. The self-harmer tries to annihilate her mental pain by inflicting physical pain on herself. She also indirectly attacks those around her, who have failed to protect her or help her to manage unbearable memories and feelings, so that she feels forced to enact them on to her own body. This aggression may be fuelled by the anger that she feels towards her once idealised carers, and may also be an attempt to protect them from this rage by turning it on herself.

THE PSYCHIATRIC MODEL

Self-harm and borderline personality disorder

Self-harm has been found to be strongly associated with the diagnosis of borderline personality disorder, and, to a lesser extent, with antisocial personality disorder. One diagnostic feature of borderline personality disorder is the presence of intermittent psychosis, which can be associated with deliberate self-harm in two ways: first, women may say they self-harm in response to voices; second, psychosis creates a divorce from reality and altered state of consciousness, or dissociation, in which action can take place without the usual emotional affect, physical perceptions or cognitive awareness. This may explain the sense of release from tension and absence of pain which self-harmers typically experience (Adshead, 1997).

In their study of female prisoners who self-harm, Wilkins and Coid (1991) found that self-mutilation, 'as a single variable, identified a subgroup of female prisoners with severe personality disorder and multiple impulse disorders' (Wilkins and Coid, 1991:247). This subgroup (7.5 per cent of women with a history of self-mutilation received into a London prison) were also characterised by disruption and deprivation in their early family environment, and greater experience of physical and sexual abuse than controls. Their criminal histories also differed from those of offenders who did not self-mutilate and were characterised by an early onset of persistent, serious and wide-ranging patterns of offending. The authors found that the women who self-mutilated demonstrated abnormal psychosexual development and 'polymorphous perversity'. Despite their severe psychopathology and repeated and frequent psychiatric contact, these women were subject to long periods of custody, with psychiatric hospitals being 'unwilling or unable to cope with their behaviour'.

Self-harm as a symptom-reduction strategy

There is evidence that the function of self-mutilation for women with borderline personality disorder is to obtain relief from the affective components of the disorder, i.e. their mood, and that the deficit in impulse control is associated with other disorders of impulse control (Wilkins and Coid, 1991). They conclude that the underlying disorder is the intensity of the depressed and anxious feelings, rather than a behavioural disorder. They suggest that the most important factor in generating and maintaining self-injurious behaviour is the release of tension, anxiety and depression which the women report, and consider this to be of greater significance than environmental factors. Wilkins and Coid (1991) find support for the hypothesis that a history of self-mutilation in women prisoners indicates severe and extensive psychiatric pathology and does not merely reflect the institutional environment alone. Their study involved screening all women remanded in custody by nursing staff for a history of self-mutilation and also included checking for evidence of scarring during the routine physical examination. Controls were sixty-two women selected at random from the remaining pool of prisoners.

In a later study Coid *et al.* (1992) used cluster analysis of phenomenological variables and the associated symptom profile of self-mutilation in seventy-four women remanded in custody. They identified a subgroup of women who injured themselves in order to relieve the symptoms of their underlying severe mood disorder; this subgroup of women also received a diagnosis of borderline personality disorder.

There were distinct differences between this subgroup of self-injuring women and those who self-injured reactively, i.e. not as a result of a disorder of mood but as a reaction to life events, psychotic illness or as a suicide attempt. For the women diagnosed with borderline personality disorder, the central function of self-mutilation was relief from mounting feelings of tension, depression, anxiety and anger, which built up as the day progressed and for which no particular external triggers could be identified by the women themselves. These women described the lack of physical pain accompanying self-mutilation and the successful reduction of symptoms of affective disorder. They also found that self-harm caused the cessation of experiences such as depersonalisation and derealisation; that is, that the use of self-injury resulted in release from distressing psychological experiences and facilitated the return of 'feeling real'.

Reactive self-harm

The women who self-mutilated in response to underlying feelings of tension, anxiety and depression were in stark contrast to another group of women, who could clearly identify triggers in the external world which preceded the decision to self-harm, and who were not diagnosed with borderline personality disorder. This group was identified as self-injuring in reaction to external events rather than because of 'internal' disorders of mood and the resulting symptomatology, and was found to have a different pattern of self-injury. They did not self-mutilate more in the evening and at night, unlike the women diagnosed with borderline personality disorder, who appeared to be responding to an accumulation of symptoms; their motivation for self-injury was different. They did not rely on self-mutilation as a symptom-reduction strategy and, indeed, appeared to be free of the symptoms found in the borderline personality disorder group.

The groups were clearly differentiated by the phenomenology of their self-injury, their psychiatric history and their criminal histories. The women with borderline personality disorder diagnoses were also found to have much more extensive psychiatric and criminal histories than the other group of women who appeared to be using self-harm as an intelligible and discrete response to particular environmental stressors. The role of the disturbed early environment was identified as a significant factor in differentiating between these groups of women who self-harm.

Self-harm and a deficit in impulse control

The studies cited above differ from previous research in terms of highlighting the positive function of self-mutilation in women with severely disturbed personality organisation. Coid and his colleagues emphasise the role of underlying mood disturbance rather than lack of impulse control or a primary disturbance in behaviour, as stressed by Pattison and Kahan (1983), and emphasise the need for therapeutic intervention, rather than the 'therapeutic nihilism' often associated with the diagnosis of personality disorder.

Lacey and Evans (1986) identified a group of patients with multiple disorders of impulse control, poor prognosis for treatment, and frequent presentation at the psychiatric services, and suggest that this is evidence for a 'multi-impulsive personality disorder'. The types of impulse disorder which can co-exist with self-injurious behaviour include compulsive sexuality, kleptomania, eating disorders and anger-control difficulties. Coid et al. (1992) also suggest that different forms of destructive behaviour can replace self-mutilation and that in the personality disordered group of women in their study the presence of other 'impulse disorders' was usual; the non-personality disordered group of women did not usually manifest these impulse disorders but self-harmed in reaction to external events. Coid et al. do not view a deficit in impulse control as being a sufficient cause for the self-harm behaviour, in the absence of underlying depression or anxiety, viewing these 'affective disorders' as an integral part of the self-harm syndrome:

> Lacey and Evans contrast with us in emphasising the primary problem as a deficit in impulse control closely related to difficulty in coping with depressive emotions and anxiety rather than the severity of these symptoms themselves. We would argue that this deficit in impulse control is combined with a severe underlying affective disorder . . . the disastrous combination of the two has led to their inclusion in a prison sample and the poor prognosis.
>
> (Coid et al., 1992:11)

It is worth noting that the effects of incarceration can result in high rates of self-harm, and may reflect an institutional dynamic, in which self-harm is accepted as the currency of communication within an organisation. The high rates of self-harm among women in prisons, special hospitals and psychiatric units point to the possibility that incarceration can itself predispose women to self-harm.

The research conducted by Coid and colleagues is important in its elucidation of the complex multifaceted nature of self-harm, and the need to identify the particular function which it serves for an individual in terms of her particular constellation of psychological difficulties, and her social context. It highlights the significance of underlying psychological distress for particularly disturbed women, and indicates the powerful role of self-injury as an effective strategy for symptom relief. The study of self-injury within a custodial population, and the comparisons between the groups of women in terms of their patterns of injury and factors in their own current psychological presentation and background history, provide a useful starting point for further research, identifying and distinguishing between types and functions of self-injurious behaviour.

The psychiatric debate centres on whether self-harm is predominantly a function of an 'impulse deficit' or symptom relief from an 'affective disorder'. There are strong links between borderline personality disorder and self-harm and it is suggested that the subgroups of women who are diagnosed with borderline personality disorder and who self-harm do so as a result of the intensity of their underlying 'symptoms' rather than in reaction to particular external events or 'triggers'.

Critique of the psychiatric model

There are certain methodological limitations of the studies discussed, one of which is that they place emphasis on self-injury as an expression of severe psychopathology, placing it on the far end of the continuum of 'normal' distress, and therefore situating it at some remove from the ordinary experience of women. It is a medical model which emphasises individual psychopathology over social factors and the effects of confinement. Coid *et al.* (1992) apply a traditional distinction between endogenous and reactive affective disorders to the onset of self-injury and consider the institutional context to be secondary to severe psychopathology of the individual. This emphasis somewhat minimises the profound effects of incarceration and largely ignores the communicative function of self-harm.

Additionally, Coid *et al.*'s study highlights the central role of psychopathology rather than elucidating the 'common pathway' which may lead both to personality disorder and to self-mutilation. The authors make a distinction about endogenous versus reactive self-mutilation based on the women's difficulties in identifying current triggers for self-harm. It may be the case, however, that such triggers exist but that the more emotionally abused and traumatised women feel unable to make these links explicit. Early traumatisation may have prevented verbal articulation and symbolisation. Incarceration in a custodial setting may itself act as a trigger for recurrent self-harm in its evocation of earlier experiences of being humiliated and powerless. The feelings of depression, anxiety, tension and depersonalisation may be a response to the situation of being incarcerated, which resonates with painful memories. The whole custodial situation may act as an unconscious trigger for the woman, in releasing painful and overwhelming feelings, which she attempts to manage through self-harm. In other words, the failure to identify a particular external trigger for self-mutilation is not strong evidence of an underlying, endogenous mood disorder. The feelings described as 'symptoms' could be understood as intelligible responses to situations of degradation and humiliation, which evoke painful memories of similar experiences in early life.

This model of conceptualising self-harm seems to reflect the language of psychopathology and the medical model of understanding the behaviour as indicative of personality disorder, and as such is an impoverished and, I suggest, ultimately limited approach. It tends to focus on the pathology rather than the meaning of behaviour, and to locate the reasons and motivations of the self-harming women in the psychiatric classification which best fits them. This creates a constricted and dehumanising model of understanding the symbolic, as well as the immediate, function of self-harm. It is a retreat to the realm of female madness and itself reflects the process of splitting: according to this model self-harm can be located in 'mad' women rather than recognised as an intelligible response to intolerable situations.

Case illustration: Patricia: Deliberate self-harm in an incest survivor

Patricia was 23 when she was arrested and charged with assault occasioning grievous bodily harm, to which she pleaded guilty, after her initial charge of wounding with intent to kill had been reduced in the plea-bargaining process. She had stabbed her boyfriend in the chest with a knife, following what appeared to be a trivial disagreement between them. She had narrowly missed his lungs and disclosed that she had, at the moment of stabbing him, felt like killing him. Her motivation for this had not been clear to her at the time and she had not planned to kill him before the meeting, or brought along a weapon with the intention of stabbing him. She had carried a knife with her at all times to make her 'feel safe'. She had not used it against anyone other than herself before this occasion; she revealed that she had used it to cut herself, inflicting tiny wounds in places which no one else could see, like her inner thighs, her breasts and the soles of her feet. She had been remanded to a regional secure unit for the preparation of psychiatric reports following an episode of serious depression in prison, where she had initially been held for two months before being transferred to hospital. Her serious self-harm attempts in custody had alerted the prison authorities to her vulnerability and she had been transferred to the hospital wing of the prison prior to her admission to a regional secure unit. She was eventually sentenced to a hospital treatment order at the regional secure unit under section 37 of the Mental Health Act and a restriction order, section 41 of the Mental Health Act, imposed in the interests of public safety.

At initial presentation on the admission ward she appeared withdrawn, thin and child-like, and had difficulty making eye contact. She complained of difficulty sleeping, saying that she had nightmares but was not able to describe their content. She was nervous in the presence of male staff and other patients, particularly men, and seemed to find it hard to trust anyone. On one occasion when she reported having a nightmare a male nurse put his arm around her shoulder, in a gesture of comfort; he was startled when this triggered an angry and frightened outburst from Patricia, who accused him of 'rape'. After several weeks on the ward Patricia and a female nurse had formed a very close relationship and she always asked to speak privately to this nurse, to whom she disclosed secrets.

The psychiatric assessment at the prison had been thorough and Patricia had disclosed that she had been sexually abused in her early adolescence by her father and had a history of drug abuse, anorexia, running away from home and deliberate self-harm. Patricia had four older brothers, the eldest one being six years her senior while the youngest was only 18 months older than she was. As the only girl, and the youngest child, Patricia had enjoyed special privileges. She described herself as a 'Daddy's girl'. Her father had spent time alone with her in her childhood, taking her out to visit relations in other cities and helping her with her homework. She described her mother as a 'weak' woman who had worked long hours in a cleaning job and was not readily available to spend time with the children. Throughout Patricia's childhood her mother had suffered from asthma and chronic fatigue, often being confined to bed for several days at a time. Although she had never received psychiatric treatment it appeared that she had suffered from depression. Patricia remembered the distress and anxiety it caused her to see her mother so weak and frail. She had held a secret conviction that her mother had a form of cancer which would eventually kill her, leaving Patricia totally responsible for the household and forced into the role of surrogate wife to her father. She was attached to her maternal grandparents who lived next door.

Her father had repeatedly sexually abused Patricia from the age of 11 and she vividly recalled how he had followed her into her room after school one afternoon, when no one else was in the house, watched her as she changed out of her school uniform, and then raped her. It was following the first occasion of sexual abuse that Patricia cut herself, in secret, on the soles of her feet. She later began to cut her inner thighs, and on a few occasions had also made tiny cuts on her genitals. She described this as being a sign to herself that something awful and damaging had happened to her; she believed that she had somehow provoked her father's sexual interest because he had first abused her shortly after she began wearing a bra and started her periods. He had accused her of 'showing off' to him, and she had accepted this criticism as a reason for his continuing to have violent sexual intercourse with her several times a week.

When I first saw her on the ward, at the urgent request of the ward staff, she seemed like a little girl. Patricia had difficulty making eye contact but would occasionally look up and smile at me, which was unexpected and engaging. She appeared like a child who had been dressed in a hurry by a distracted mother, and wore ill-fitting and torn clothing; her messy black hair was held back in a ponytail. She was very slight with a thin, flat-chested body and walked with a boyish swagger. Her face was very drawn and thin and she had deep hollows under her eyes.

Prior to meeting with me Patricia had begun to work with a female clinical psychologist to address issues relating to her childhood sexual abuse. This therapist had left the secure unit after ten months of working with her. She had been available to see her in emergencies and on several occasions Patricia had been found almost unconscious with a ligature tied around her neck; after having the ligature removed and regaining strength she would be asking to speak to the psychologist. The nursing staff would always contact the female therapist immediately, even at nights or at weekends. She lived near the hospital grounds and had offered Patricia time for discussion outside of the allocated thirty-minute sessions which they had scheduled for twice a week.

When I began to see her for regular appointments I made it clear that I would not be available to offer emergency meetings because I would not see Patricia outside of our allocated weekly session. I felt that this was necessary to preserve the strict boundaries of the psychotherapeutic work and also because twice-weekly meetings could cultivate a strong transference in Patricia which might be overwhelming for her. I did not want to encourage a deep dependence on me at the expense of her developing a sense of autonomy. I did not want to act out the role of rescuing angel, difficult as it was to resist. The urgency of the referral appeared to be related both to Patricia's perceived need to have individual psychological treatment and the nurses' feelings of helplessness and abandonment following the previous psychologist's departure. Patricia had been in the unit for nineteen months when I met her and her self-harm had, if anything, escalated during this time.

Patricia self-injured regularly using bits of material that she had in her room, which could be torn from clothing or her bedclothes. These pieces of material were used as ligatures by Patricia in attempts to strangle herself. She secreted these bits of material in her room although she would occasionally hand one in to staff, saying that if they did not confiscate it she would use it. She said that she always let go before she asphyxiated and that she never intended to die. She would generally let staff know that she had tied a ligature around her neck and would tell them that she had felt unable to resist the urge. On a few occasions she had been discovered in her room, weak and faint with a ligature still tied around her neck. As a result of the self-strangulation she developed bruises on her neck and the areas around her eyes were often the sallow colour of bruising. Partly because she looked like a helpless, battered child it was difficult for both nursing staff and me to remember that she was actually an adult woman. Her self-strangulation and child-like demeanour evoked feelings of protective outrage in some staff who felt that she must be observed one to one constantly for days to prevent further 'incidents'. Others felt furious with her for demanding so much time and attention when other, less demonstrative patients were overlooked despite their severe mental illnesses.

Patricia explicitly linked her self-strangulation and her history of self-cutting, which had started after the first occasion of incest. Her confinement in the secure unit had deprived her of the opportunity to cut herself. Cutting her feet signified her sense of violation and was her attempt at self-punishment and a way of marking, in secret, the fact that the abuse had taken place. She described cutting herself in secret, in places on her body which no one else would see, except possibly her father, who would be too aroused to look carefully at his frightened daughter and the injuries that she had inflicted on herself. She was, however, physically unable to cut herself in the regional secure unit because of the careful supervision of her and the restriction of access to sharp weapons. She had decided that she would tie herself with a ligature at times when she felt like cutting herself, e.g. when she would be flooded with memories of her sexual abuse or when she felt particularly disgusted with herself. She reported that while cutting relieved tension, suffocation blocked out sensation altogether, which offered a great release from anxiety and torment.

Progress of therapy

In the first few weeks of therapy the focus of the sessions was Patricia's sense of loss in relation to the previous psychologist leaving and how hard it would be to 'start all over again'. She had told the other therapist things about herself which she had not previously disclosed and had developed trust in her. I was treated with a degree of suspicion and it appeared likely that the anger which she had felt about being left by the other psychologist was directed at me; she had not expressed her anger towards this previous therapist. She acknowledged these feelings of anger towards me and let me know that, while I could never replace the other therapist, I might be allowed to help her understand herself and control her self-destructive behaviour. The mourning period for the previous therapist had been cut short by my arrival on the unit and because of the anxiety of the staff, who did not want Patricia to be left without support for more than a few weeks. Additionally, the psychologist had only given Patricia relatively short notice (six weeks) prior to leaving, for fear of destabilising her. I did not agree with this decision and felt that Patricia needed a longer time to address the process of separation, and anticipatory mourning for the loss of this valued relationship. Despite my awareness that Patricia needed a longer break between the other psychologist leaving and my beginning to work with her, I was also drawn into the powerful fear of upsetting her, and did not feel able to refuse this referral; to do so would have been perceived as cruel and irresponsible. I found it impossible to resist the compulsion to help.

In the first few months Patricia often ended the sessions early, finding it very difficult to concentrate for more than half an hour. She sometimes stared vacantly around the room, as though she were trying to locate her thoughts in the external environment, or identify where she was. She used my first name frequently, checking to see that I was still listening to her, sometimes demanding reassurance that she was understood through her repeated question, 'Do you know what I mean?' I thought that underlying this was the more alarming and hopeless question, '*Can* you ever know what I mean, or what I feel?' She considered her experience of incest highly unusual, beyond what could be thought about or understood and felt that she was a 'freak'. Despite her sense of isolation, it became easier to talk to her about feeling alone and her difficulty believing that her experiences were communicable in words. Her fear of the destructive impact of her feelings emerged.

As therapy with Patricia progressed she began to discuss in detail the feelings and thoughts which preceded her deliberate self-injury. She had recurrent images of her father undressing before having sex with her, and a specific memory of the expression on his face the first time that he raped her. She reported that this memory would often intrude upon her thoughts and affect her peace of mind. She would begin to feel afraid and disturbed, as though he were still in the next room to hers and could enter her bedroom at any moment. Certain noises, like the sound of a light being switched on, could set off these memories, as she associated these sounds with her father approaching her bedroom door. Although she would begin to feel anger towards her father when these images and memories occurred, she had learned to empty all the feelings out of her mind because she was afraid that they might overwhelm her. Her anger at her boyfriend at the time of the index offence had followed her refusal to have sex with him; he had become angry and aggressive in his demands that she have intercourse with him. The experience of coercion had, she said, brought back a kind of blind panic and rage, which she related to her earlier experience of incest.

Her sense of confusion was evident as she described how her father, whom she had loved and trusted, began to terrorise her systematically with his sexual demands. She reported feeling guilty about becoming angry with him, and felt that she should not be talking about the abuse, that she must have invited it, encouraged and deserved it. At the same time she knew that her father had been wrong and had somehow changed from being loving to being predatory and frightening, like an animal. The physical sensations that she remembered left her feeling totally overwhelmed and terrified, literally trapped. She felt guilty, suffocated and scared at the same time. She had a clear recollection of being afraid that she would not be able to breathe because of her father's weight on her. She also remembered his heavy, quick breathing.

Patricia had developed a variety of techniques to cope with these memories and defuse the aggressive impulses that she felt she might enact. One of these strategies was to make herself go numb, and simply observe the images/memories as though she had not been a participant. She had become accomplished at reaching this state of emotional numbness but was aware of a negative consequence – that it made her feel similarly disconnected from events and interactions in her present life. She would be left feeling depersonalised and 'unreal', as though she was an observer in her own life. After some time in this calm but estranged state she would need to 'get back to normal' and found that tying a ligature around her neck, or cutting herself if she had the means, would bring her back, allowing her to 'feel real' again. She had an elaborate ritual for self-injuring and believed that methodically and carefully going through this ritual also allowed time for the intrusive and disturbing memories to fade, so that their destructive power would be reduced when she once again engaged with the world.

As she became aware of the times when she would be most likely to self-injure she developed a clear idea of its functions. She understood her self-strangulation to have five main functions: first, to allow her to feel 'real' again once she had numbed herself in response to unwanted thoughts and feelings; second, to distract her from the pain of intrusive memories of childhood sexual abuse; third, to alert staff members to the danger that she felt she was in, and her need for support and understanding; fourth, to express anger and outrage; five, to gain control at times when memories and current events made her feel powerless. Taking each function in turn she was able to outline strategies other than self-harm which would achieve the same end. Although it initially appeared to be a weak alternative, Patricia developed the capacity for mental imagery and relaxation which she used to distract herself from the memories of abuse and to reduce tension and anxiety.

Eleven months into the therapy Patricia informed me that she was starting to keep a diary about her memories, and the thoughts and feelings which led to her self-harming. She appeared to be wanting to transform her mental anguish into something tangible and she could, in a sense, redirect her need to physically attack herself to doing something else with the feelings, writing them down. This seemed to be a highly significant move; she had shifted from writing on her body to writing about her body. Writing gave her an alternative method of distancing herself from the memories and also enabled her to identify patterns in her self-harm. She did not always wish to show me everything that she had written, showing how exposed she felt in relation to me, conflicting with her desire to unburden herself to me.

She slowly began to allow herself to express anger at her father, and the rest of the family, whom she blamed for not protecting her from serious sexual abuse. This shift from blaming only herself for the abuse had developed very slowly. As this emerged she recognised that she did not need to remain emotionally numb; that it was possible to allow herself some strong feelings about her abuse, and her role in her family.

Therapy continued for almost eighteen months but Patricia still felt alienated, dissociated and desperate at times throughout this period. She described these experiences as similar to the feelings that she had cultivated at the time when the abuse was going on. She recognised that the ability to 'go dead' and become alienated had been necessary for her as a young incest victim, but also that it no longer served a useful function for her, and actually blocked the expression of her current feelings. She wanted to find other ways to let staff know when she felt pressured or ignored, and was aware that her self-injurious behaviour curtailed her degree of freedom on the ward, re-creating a situation in which she was controlled and infantilised. Although at some level this met her need for protection and concern, at another level she craved greater freedom and a degree of autonomy.

Although she often felt depressed about the past she retained some hope for change. She had increasing insight into how she unconsciously re-created abusive situations, for example, through allowing sexual activity to take place with exploitative men on the ward, and through indiscriminate disclosure of very intimate details. She felt that through her sessions with me she was increasingly able to contain her communicative needs and 'save' them for the sessions rather than alerting the entire ward staff to her situation. In the past she had related details of the incest to various nurses and junior doctors, eventually experiencing this as another abusive situation. Revealing painful material to several people left her feeling anxious and exposed. It also blurred the boundaries between staff members and me, her therapist, leaving Patricia confused about who could be relied on to know about and contain the anxiety and horror evoked by her experiences. There was also a seductive element in her choosing to confide in 'special' people.

Transference issues and breaks in therapy

I was aware of the danger that Patricia would enact her distress and anger about the breaks in therapy through self-harm. I emphasised the need for her to articulate her anger and disappointment in me. It was, at times, difficult to understand which significant figure in her past I became in the transference, and what kind of object I was for her. At times, particularly when there were breaks in therapy owing to holidays, I seemed to be an unprotective and abandoning mother or a confusing father who, on the one hand, offered love and interest and, on the other, appeared violent and uncaring. Patricia often praised and flattered me, revealing a highly idealised picture of me. At other times she expressed great disappointment and anger, believing that I would not keep seeing her, that I would leave her to her own devices because she was not 'doing well enough'. I appeared at times to become a persecutory, demanding and unreliable object.

In some ways even the privacy of therapy mirrored the abusive experience in its intimacy and removal from the other members of the ward. It was therefore essential to allow Patricia to discuss this and to clarify to her that the individual psychotherapy sessions were not secret, that is, that they formed part of her treatment programme on the ward and that the progress, though not the intimate details, of this work would be communicated to others involved in her care. The limited nature of confidentiality and the role of the psychologist in relation to the rest of the multidisciplinary team was made clear to her all along. It was essential that therapy was *private* but not *secret* and that I resisted Patricia's attempt to turn me into a special person for her whom she could seduce and be seduced by. This allowed Patricia the opportunity to have an intimate therapeutic relationship which would be non-abusive but where I would not be compelled to silence. At times Patricia relied on me to communicate for her to others and it was clear that protecting her physical and mental health meant being able to tell other members of the team how she was feeling. My countertransference feelings for her were primarily protective but she also occasioned disappointment and anger when she self-harmed. I felt at those times that I had let her down and that she was actually attacking me.

In the transference I had become the unprotective mother who could not prevent Patricia's body from injury and, in a sense, I was being attacked; Patricia psychically split off her body from herself, identified her female body with mine, the symbolic maternal body, and then attacked it through her self-strangulation. My sense of being attacked was a powerful communication about the motivations for Patricia's self-harm. I interpreted this in therapy as Patricia being angry with a weak mother who could not and did not stop the sexual abuse, just as I was not always available and able to stop her self-harm. By telling me about her self-harm she was both punishing me for my impotence and, more hopefully, letting me know that she was at risk, so that I could help her.

Outcome of therapy

Patricia did not stop self-harming altogether during the course of psychotherapy but there were fewer instances recorded during the time when she was engaged in therapy and over the course of the first year after ending therapy. She developed the confidence to let staff know when she was distressed or anxious, and to say when she did not want to go into details about her memories and experiences. She began to take more care of her physical appearance, washing her hair regularly and gaining some weight, although she still went through periods of 'forgetting' to eat. She was significantly more assertive in her interactions with staff and patients. She made direct eye contact with others and her speech sounded more distinct and adult, less like that of a self-conscious young girl. She was eventually discharged from the secure unit to live in a hostel. It was reported by hostel staff that she still self-harmed at times of crisis but the frequency of these occasions was much less than when she had first been admitted to the secure unit. Although we had continued to meet during her preparation for leaving, Patricia chose to see me only infrequently once she had left the unit, feeling that to return for regular outpatient appointments would stigmatise her and tie her to secure services. At follow-up she continued to maintain progress although she had not entirely given up self-strangulation at times of acute stress.

For Patricia to relinquish her self-strangulation completely would have meant sacrificing one of her most powerful forms of expression. It appeared that while she could reduce her reliance on self-harm she could not altogether abandon it. Such acting out might be viewed as a contraindication for treatment in traditional psychoanalytically informed therapies; in the context of the containing environment of the regional secure unit I did not take this view and attempted to work with her to understand the meaning and function of her behaviour, and to develop other ways of coping with and expressing anger and despair. The intensity of the feelings of depression and anxiety giving rise to self-harm abated considerably during the course of therapy as Patricia was able to work through her experience of childhood sexual abuse. I was informed by a psychodynamic model of understanding her unconscious communications and their effect on me and the rest of the multidisciplinary team. I considered her self-harm to be linked powerfully to her experience of incest, expressing her sense of guilt, anger, helplessness and depersonalisation.

DISCUSSION

Feeling real: an attack on depersonalisation

Miller and Bashkin (1964) describe this function of self-harm in an account of depersonalisation in patient F: 'F mutilated himself to rapidly terminate states of acute depersonalisation characterised by feelings of unreality, deadness and depression, of being outside himself and not in full control of his actions' (Miller and Bashkin, 1964:641). One of the central functions of self-harm is to regain a feeling of 'being real' in people who feel that they are no longer engaged in the world, and who have lost the sense that they are experiencing sensations and emotions. They feel numb and detached from others, describing the return of sensation as being one of the most important aspects of their self-harm. Psychic withdrawal from the world can be defeated through physical engagement, which self-harm provides. In a sense, the act of self-harming is a hopeful one, indicating a desire to return to the world and to restore the capacity to feel, not least by finding a symbolic method of communicating distress.

It has been suggested that for some self-harmers the sensation of pain is greatly reduced or negated altogether; this has been corroborated by women's own descriptions of self-harming. For others, the experience of sensation, even if painful, is a significant attempt to restore their sense of feeling and reaffirm their own existence. For those who have been traumatised in childhood, depersonalisation, the experience of feeling not real, not inhabiting one's own body, has served the essential function of affording escape from potentially intolerable situations. At times of stress and unhappiness in their current lives this defence may be reawakened, with the resulting feelings of being unreal and unable to engage with others. This defence may be useful for a short period of time but may become deadening, and seem inescapable. It is at this point that self-harm may serve to effectively bring the person back to life.

The function of self-harm, and its communicative validity, should not be overlooked in the attempt to prevent it. The behaviour cannot simply be dismissed as a pathological example of an inability to cope, or a masochistic perversion. Patricia often described feeling unreal and confused, sometimes wondering if she was still a little girl or a fully grown woman; she had feelings of being ill at ease in, and uncomfortable with, her body, and this sense of a split between her mental and her physical state was unpleasant and disturbing for her. Self-harm allowed her to feel that her mind and body were connected. As a child she had relied on this capacity to split off mentally from what was happening to her body and to 'float away' to other places, to dissociate herself from the intrusion, distress and pain of her father's sexual assaults on her. As an adult she employed the capacity to separate herself mentally from her environment in order to cope with stressful situations, but then found this psychological distance frightening and confusing, intensifying her sense of isolation and alienation. The strategy which had been crucial for survival in childhood had become confusing and frightening in adulthood. Self-strangulation was her chosen antidote, enabling her to feel that she could re-engage in the world and that her body was under her control.

Distraction

Patricia found the planning and execution of self-injury helpful in distracting her from emotional pain. It also helped her to unify body and mind. By focusing on her physical pain she felt relieved of mental pain and reassured that her body was hers, that it could be controlled and manipulated by her mind and that it could experience sensation. At times when she felt most depressed and anxious she became tempted to self-harm. She focused on the images of the act. The ideas of going to her room, ripping some material, tying the ligature and gradually increasing the pressure became powerful preoccupations; at times of intense anxiety she said she thought of little else, imagining precisely how she would harm herself. Acting on this fantasy brought mental relief and physical sensation together, allowing her to feel that she was 'normal' and real, that she existed. It would also bring a tremendous sense of relief from the tension, anxiety and depression she frequently experienced, particularly when images of the sexual abuse intruded on her. The long periods spent alone on the ward were times when the memories became particularly oppressive and frightening.

Communication

The communicative function of Patricia's self-injury was clear; she was informing staff that her current feelings of anxiety and unhappiness endangered her. She was also communicating the fact of her experience of pain, related to the memories of the incest, inscribing her suffering on her body, using the language of violence and mutilation. Susan Bordo describes the gesture of protest which such violence constitutes: 'a steady motif in the feminist literature on female disorder is that of pathology as embodied protest – unconscious, inchoate and counterproductive protest without an effective language, voice or politics but protest nonetheless' (Bordo, 1993: 97).

Patricia's self-harm was, in part, an expression of anger at the staff and those close to her who betrayed, disappointed and hurt her. This anger was too dangerous to be expressed to them directly and she displaced it instead on to herself, thus finding an indirect mode of communication. When she tied ligatures around her neck or cut herself she was making a public statement. In the past her father had hurt her in secret, making it impossible for her to let anyone know what was going on. She was making public her private experience and showing that she was, literally, a damaged object who needed care and help. The nursing staff response to her self-harm provided important information about the nature of Patricia's communication, as expressed through self-harm. This will be discussed further in the section entitled 'Countertransference issues'. See pages 178–81.

Self-injury as expression of anger: displacement

Patricia's self-injury expressed the anger that she harboured towards her father who had abused her, psychologically, physically and sexually, and towards those family members who had failed to notice her abuse or protect her from it. The significant figures in her current life who failed her also generated considerable feelings of anger, to which she rarely gave voice. Her frequent self-harm attempts reflected her degree of self-blame and anger at herself for allowing the abuse to take place and, she believed, for being the kind of person who had attracted this sexual activity and interest. She accepted her father's distorted reasoning that she was responsible for the abuse. She often blamed herself for the incest, reproaching herself for wearing nice clothes, scent and pretty underwear. She called herself a 'dirty slut, a whore', as her father had done while abusing her. She described these statements as critical intrusive thoughts which preoccupied her. Deliberate self-harm followed apparently trivial disappointments and perceived rejections. She self-injured at times when the intrusive and negative thoughts became very intense and persecutory. This allowed her to punish herself for being a 'dirty slut' as well as channelling the anger that she felt towards others, so that her father, mother and brothers could survive. Self-injury attempts also followed disagreements with ward staff which evoked fears in Patricia of what her anger could do to people on whom she relied. On occasions when she felt let down and hurt, her anger was so intense that she found it necessary to deflect this anger on to herself, on to her own body which she felt had already been defiled and violated. Her self-harm could be viewed as manifesting the defence of identification with the aggressor. In order to alleviate the pain of victimisation Patricia identified with her father, using her own body as an object to be treated with contempt and violence, as he had.

Patricia's use of violence against herself did not preclude the use of violence against another person, as illustrated in her index offence, which occurred when her boyfriend was 'hassling' her sexually. Although she *mainly* turned anger against herself she had stabbed this sexual partner, in an apparent displacement of the rage which she felt at her father, and in the context of alcohol abuse. That she stabbed her boyfriend, penetrating him with a knife, has obvious symbolic significance. It reflected her profound difficulties in sexual relationships and her confusion of her boyfriend with her father: she associated her sexuality with deviance and shame. There was also a homicidal aspect to her destructiveness; the homicidal urge which underlies suicidal behaviour was manifest in her index offence.

Her feelings of guilt and self-blame for the abuse still plagued her. She worried about how her disclosure might destabilise the family to the extent that she did not want her mother to know that incest had taken place, wanting to preserve the illusion of a happy family. Her placement in a secure psychiatric unit, however, stigmatised the family and raised questions about its functioning, drawing attention to the fact that something awful had happened within this apparently happy family.

Assertion of control

In some ways Patricia felt that through self-harm she was branding herself, and asserting the fact that her body, if not her mind, was her domain, over which she could exert control. It was an attempt to reclaim ownership and control over her body and to assert that she, not anyone else, had the right and power to touch it. She displayed her bruising with a degree of pride that conveyed this, and did not believe that her self-injuring was out of her control or a suicidal gesture. She felt that it literally tied her to reality and also brought tremendous and necessary relief from the psychological pressure that she faced. Her anger, she felt, was justified and needed to be demonstrated. Interestingly, this particular expression of anger was a potent symbol for the whole staff team, who became preoccupied with preventing her from self-harming, while finding it difficult to think about what it symbolised for her.

Countertransference issues

The nature of the institutional response to Patricia's self-harming, like the nature of the communication, was not primarily verbal but found its expression through behaviour and through the emotional quality of the interactions with Patricia. She became a central figure, who would require much discussion in ward rounds and staff handovers, generating heated debates about how best to manage her self-injurious behaviour.

Her self-harming behaviour, coupled with her vulnerability and dependence, contributed to a powerful re-creation on the ward of her earlier experience of abuse. Her behaviour and her psychological functioning had a powerful effect: the nursing staff responded by taking on roles in relation to her which mirrored her earlier experiences. The nurses, Patricia's main carers, became either the punitive aggressors, who could not see her pain, or, if they could, blamed her for it, or the unprotective mothers who could be vigilant *only after* their child was hurt. The nursing staff who wanted to be with Patricia and observe her every action were behaving like the guilty mother who has failed to see what is happening to her child and whose protectiveness comes too late. The constant presence of nurses was also intrusive, reminiscent of the father who had not allowed her any privacy. The male staff felt uncomfortable with Patricia, alternating between feeling over-protective of her or becoming drawn into a flirtatious relationship with her.

The defence mechanism of projective identification was illustrated in the way that the nursing staff were not only receptacles for Patricia's powerful projections, but also integrated these projections into themselves and behaved accordingly, becoming the persecutory figures which inhabited Patricia's internal world. The staff members may have had benign and helpful motives in relation to her, but without the necessary opportunity to reflect on their responses they reinforced Patricia's disturbance, mirroring earlier experiences, without helping her to gain insight into it. The pull of her distress was simply too great to resist. She successfully evacuated her anxiety into staff, as she evacuated her mental distress into and on to her body. In an important sense her self-harm contained a significant degree of aggression towards those who were required to manage it, and who were reminded of their inability to do so whenever she self-harmed.

The staff group was dramatically split in their understanding of and attitude towards Patricia. An example of this was found in the ongoing disagreement between the Consultant Psychiatrist and the Registrar attached to his team about how best to manage her self-harm attempts. The Consultant was in favour of ensuring that one-to-one observation continued for twenty-four hours a day, for an indefinite period of time, while the Registrar believed that this was unhelpful and infantilising; she felt that Patricia should be referred for specialist psychoanalytic psychotherapy outside the unit. Decisions were often postponed while staff at all levels argued about appropriate policies in relation to managing her self-harm and ensuring her safety. Protection and control were concerns which could not easily be reconciled with Patricia's need for privacy and increasing levels of freedom. It became difficult for staff to feel confident enough to test out whether she had gained sufficient control of her behaviour and mood to make it possible to consider her progress through the unit. For weeks no specific policy or decision would be made as the debates continued. The splits in nursing and professional staff can be read as clues about the patient's disturbance and seen as the externalisation of the fragmentation of her own internal world.

Patricia rendered the ward staff impotent because she was able to re-create the family dynamics in which sexual abuse of a child can occur, where the secrecy and silence surrounding the activity render those who *could* help paralysed and ignorant. Patricia was symbolically asking the staff member whom she had told about her self-injury to take notice of her pain and help her to manage it. She was not simply reproaching the staff but *warning* them to be aware of her fragility and difficulty in managing her fear and anger. She was also giving them an opportunity to repair her psychic damage. If they could be vigilant enough to see when she was distressed and speak to her instead of ignoring her, they could help her to articulate her despair rather than enact it through self-injury. In this sense the act of self-injury in the context of the secure unit was a hopeful gesture, inviting staff to help her to understand and contain unhappiness and anger.

Patricia did not always disclose that she had hurt herself immediately but on those occasions when she did she was symbolically violating the secrecy of the incest situation. The function of her self-harm was that she could re-create the relationship between her childhood self and her father in the current relationship between her body and herself, only now she could become the aggressor. Once she had self-harmed she was able to show other people evidence that she had been harmed, in the hope that they might help her and protect her from further pain. She was mastering her earlier trauma, playing an active rather than a passive role in relation to her body. She was, literally and figuratively, writing on, and with, her body.

Patricia's compulsion to self-harm was multiply determined. She responded to boredom, frustration and conflict in her environment and also to feelings of unhappiness and anxiety generated by her thoughts. It reflected her need to re-create the abusive situation in order to master it in adulthood; self-harm provided a means by which staff could be transformed into significant figures from her childhood. By simply listening without attempting to punish or protect her, the nursing and medical staff could help Patricia to come to terms with what had happened to her. This perspective was very difficult for staff to maintain when confronted with their feelings of inadequacy and distress about not preventing her self-harm. It was easier for staff to respond actively to the behaviour than to reflect on it, because of the degree of anxiety which her self-mutilation evoked; this type of task-orientated response to anxiety has been powerfully described by Menzies Lyth (1959) in her exploration of social norms in nursing as a defence against the anxiety of getting too close to the patient's painful experiences. Some nursing staff also perceived triumph and hostility in Patricia's disclosures that she had self-harmed in secret and they had been powerless to prevent it. This seemed to them to be a sadistic reproach, an accusation that they had failed her.

Staff response was either to become angry and punitive towards her or to become over-protective and anxious, checking on her every move, therefore infantilising her. The split in the staff group mirrored the split within Patricia and the difficulty that she had integrating the aggressive and dependent aspects of her personality. The difficulty that both Patricia and the medical and nursing staff had in understanding the contradictory aspects of her personality reflected the psychological consequences of her sexual abuse in childhood. In some ways Patricia seemed to be developmentally fixed at age 11, as though the trauma of sexual abuse had interfered with the emergence of an adult personality. On the ward she behaved and was treated like a vulnerable child or adolescent rather than an angry and powerful adult woman. Being infantilised created a situation in which she could not acknowledge her feelings of rage against her father. She continued to turn this anger against herself and used herself, specifically her body, as the receptacle for her violent impulses and only very gradually gained insight and control into the reasons for her self-harm. She could then develop another voice, becoming able to articulate her thoughts and memories rather than enacting them.

THE EFFECT OF DELIBERATE SELF-HARM ON NURSING STAFF

The countertransference feelings towards women who self-harm are very powerful and it is essential that supervision is provided in which the clinician can address this. The urge to protect self-harmers, and, alternatively, punitive feelings towards them, are to be expected in undertaking treatment with this client group.

The impact of a self-injurious action on nursing staff can be profound. A central question for any staff team is how to deal with and appropriately manage self-injury. The crucial importance of the relationship with health care professionals relates to the needs of the patient for ideal care and protection, which were not available in her early life, and which are invariably disappointed by the carers. The carer is idealised and then denigrated, particularly if the carer responds to the patient's vulnerability by colluding with and maintaining a 'special' relationship in which boundaries are overstepped (Adshead, 1997).

Staff working with women who self-harm may feel alternatively drawn towards them in a protective capacity and horrified and repulsed by them. They will often feel helpless, anxious and incompetent as a result of the patients' projections. Those members of the nursing staff who have to stitch a patient's wounds, or find her in a nearly strangled state, will often feel physically affected themselves; to some extent the staff can also be viewed as victims in the self-harm attempt; they are assaulted with the horror and pain which patients who self-harm are not able to contain themselves and have projected on to and into the staff who treat them. Such patients may also create situations in which they are themselves treated sadistically, often because of the strong feelings which self-harm creates in those around them. In this case they become victims of their own and others' sadistic impulses and re-create the situation of their original trauma. This can be understood as the compulsion to repeat, which demonstrates that an underlying conflict has not yet been resolved, or, more benignly, as an attempt to master the trauma through re-creating the original situation but hoping for some resolution of the conflict.

SUMMARY OF TREATMENT MODELS

A psychological model of self-harm should highlight the significance of the development, function and maintenance of self-harm for a particular woman, within a particular context. I have given an extended case study to show the complexity and over-determination of such cases, and to highlight indirectly how different kinds of violence can co-exist. Patricia had suffered from anorexia in adolescence, which coincided with the onset of her self-mutilation, went on to stab her boyfriend, and became dependent on self-strangulation when an inpatient in a medium secure unit. The scars she had from cutting into her skin might serve as memories which she needed to record and inscribe. The secondary gains achieved through self-harm, and the absence of alternative modes of self-expression, may be important factors in maintaining the behaviour. Self-harm may occur as a response to intrusive and frightening thoughts or memories, or even in response to a command hallucination in a psychosis.

Cognitive behavioural therapy and dialectical behaviour therapy

A psychological model has been proposed which stresses the significance of obsessive thoughts in the generation of self-harm and applies cognitive behavioural techniques to the treatment of self-injurious behaviour and dissociative symptoms. This model emphasises the cognitive processes leading to self-harming and advocates the woman's own identification of the thoughts which lead to such behaviour, helping her to identify alternative methods for coping with stressful intrusive thoughts. Kennerley (1996) outlines this approach, describing the treatment of self-mutilation and dissociation through cognitive behavioural therapy. Linehan (1993) has developed a cognitive behavioural treatment approach, dialectical behaviour therapy (DBT), designed for use with self-injuring women, which has proven efficacy in treating individuals with borderline personality disorders.

Linehan's approach challenges the therapeutic nihilism which has met the diagnosis of borderline personality, which so often accompanies self-injurious behaviour. She argues that the diagnosis of borderline personality disorder (BPD) is one which does not preclude the possibility of making changes in the behaviour of those individuals, challenging the critique which has been made of the notion of borderline personality as a pathologising of those women who have experienced trauma, and who express these effects in their behaviour. The strong link between childhood sexual abuse and the diagnosis of BPD has led critics of the diagnostic term to suggest that another diagnosis is given, which emphasises the association of the traumatic experience and the development of behaviour such as self-injury and severe disturbances in interpersonal relationships with difficulty in retaining a stable sense of identity. Such a diagnosis might be 'post-traumatic syndrome'. Linehan notes an important overlap between self-injury and the diagnosis of BPD: 'most individuals who engage in non-fatal self injurious behaviour and most individuals who meet criteria for BPD are women' (Linehan, 1993:4).

The cognitive behavioural treatment programme which she has developed for individuals with borderline personality, DBT, is primarily directed at women who display self-injurious behaviour, using a wide range of cognitive and behavioural strategies to address the problems of BPD, including self-injurious behaviour. Techniques such as problem-solving, exposure techniques, cognitive modification, skills training and contingency management form the core procedures in treatment, which has the advantage over other therapeutic endeavours of being empirically evaluated: it was found that there were significant gains over one year, many of which were maintained at follow-up, but Linehan is herself cautious about the strength of these findings, based only on a sample of seventy-two women:

> Our data do not support a claim that one year of treatment is sufficient for these patients. Our subjects were still scoring in the clinical range on almost all measures. Second, one study is a very slim basis for deciding a treatment is effective . . . much more research is needed. Third, there are few or no data to indicate that other treatments are *not* effective . . . no other treatments have ever been evaluated in a controlled clinical trial.
>
> (Linehan, 1993:24)

The techniques of DBT have been outlined in training manuals, and Linehan and her colleagues offer workshops to clinicians who are interested in attempting to work therapeutically with those diagnosed with BPD. While the therapeutic optimism of the approach, and its openness to empirical testing and evaluation, are valuable aspects of this approach, it remains open to the criticism that it situates self-injury within the psychopathology of BPD, locating it within a particular psychiatric paradigm and ignoring its traumatic roots. To locate it thus is to miss the complexity and symbolic quality of this form of self-expression.

The psychiatric model

The psychiatric model emphasises the role of personality disorder, which develops in response to particular developmental difficulties and disturbed early environment. The competing hypotheses of self-harm as a symptom reduction strategy and as the manifestation of poor impulse control are offered, and it has been suggested that there are distinct population groups for whom self-harm serves different functions. For the group diagnosed with BPD self-harm occurs primarily in response to internal problems, i.e. symptoms of anxiety or depression, while in another, less disturbed group, self-harm occurs in response to external triggers. The main criticism of this model is that it emphasises individual psychopathology at the expense of recognising the profound meaning and communicative function of self harm and its cultural context.

Psychodynamic psychotherapy

Psychodynamic perspectives highlight the elements of secrecy, risk-taking, guilt and ritual which are powerful factors in deliberate self-harm and in other perversions. Self-harm is a defence against intimacy, binding a woman to her own body to the exclusion of others. These aspects of ritual, excitement and secrecy, as well as the short-lived but powerful sense of well-being immediately following an episode of self-harm, serve as important and intoxicating ingredients which perpetuate the cycle. This model also emphasises the role of early experience in the development of later disorder, and the symbolic meaning of self-harm; its role as the embodiment of trauma is seen as central. In psychodynamic psychotherapy conflicts relating to early experiences can be articulated, understood and resolved.

The psychodynamic treatment of self-harm in a ward setting

Interventions intended to increase therapeutic engagement with patients and cause a reduction in their self-harm behaviour are described by Cremin *et al.* (1995) who used a psychodynamic treatment perspective to address self-harm in a unit specialising in the treatment of people with personality disorders. This unit was intended to address the needs of people aged 17–30 with an entrenched pattern of impulsive and self-destructive behaviour. The authors noted that self-harm escalated following admission and that nursing attempts to increase surveillance and curtail freedom simply resulted in 'a hostile stalemate. It was as if the patients' sole ambition was to defeat the staff by dangerous gestures approaching a final act of freedom, the threat of suicide' (Cremin *et al.*, 1995:237).

Instead of persisting with this approach to treatment, with which patients were dissatisfied and staff frustrated, a new programme was introduced. A psychoanalytic perspective on self-harm, viewing it as a compulsion to repeat, was chosen as the theoretical foundation on which to base a treatment intervention. This intervention involved a preliminary pre-admission assessment in which the admitting team would, under the supervision of a psychotherapist, arrive at a psychodynamic formulation of the self-harming behaviour. This formulation was used to inform the meaning of further acts of self-harm and to anticipate the probable effects on and reactions of the staff, primary nurse and team. This approach identified various functions of self-harm for the patient and anticipated the roles which the nursing staff would be tempted to enact, fulfilling the patient's unconscious needs and repeating aspects of her history. By identifying these prior to admission, the patient's attempt to re-enact or repeat aspects of her early life could be thwarted and alternative solutions to the patient's difficulties presented.

This treatment intervention was based on a recognition of the psychological make-up of people with BPD and the effect which such people can have on the organisation in which they are placed. The defences employed to defend against psychic pain, including splitting of the ego (Freud, 1940) and projective identification (Klein, 1946; Bion, 1959) are described and the effects of this on the nursing system anticipated. The authors describe how these individuals create powerful and destructive relationships with others:

> The means by which a person may defend him or herself from feelings of rage, helplessness and betrayal can lead to sado-masochistic relationships with significant others, including nurses. Such relationships tend to be highly addictive as the person employing these defences becomes excited and triumphant, but also unconsciously frightened of the consequences of their actions and therefore cannot give them up. So, for example, relentless, escalating, cruel attacks on the nurses' concerned attempts to offer help and care not unnaturally drive nurses to despair and to hate the patient (Winnicott 1949). Thus, defences, initially intended to protect the patient from psychic pain, can give rise to dangerous situations spiralling out of control.
>
> (Cremin *et al.*, 1995:238)

The transference relationships created by the unconscious needs of these patients, rather than being seen as obstacles to treatment, were used to develop an understanding of the patients' internal world. Even splits in the nursing staff, which may be created by the task of caring for patients who employ these primitive defences, can contribute to an understanding of the patients' psychological functioning. In Cremin *et al.*'s study the nursing staff were given intensive training and education in understanding the genesis and function of self-harm, using a psychoanalytic model, and were guided in developing a comprehensive picture of the various roles which they were invited to play. This is a valuable example of a sensitive and informed treatment approach.

A feminist approach: understanding the reasons for self-harm

Deliberate self-injury often requires an immediate medical or nursing intervention but the staff team may fear that responding too readily to self-injury may actually reinforce the behaviour and escalate the self-harm. This fear can be alleviated through a sensitive understanding of the motivations behind and functions of self-harm for a particular individual. Important feminist research has been undertaken in Special Hospitals by Liebling and Chipchase (1992) and Liebling *et al.* (1994) who have examined the reasons why women say that they self-harm and staff perceptions of self-injury and its function. They state that while the problem of self-injurious behaviour in women has been well documented 'the understanding of this behaviour is minimal and effective treatment and management programmes are lacking' (Liebling and Chipchase, 1992:19). Such behaviour is often dismissed as 'attention-seeking' and 'manipulative' and therefore not requiring serious psychotherapeutic treatment.

Self-injurious behaviour by female patients is a frequent problem in Special Hospitals in general (Burrow, 1992). Liebling and Chipchase (1992) had provided invaluable data about the prevalence, assessment and treatment of self-harm in female patients in Ashworth Special Hospital. Sellars and Liebling (1988) compared male and female patients in Broadmoor Hospital, all detained under section 3 of the Mental Health Act. This study revealed that 88 per cent of the women compared with 15 per cent of the men had exhibited some form of self-injurious behaviour during their stay at Broadmoor. This raised questions about whether the difference in self-injury rates reflected a difference in levels of depression or clinical disturbance in men and women, or whether there were other factors at play, such as gender differences in the expression of distress.

Cookson (1977) studied female prisoners and identified a number of factors as possible risk factors for self-injury. She argued that for some 'intro-punitive' women, self-injury generates a punitive social response which would in turn encourage further self-injuries. This social response was seen as positive. Self-injury both distracted the individual from profound psychological distress and provoked a response from her environment. This allowed women to gain a sense of control that reduced their feelings of helplessness and depersonalisation. The pilot study conducted by Liebling and Chipchase (1992) showed that staff perceptions of the motivations and functions of self-injury largely correlated with those cited by the self-harming patients themselves. Their research into the backgrounds of female self-harmers in Special Hospitals revealed the extent of the abuse, both sexual and physical, in the backgrounds of these women, highlighting the link between childhood abuse, particularly childhood sexual abuse, and self-harm. They describe the various losses which these patients had experienced since being admitted to the Special Hospitals, including their removal from social support networks, families of origin, relationships, and, often, the removal of their children from their custody because of concerns about possible risks to the children posed by these women. In the context of tremendous losses and helplessness, self-harm may be the only means by which some degree of control can be reclaimed by the women, and some ownership of their own lives asserted. The authors emphasise the importance of working with staff groups to educate them about the causes of self-injury and to offer support when dealing with emotionally distressing and physically abhorrent injuries. In terms of treatment options for the self-harmers, the model of a supportive psychotherapy group is favoured and the emphasis is on enabling the women to discuss why they self-injure and helping them to develop alternative ways of coping with unmanageable feelings.

Liebling and Chipchase (1996) outline the significance of working supportively with the staff who work with women who self-harm, providing them with opportunities to discuss their feelings, and helping them to understand the motivations for self-injury. The therapeutic approach to working with self-harm should address the underlying problems which lead to the self-harm behaviour, rather than simply focusing on the self-harm itself. A thorough assessment of the problem is a prerequisite, as is the importance of staff remaining non-judgemental and accepting of self-harm behaviours. Focusing on the underlying distress which leads to self-harm allows staff to keep moral judgements in check. Self-harm should be viewed as a meaningful communication about psychological distress and therefore it serves a valuable function. This view is not always easy to accept, particularly for staff who treat the results of self-injury, but it may be the first step towards helping the woman to deal with underlying unhappiness and distress in other ways.

Liebling et al. (1997a, 1997b) stress that treatment for self-injury should be based on understanding why women self-harm and what factors maintain this behaviour. They have drawn up a semi-structured question-naire which can be used as a guide in drawing up care plans and identifying treatment aims. They ask the women the following kinds of question:

1   When did you start self-harming? What was happening in your life at that time?
2   How did self-harm help you to cope with your life at that time? How does self-harm help you to cope now?
3   What situations currently lead you to feel like self-harming?
4   How do you feel before you self-harm? What thoughts run through your mind at these times?
5   How do you feel after self-harming?
6   What helps you to cope with feelings to self-harm?

(Liebling, 1995)

Underlying these questions is an acceptance of self-harm as a way of coping and a desire to enable women to identify alternative ways of communicating feelings. Liebling and her colleagues found that the therapeutic needs of women who self-harm were not being adequately met. They identified nurse training as an important area to focus on in the development of comprehensive and sensitive therapeutic programmes for women in Special Hospital settings (Liebling *et al.*, 1997b). Liebling *et al.* evaluated group therapy for women who self-harm, expressing the view that this type of treatment, based on qualitative information about the development and function of self-harm for individuals, was helpful for women in Special Hospitals.

CONCLUSION

The need for a psychological treatment model

A psychodynamic understanding of the meaning and origins of self-harm will enhance a psychological formulation of the problem by drawing attention to a woman's underlying distress rather than simply focusing on preventing the behaviour. It is essential to view self-harm, including anorexia, as a solution to a particular psychological conflict or crisis. Therapy can assist the woman who relied on this solution to develop other, less destructive, ways of resolving her crises and articulating her distress. Therapy should be informed by a sensitive, non-judgemental attitude to the behaviour, regardless of the theoretical orientation of the therapist. The feminist research provides an invaluable guide to understanding the meaning of self-harm, avoiding the discourse of psychiatric pathologising. Any thorough psychological formulation must identify factors in the background and current situation of the woman who self-harms in order to understand the function of self-harm in the present and the historical antecedents which gave rise to the underlying thoughts and feelings.

Psychological treatment, whether along psychotherapeutic or cognitive behavioural lines, requires a comprehensive understanding of the particular occasions which give rise to self-harm, and how it is manifested. The feelings which produce self-harm will be explored and the woman who self-mutilates will be encouraged to express her feelings verbally and to identify underlying thoughts about deserving to be punished, or needing to keep her suffering silent and secret. There is a vital role to be played by organisations such as the Bristol Crisis Service for Women, which provides a telephone crisis line to support self-harming women in the community and information for their friends and relatives. It is clear that therapists, nurses, social workers, probation officers, youth workers, psychiatrists and general practitioners would also benefit from informed, compassionate training programmes to enable them to identify and treat self-harm, both in the general population and in prisons and psychiatric hospitals. Clinical psychologists also have an important role to play in psychiatric units, where they can offer nursing staff training, assistance and supervision in understanding self-harm, assessing the etiology of the problem for particular individuals, and designing treatment programmes and ward policies for dealing with self-injurious behaviour.

The woman's use of her body, her secret weapon, can eventually be talked about explicitly in therapy. The opportunity to discuss her feelings can be helpful in reducing her need to show her pain and relieve her anxiety and tension through self-mutilation. She can be helped to find other ways of articulating her distress and other methods of relieving anxiety, depression and anger. The therapist should also take into account the environment in which the woman finds herself, and the particular function which self-harm serves within this setting. The issue of control within an oppressive institution can be explored within a psychological model of self-harm. Psychological therapy can be either individual or group.

Countertransference responses to the self-harming, or anorexic, patient will be powerful as therapists working alone, or a ward-based team, become witnesses to the violence that these women inflict on themselves. Close supervision and proper training of nursing staff are essential when working with self-harming women, who generate both powerful protective and punitive feelings in therapists, which threaten their capacity to think clearly about how best to approach them.

If the communicative function of self-harm is to show what cannot be spoken about, this must be recognised and responded to. In order to build a therapeutic relationship with the patient it is crucial to convey to her that her pain is recognised and can be understood. This may be the first step towards the woman being able to articulate her feelings as it generates faith in the possibility of communication. Women who were sexually abused, and had to bear the burden of secrecy, may have lost hope that their experiences can be spoken about to others. They may feel unable to think or speak about their histories of abuse, and instead enact them.

Women locate their sense of identity in their bodies, which may be their most powerful tools of self-expression. For many women, painful experiences are literally inscribed on their bodies. Their histories of abuse, neglect and trauma may be written on their bodies: these narratives must be decoded and understood.

Chapter 6

Anorexia nervosa

One of the cruellest forms of attacking the body is to starve it, depriving it of the nutrition which it requires for life. My understanding of this deliberate starvation is that it expresses violence towards the self: the object of hostility in this case is the woman's body, representing the mother's body. As Welldon states:

> In female perversion not only the whole body but also its mental representations are used to express sadism and hostility. Women express their perverse attitudes not only through but also towards their bodies, very often in a self-destructive way. If we look at the psychopathologies most frequently associated with women, we find syndromes of self-injury associated with biological or hormonal disorders affecting the reproductive functioning. Such is the case with anorexia nervosa, bulimia, and forms of self-mutilation, where the menses, their absence or their presence, may act as indicators of the pathological condition. These women experience a feeling of elation from the manipulation of their bodies when they are starving, and which disappears when they start to eat again. They experience a sense of power through being in control of the shapes and forms their bodies assume as a result of the physical injuries and abuse they inflict on themselves.
>
> (Welldon, 1992:34)

Like other manifestations of self-harm, anorexia nervosa can be viewed as a communicative attempt, and as a solution, no matter how maladaptive, to a central conflict or difficulty. For those women who are required to be very thin, because of their professions or aspirations, for example, modelling, ballet or athletics, anorexia may develop out of the need to limit eating to a great degree, eventually leading to dietary restriction and the control that it apparently affords becoming an end in itself. Anorexia nervosa is generally considered to be multifactorial in etiology and it is construed as a disorder which is self-perpetuating, in that factors which were not central at the outset eventually assume a significance which contributes to its maintenance, such as the powerful sense of mastery afforded by 'successful' starvation and weight loss.

In this chapter I focus on the understanding of anorexia as an expression of female violence against the self. I will also discuss the cognitive behavioural approach and its treatment implications as well as considering systemic and feminist understandings of anorexia nervosa. Treatment of anorexia nervosa is known to be difficult, as the anorectic will often not recognise weight loss as a problem and will resist treatment of the disorder. I will briefly describe the main psychotherapeutic models of treatment, namely individual psychotherapy, cognitive behavioural therapy and family therapy, as well as drawing attention to particular difficulties faced by therapists who work with anorectic women.

Eating disorders in general are found far more frequently in women than in men, and the average age of onset of anorexia nervosa has been found to be 18 (Crisp, 1995:22). It is a disorder which often begins in adolescence, occurring much more commonly in females than males, and has been conceptualised as a response to the changes in body shape and weight which occur in puberty. Its description in the *Diagnostic Statistical Manual* (Fourth Edition) (DSM IV) specifies that the absence of menstrual periods is one of the essential criteria for diagnosis of the disorder, as is the refusal to maintain body weight within the normal range.

DSM IV (1994) CLASSIFICATION OF ANOREXIA NERVOSA

Anorexia nervosa is a recognised syndrome which has been classified in the DSM IV according to the following criteria:

a) Refusal to maintain body weight at or above a minimally normal body weight for age and height (e.g. weight loss leading to maintenance of body weight less than 85% of that expected: or failure to make expected weight gain during period of growth leading to body weight less than 85% of that expected).

b) Intense fear of gaining weight or becoming fat even though underweight.

c) Disturbance in the way in which one's body weight or shape is experienced, undue influence of body weight or shape on self-evaluation, or denial of the seriousness of the current low body weight.

d) In post-menarcheal females, amenorrhoea, i.e. the absence of at least three consecutive menstrual cycles (a woman is considered to have amenorrhoea if her periods occur only following hormone, e.g. oestrogen, administration).

Specified type:

restricting type: During the current episode of anorexia nervosa, the person has not regularly engaged in binge eating or purging behaviour (i.e. self-induced vomiting or the misuse of laxatives, diuretics, or enemas).

binge eating/purging type: During the current episode of anorexia nervosa the person has regularly engaged in binge eating or purging behaviour (i.e. self-induced vomiting or the misuse of laxatives, diuretics, or enemas).

(DSM IV, 1994:544–5)

ANOREXIA AND FEMALE VIOLENCE AGAINST THE SELF

Anorexia can be considered an act of violence against adult female sexuality in its creation of an amenorrhoeic state: it is a denial of women's reproductive capacity and a refusal to relinquish the comparative androgyny of childhood. It reflects an attempt to defy the natural processes of ageing which psychoanalysts have linked to a disturbance in the process of separation from the mother:

> I would say that anorexia nervosa is more than a disorder in the psychological meaning of body weight or a disorder in relation to food. It is an attempt to annihilate the very nature of human existence – inequality, progression through the life cycle, death . . . one component of this state of affairs lies in a disturbance in the areas of symbolisation connected with a lack of a 'transitional space' with the primary object.

(Birksted-Breen, 1997:118)

Through self-starvation women can carve their bodies into objects of desire and trophies testifying to their self-control and self-sacrifice. The weapon of this act of destructive self-control is the body. Her control over her appetites offers the anorectic woman a sense of power and mastery within the private sphere of her own body. It often develops at a point in the life cycle when teenage females are struggling to individuate themselves from their mothers, in families in which their bodies are actually not considered to belong to them, in enmeshed family systems where boundaries between parents and children, and between siblings, are blurred. It can be a powerful weapon and means of control within this family. Anorexia appears to express internalised rage and is a form of assault on the self; it is a clear illustration of the model of female violence proposed by Welldon (1992). The virtual addiction of some women to self-starvation is a powerful mode of self-expression.

The link between anorexia and aggression has been well described. Anorexia nervosa is potentially a life-threatening condition. Hughes warns:

> patients with anorexia nervosa show real and alarming behaviour to the point of self murder, and it is important that both the impulse to damage the self and to sabotage the therapy are addressed. These are not idle worries: one in six anorectics dies either from illness resulting from starvation or by committing suicide . . . this patient's therapy is a life and death matter.
>
> (Hughes, 1995:48)

Anorexia and the model of female perversion

Once again, I must stress that the notion of perversion is not a moral one, nor a condemnation, but is descriptive of a mode of functioning which essentially precludes the possibility of intimacy with another person.

The cycle of perversion described by Welldon (1992) takes as its starting point a woman's low self-esteem and sense of guilt which engender feelings of worthlessness, depression and and a pervasive sense of emptiness. These feelings are managed partly through a retreat to a fantasy world of imaginary activities. When the depressive feelings threaten to overwhelm her, a woman may act out these fantasies; acting out the fantasies temporarily provides an exhilarating escape from distress and emptiness. These are essentially forbidden activities, prohibited by the ego and by social norms, which may have been internalised in the superego, or conscience; there is a sense of a compulsion to act despite some awareness that to do so will be dangerous.

The activities are performed secretly, with the secrecy itself creating a particular thrill and excitement. There is hostility inherent in this compulsive activity, which can be considered a perversion. The hostility is directed towards the self, towards the mother, as she is symbolically embodied in the woman's own body, and towards others, who are kept away through the narcissistic immersion in anorexia. Underlying this aggression is the fear of being submerged or engulfed in an intimate relationship. The perversion is essentially narcissistic, in that the woman is immersed in her own fantasies, and activities, to the exclusion of anyone else. It has been suggested that this escape from intimacy is one of the main functions of perversions (Glasser, 1979) and that anorexia nervosa enables its sufferer to retreat from the terrors of sexual relationships and anaesthetise the self against painful emotions (Malan, 1997). The object of a perversion is tortured and kept at a distance: in the case of anorexia this object can be identified as the appetites of the body itself, symbolically represented through food.

The anorectic may engage in a complex deception in which she either pretends to eat, when watched, or actually eats, but later, in secret, purges, literally emptying herself of the food. Purging does not necessarily accompany anorexia, but as the DSM IV description makes clear, it is a feature of one type of anorexia: it has been suggested that diagnosis of anorexia nervosa without this type of dietary restriction is increasingly rare. The anorectic may occasionally binge eat, and then purge. She may also hoard food, without actually eating it, surrounding herself with forbidden objects (Crisp, 1995).

DISTINCTION BETWEEN BULIMIA NERVOSA AND ANOREXIA NERVOSA

In bulimia nervosa, the distortion of body image and amenorrhoea, which are characteristic of anorexia nervosa, are absent. Bulimia nervosa is characterised by an excessive intake of food followed by purging, through vomiting and/or laxative abuse. Bruch (1985) suggested that bulimia nervosa should not necessarily be considered a clinical entity in its own right: 'I have grave doubts that bulimia is a clinical entity. Compulsive overeating may occur in different conditions and with different severity (Bruch, 1985:12). This approach has shifted dramatically and bulimia nervosa is now recognised as a separate clinical entity. As the DSM IV classification of anorexia nervosa makes clear, purging can also be part of the anorexic syndrome. Bulimia nervosa can exist as a separate disorder, in which the body image distortion is absent. Like anorexia it is characterised by an over-valuation of weight and shape, and an engagement in dietary restriction, which in the case of bulimia is an alternation of binge eating and purging. Wilson describes bulimia as a loss of control over eating and the expression of 'chaotic dietary habits . . . with binge eating and compensatory purging' (Wilson, 1999:582).

Bulimia nervosa is further distinguished from binge eating disorder, which is characterised by recurrent episodes of binge eating without the extreme attempts at dietary restriction seen in anorexia and in bulimia nervosa. Generally, bulimia nervosa is not considered to be as dangerous a disorder as anorexia nervosa, which is associated with mortality and, as such, is a potentially fatal condition. In one sense, anorexia nervosa can be construed as an attempt to annihilate or kill off the body, through denial of its needs, as expressed through hunger; bulimia nervosa can be seen as an ongoing abuse of the body, a kind of sadistic alternation of gratification and deprivation of the body, in which food is rammed into the body in a frenzy and then violently removed, through a purge. The guilt of eating is expiated through the purging, which may occur in secret, so that the bulimic may give the appearance of enjoying food and eating 'normally'. Bulimia can therefore be understood in relation to the model of female perversion, with its characteristic secrecy, deceit and violence directed towards the self.

In bulimia and binge eating the gorging of food, cramming it frantically into the body, without a sense of internal limits, and little awareness of the feeling of being full, can be likened to a sexual frenzy, in which the climax is indefinitely postponed. This is an example of acting out perverse fantasies which appear to offer an escape from depression and feelings of worthlessness. Although the excitement of enacting the perversion offers short-lived euphoria, this soon subsides and gradually the sense of depression returns, with an intensified sense of guilt and self-loathing as a result of having enacted the fantasy. The starting point of the circle, the deep sense of self-contempt, has been reached again and the perverse cycle is reinforced.

ANOREXIA AS A DISORDER OF ADOLESCENCE

Anorexia nervosa often begins in adolescence, and is much more common in girls than boys, reflecting the adolescent girl's struggle to retain her childlike state and to assert control over her body, and, indirectly, over those around her, who become witness to her self-starvation. The cultural ambivalence towards women's bodies and their procreative capacities, which are both idealised and denigrated, is a significant reason for female anxiety about weight and size (Maguire, 1995:186).

Laufer and Laufer (1984) suggest that adolescence is a time when hormonal changes create an excited longing for sexual and physical intimacy, which may feel overwhelming for vulnerable individuals, who may perceive their bodies as being out of their control. The deep fear of these young women is that these strong desires become 'indistinguishable from a desperate longing for regressive intimacy with the parent, in an idealised fusion with the parent, which is both desired and dreaded' (Hughes, 1995:48). The attempt to starve herself is a young woman's attempt to kill off the longings of the pubertal body, and return to the comparative safety of the child's body. The force of the adolescent's longing for sexual intimacy comes from her infantile wishes for her mother's body, and her murderous feelings towards the mother who frustrates these desires. It can also be conceptualised as an unconscious punishment for violent fantasies relating to the mother and, as such, stems from guilt feelings.

Essentially, adolescence is a time when biological, hormonal changes create an intense need for physical contact, reawakening infantile needs for intimate contact with the parent. It has been referred to as the second phase of individuation, in that, once again, the child must negotiate the task of separation from the parent (Blos, 1967). Separation difficulties frequently occur in women with eating disorders including anorexia. Contemporary object relations analysts link somatising pain to the dilemma of the young woman who must differentiate herself psychically from the mother with whose body she identifies. This process of psychic separation is lifelong and unresolved conflicts in relation to the mother will resurface and intensify at crucial points of the life cycle, that is, puberty, pregnancy and the menopause (Pines, 1993). Birksted-Breen describes the central conflict for the anorectic woman:

> the anorexic's wish for, and fear of, fusion with her mother . . . anorexia can be seen as a girl's attempt to have a body separate from her mother's body, and a sense of self separate from her mother, the pathological nature of this attempt arising from the very lack of achievement of such separateness prior to adolescence.
>
> (Birksted-Breen, 1997:105).

A young woman's abuse of her body expresses her ambivalence about identifying with her mother's body: starving herself can be seen as a symbolic assault on the mother's body. Williams describes anorexia as the young woman's refusal to allow a foreign object into her body and links this with an earlier experience of being used to contain a parent's anxieties (Williams, 1997). Rather than the parent containing and making manageable the difficult psychic experiences of the child, the child has been used to perform this function for the parent. Because of her developmental stage, and the fragility of her own psychic apparatus, she is unable actually to contain these projections: she does not yet have the capacity for containment. The child is used as a receptacle, a dumping ground for her parent's anxieties:

> A pervasive symptomatology with a 'no-entry' quality can represent a defensive system developed by a child who has perceived himself/herself (early in infancy) to have been invaded by projections. These projections are likely to have been experienced by him or her as persecutory foreign bodies. The 'no-entry' syndrome performs the defensive function of blocking access to any input experienced as potentially intrusive and persecutory.
>
> (Williams, 1997:121)

Malan (1997) considers one of the most significant psychic functions of anorexia nervosa to be the repression of sexual drives through the rigid control of appetite; in this sense sexual feelings are represented by hunger, and successful mastery of both uncontrollable appetites is attempted through anorexia nervosa. Additionally, anorexia reflects a retreat from the frightening world of relationships and provides an escape from intimacy, albeit into the claustrophobia of obsession. Malan identifies the possible sources of the self-destructive impulses associated with anorexia in terms of id, ego and superego aspects. He suggests that self-destruction is not the primary aim of anorexia nervosa, which, in fact, provides a solution for psychic difficulties, although one which will ultimately fail. He outlines certain psychodynamic aspects of anorexia which include the threatening quality of intense needs for physical closeness and satisfaction from others, the use of eating as a substitute for intimate relationships in that it is under the anorectic's control. One of the most significant functions of self-starvation is to anaesthetise the anorectic against the turmoil of emotions, which threaten her psychic equilibrium:

> Hunger as an emotional anaesthetic. Its aim is to defend against the hope of having these needs fulfilled, in order to avoid the disappointment and despair consequent upon their being left unfulfilled. In other words, hunger functions as a defence against all aspects of close relationships.
>
> (Malan, 1997:95)

Malan describes the destructive aspect of anorexia, in its demolition of potential fulfilment through obsessional rituals. This destructive deprivation enables the anorectic to express guilt as self-punishment for sexual and aggressive impulses as well as serving as 'the expression of self-directed rage about disappointment in the past' (Malan, 1997:95). He does not consider the desire to kill oneself to be the primary motivation in anorexia, viewing suicide as an unintended consequence of this condition, which develops as a solution to a psychic problem.

THE LINE BETWEEN SHOPLIFTING AND ANOREXIA NERVOSA

In the forensic population, anorexia nervosa, or a history of anorexia, can be found in women who commit relatively minor offences, such as shoplifting and theft, and also in women who commit acts of violence against others and inflict harm on themselves (Crisp, 1995; Maden, 1996). It can feature as part of the complex set of behaviours which are found in those women classified as 'personality disordered' and also occurs in the general population of young girls and women who are desperately striving to achieve an ideal state of thinness. It can coexist with other forms of self-harm, and dramatically illustrates a refusal to allow anything good or caring to enter into the woman's internal world, behaviourally enacting the psychic state in which rejection and defence are the main strategies for survival.

Crisp (1995) discusses the link between hoarding and anorexia nervosa; there appears to be an important association between the act of stealing and the self-starvation of anorexia. Both stealing and punishment-seeking may be associated with anorexia nervosa, as though eating itself is considered to be bad and greedy, whereas deprivation of the self is seen as good, demonstrating strength and control. The anorectic can create a state of tension between fulfillment and deprivation of desire. At an unconscious level the anorectic shoplifter's act of theft may serve to guarantee punishment for the crime of greed. This punishment will temporarily alleviate the guilt an anorectic feels when she eats, or otherwise desires. Stealing food has clear symbolic significance.

Case illustration: Ruth: Shoplifting and anorexia in a 32-year-old woman

Ruth was referred to me for assessment of her suitability for psycho-therapeutic treatment. She was a slim, anxious-looking woman of Central European parents, who spent much of the first session in tears, as she described her sense of loneliness and failure, and her guilt about stealing. Although in her early 30s she dressed more like an adolescent, in trainers, flared leggings and a tee shirt. She mainly stole food from shops, and, even more significantly, only stole bags of sweets, which she would then devour. She had been caught shoplifting on at least half a dozen occasions and came to me for assessment following a referral by her probation officer, whom she was seeing regularly as part of her probation order. She had never received a custodial sentence for her offences.

It appeared that Ruth was suffering from an unresolved grief reaction following her father's sudden death when she was 16. She felt guilty about having left home shortly before his death and for beginning to have sexual relationships in the few months before he died. She felt guilty much of the time and described a sense of relief when she was caught for her shoplifting, explaining that this seemed to make her feel, temporarily, less guilty.

Three months after her father's death she had developed anorexic symptoms, which had resulted in serious illnesses on three occasions. Over the past two years her weight had been stable at just below seven stones and was regularly monitored by a nurse at her general practitioner's surgery. Her shoplifting had increased just as her weight had begun to stabilise. Although her weight had not reached dangerously low levels in the past three years, she continued to starve herself for at least two days out of every week, but would then make sure that she took in just enough not to lose too much weight. She exerted punitive control over her appetite, depriving herself of 'luxury items' like sweets, and occasionally chocolate, but never stole anything other than this.

Ruth had a younger brother with whom she had a long history of conflict and antagonism, exacerbated by her envy of his emotional detachment from his mother and his apparent enjoyment of his independent life and his own family. Ruth felt that she had been left to care for her mother while her brother was allowed the freedom to become an adult, with his own independent interests and new allegiances. Her perception was that sons were allowed to leave home while daughters were obligated to act as carers and companions for their parents, and were subject to strict control by them. She felt that she had never been allowed to leave home, and had developed few friends, interests or hobbies. Anorexia gave her a mode of expression of her anger at being so harshly restricted and confined.

Despite her rigorously restricted social life Ruth was fulfilled in her work as a medical secretary and formed deep attachments to the doctors in the surgery, one of whom had encouraged her to seek help for both her compulsive shoplifting of food and her self-destructive dieting. She took great pride in her work and was extremely conscientious about it, conveying the extent to which she was capable of a high level of functioning, and the degree to which her behaviour was shaped by a fear of losing control or getting things wrong. Just as she cleaned her house several times daily, for fear of germs and contamination, she also checked through reports and letters written for the doctors repeatedly, sometimes staying in the office for hours after the practice had closed to check through her work.

At the conclusion of my three-session assessment of her suitability for psychotherapy I prepared a report for the Court in which I emphasised the underlying meaning of Ruth's shoplifting (to receive punishment for her unconscious guilt) and its compulsive nature. When I saw her she had been charged with two counts of theft related to the sweets which she had stolen, and the Court was considering her disposal. Her probation officer was recommending that she receive a probation order. Ruth was fully aware that I would prepare a report and that following this she might be referred to a colleague for therapy, if she and I considered this to be desirable. I had not been able to offer her confidentiality because of the need to prepare a report for the Court in considering sentencing. In my report I recommended that she engage in therapeutic work addressing her underlying difficulties, and the function of shoplifting in enabling her to be punished for her forbidden impulses. It was my opinion that the best method for reducing the risk of re-offending and alleviating her psychological distress would be for her to be engaged in individual therapy addressing these issues, and allowing her to make links between her bereavement and her desire to punish herself through self-starvation and stealing.

Ruth was sentenced to a two-year probation order without the condition to attend for therapy, as I had indicated that the work would be more effective if she attended out of her own volition. It was clear that to subject Ruth to a condition of treatment would be, once again, to inflict harsh parental authority on her and deprive her of the opportunity to make choices and express rebellion.

Ruth attended therapy with my colleague reliably for over two years and did not re-offend during this time, although she continued to starve herself at times of stress and during the therapeutic breaks. She found it hard to attend for more than three sessions consecutively, and would miss the following session, as though therapy, like food, was something that she needed to control, and of which she would deprive herself. Nonetheless, she used the therapy to explore her sense of anger, abandonment, guilt and confusion following her father's sudden and devastating death. It appeared that her attack on her own body was, in part, an attack on this unreliable internal object, as well as an attempt to keep him alive, through a painful process of mourning in which healing could not occur and the loved lost object would not need to be relinquished. This process has been described by Freud in 'Mourning and melancholia', in which he explores how, in suicidal patients, aggression towards the lost object is turned inwards, on to a hated part of the self: 'the shadow of the object fell upon the ego' (Freud, 1917:258). Ruth felt that allowing herself peace of mind and bodily health would be to relinquish her father's presence, which she experienced most powerfully when she was in a state of intense pain and anxiety. She described him as having been 'strict but loving' and missed him most when she was alone. Crying seemed to heighten the experience of loss and made her father seem a closer presence, his absence more deeply felt. Her anorexia meant that she was often fatigued and exhausted, which resulted in frequent bouts of crying.

During the two years of therapy Ruth did not re-offend, nor did she fall below a critical weight. She remained at home with her mother but described her attendance at the clinic as very important to her, saying that she looked forward to sessions and felt that they gave her something for herself. She retained, however, a firm belief that she was still heavy, and eating remained a preoccupation for her, to the extent that she felt guilty after she ate anything, despite her growing awareness that this guilt stemmed from sources other than her relentless need for food. She did not enter a sexual relationship during this time but did form a close female friendship.

DISCUSSION

Understanding Ruth's anorexia

It was significant that Ruth obsessively focused on her own body, treating it with a cruel degree of control, when she had chosen to work in an area where the ill body was the focus of attention and concern. She herself wondered whether her fascination with starving herself, to see what would happen, and her interest in her job, with the morbid details of illness and death readily at hand, were an attempt to understand what had happened to her father and a symbolic attempt to gain control over inexorable processes of illness and deterioration. Although anorexia can be seen as a specific attempt to attack adult sexuality and preserve childhood, it can also be seen as a struggle to defeat the terrifying process of ageing in general, not just the reproductive development of an adult woman's body.

Ruth felt that to allow the expression of her hunger would be dangerous, linked as it was to her sexual feelings and her underlying anger about her mother's suffocating control over her. She could only allow herself to have this food that she craved, sweets, with their high calorie content, in situations where she would be punished. In this sense, her anorexia related to her fear about her own underlying impulses. She refused to take something into her body and became highly distressed when she felt that she had eaten too much; her self-starvation could be understood as a reflection of her fear that what was taken in would become an internal persecutor. The appetite which craved sweets appeared to be related to other uncontrollable and unacceptable urges and impulses, to sexual and aggressive feelings. Sweets represented indulgence, greed and childish treats, all of which Ruth felt that she must resist.

Her shoplifting resulted from an irresistible impulse to take a forbidden, pleasurable food, the kind of food used as a treat for children. Her stealing put me in mind of a small child, who feels deprived, stealing a special treat which she wanted, but felt she did not deserve. When she was caught, she felt, she said, like a naughty child, who would be taken away and kept out of harm's way, as though she were being sent to her room. A part of her craved this infantilising experience, in which she could feel that her own impulses would be kept under control, and that her dangerous desires would not lead her into trouble. She was freed from responsibility and could be temporarily cocooned in an enclosed space, without the temptation to behave like an adult. Eating sweets was, like sex, a forbidden pleasure: Ruth could only allow herself tiny tastes of these pleasures and had to create a situation where fulfilling her desires would result in punishment, maintaining this constant tension between wanting and denying. She did not allow herself to have sexual relationships, finding it very difficult to forget what she considered the catastrophic consequence of her adolescent sexual relationship – her father's death. Underlying her self-denial was a desperate sense of deprivation and a longing somehow to escape the claustrophobia of her relationship with her mother. Using her own body as an object to be tortured, denied food, and then teased with forbidden indulgences, was her only way of asserting this autonomy, and reminding herself and her mother that her life was, in fact, her own.

Relation of Ruth's anorexia nervosa to her shoplifting

It seemed that Ruth's shoplifting represented a conscious but compulsive act over which she had little control. Both shoplifting and self-starvation appeared to be motivated by an unconscious need for punishment and related to her entangled relationship with her mother, which had interfered with her capacity to separate from her and establish an adult identity.

Her guilt appeared to stem both from unresolved Oedipal feelings of sexual longing for her father, and from her complicated bereavement related to his death. She felt troubled by her sexual feelings in general and this was further complicated by his death. Being caught for shoplifting relieved her guilt feelings and need for punishment. She was able to exert punitive control over her body, depriving it of food, and then allowing herself to take the risk of stealing forbidden food, sweets, secure in the knowledge that she could be caught and chastised for this behaviour, this excursion into the land of forbidden pleasure. Her anorexia expressed her need to control her body, to enact violence against herself, particularly her sexuality, which she felt had led her astray, away from her parents. An infantile part of her had the omnipotent fantasy that her attempts to separate from her parents had somehow caused her father's death, that he could not survive without her. She had murderous, unexpressed rage against her mother which she enacted on herself. She inflicted the violence of starvation on herself with relentless cruelty, becoming wholly absorbed in the fight to restrict her food intake. She perceived hunger as a tormentor, against which she had to guard.

Her anorexia, guilt, sexuality and shoplifting seemed to be intimately connected, representing her conflicting drives and impulses. Her ongoing concerns were with staying thin, at any cost, and with pleasing her remaining parent, her mother, with whom she had a very enmeshed relationship. The process of separation from her mother had been abruptly and irrevocably interrupted by her father's death and in a powerful sense Ruth still behaved like an adolescent daughter, a 'good girl' who stayed at home with her mother rather than pursuing her own social life. Her sphere of autonomy and control was her own emaciated and deprived body.

Significance of stealing

Shoplifting can itself be understood as a symptom of underlying distress, reflecting the dissatisfaction and rebellion of apparently very compliant and respectable women, waging a private war against the hypocrisy and constraints of their circumstances. It has been described as an unconscious protest against the 'sociological false self' demanded of women:

> this facade is about being sweet natured, kind, quiet, considerate and nurturing to others. With women shoplifters this facade seems taken to an extreme and adopted unknowingly, unconsciously. Whilst most women knowingly adopt and play these roles, suffering guilt about their hypocrisy in doing so but being trapped by social expectation to continue, women shoplifters seem unconscious that their roles are merely a false sociological self.
>
> (Knowles, 1997:211)

For some women, like Ruth, group therapy may be considered preferable to individual therapy because it minimises the risk of an intense and dependent transference relationship with a therapist. One would expect that a transference to a therapist in individual therapy would replicate Ruth's enmeshed involvement with her mother, and she did in fact develop a strong relationship with her therapist, finding the breaks in the therapy very difficult to manage. As therapy within the National Health Service tends to be relatively short term compared to private psychoanalysis, this was an important issue to consider.

THE SUBJECTIVE EXPERIENCE OF ANOREXIA NERVOSA

Both anorexia nervosa and bulimia nervosa are disorders which have the capacity to possess the sufferer and become the governing principle of daily life. In her moving autobiography Marya Hornbacher vividly describes her immersion in both activities and compares the murderous nature of her anorexia with the less dangerous violence of her bulimia:

What I am about to say is tricky, and it is a statement about my own relationship with bulimia and anorexia. Bulimia is linked, in my life, to periods of intense passion, passion of all kinds, but most specifically emotional passion. Bulimia acknowledges the body explicitly, violently. It attacks the body, but it does not deny. It is an act of disgust and of need. This disgust and this need are about both the body and the emotions. The bulimic finds herself in excess, too emotional, too passionate. This sense of excess is pinned to the body . . . the bulimic impulse is more realistic than the anorexic because, for all its horrible nihilism, it understands that the body is inescapable . . . The anorectic operates under the astounding illusion that she can escape the flesh, and, by association, the realm of emotions.

(Hornbacher, 1998:93)

Throughout her memoir Hornbacher explores the complex and deeply absorbing nature of her eating disorders, describing her total immersion in both anorexic and bulimic behaviour and the power of the obsession that she developed with food and her own body, specifically the cruelty with which she inflicted starvation upon herself. She describes her awareness of her violent impulses towards herself and her risk-taking, her impulsive sexual promiscuity with great clarity and self-awareness, acknowledging the violence and the deceptive quality of eating disorders, which contributes to the ease with which their danger can be denied:

I had a clear, haunting knowledge that my eating disorder was cruelty. We forget this. We think of bulimia and anorexia as either a bizarre psychosis, or a quirky little habit, a phase, or as a thing that women just do. We forget that it is a violent act, that it bespeaks a profound level of anger toward and fear of the self.

(Hornbacher, 1998:123)

MODELS OF ANOREXIA NERVOSA

Family dynamics and anorexia nervosa: link with sexual abuse

There is empirical evidence that unwanted sexual experiences are associated with eating disorders. It must be borne in mind that these associations may be correlational rather than causal, i.e. both may occur with a high degree of frequency in the female population (Calam and

Slade, 1987). Calam and Slade suggest that the link between the development of an anorexic eating disorder and unwanted sexual experience within the family might be a form of punishment directed towards either the abusing or the non-protective parent. They propose a linear model of the causal direction of the anorexic symptomatology:

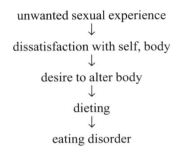

According to this model a change in eating behaviour might have an important function within the family system in that a degree of control would be exerted by the abused young woman, who would be able to create a situation in which others would be encouraging her to eat. The anger that she felt about her victimisation would be expressed indirectly at those who had enabled her abuse to take place: her own body was the conduit for the expression of anger, and her sole sphere of power.

A cognitive behavioural formulation of anorexia nervosa

Although a psychoanalyst, Hilde Bruch has been credited with laying the foundations for cognitive behavioural accounts of anorexia nervosa through her clinical observations which emphasised the importance of these patients' thinking style: she identified the 'paralysing sense of ineffectiveness, which pervades all thinking and activities of anorexic patients' (Bruch, 1973:254). The emphasis on the thinking patterns of the anorexic and the possibility of applying the principles of cognitive theory and cognitive therapy, as proposed by Beck *et al.*, 1979, were further developed by Garner and Bemis (1982, 1985) and laid the foundations for current cognitive behavioural approaches to the understanding and treatment of anorexia nervosa.

Anorexia is conceptualised by cognitive behavioural theorists as an expression of 'an extreme need to control eating' which is maintained by the rewards of self-control, so that it becomes a self-reinforcing activity, in which the physiological effects of starvation and the social rewards of thinness also contribute to the maintenance of the disorder (Fairburn *et al.*, 1999).

Fairburn *et al.* propose a cognitive behavioural formulation of anorexia nervosa which highlights the significance of anorexia as a means of gaining a sense of self-control, placing emphasis on this aspect of the disorder over other features, previously identified as key factors to be modified through treatment. This new emphasis on anorexia nervosa and self-control informs the treatment:

> Features which need to be addressed (in typical Western cases) are the use of eating, shape and weight as indices of self-control and self-worth, the disturbed eating itself and the associated extreme weight-control behaviour, the body checking and, of course, the low body weight. In contrast, we suggest that low self-esteem, difficulty recognising and expressing emotions, interpersonal problems and family difficulties, all of which are targets of the leading cognitive behavioural approach . . . do not need to be tackled unless they prevent change.
>
> (Fairburn *et al.*, 1999:10)

The cognitive behavioural treatment described above emphasises change in behaviour and thoughts about the need to control eating and weight loss; it focuses attention on the conscious function which anorexia serves for the individual, that is, the need to assert control through relentless dietary restriction. The underlying premiss is that anorexia nervosa is characterised by an extreme need to control eating, and that the feeling of self-control afforded by self-starvation is itself reinforcing. Abnormal concerns with shape and weight are not given as central a role as earlier conceptualisations of the disorder such as that proposed by Garner and Bemis (1982, 1985). This new conceptualisation would account for the prevalence of anorexia disorder in some non-Western societies in which shape and weight concerns are not part of the disorder, highlighting that the social concerns with appearance are not the only causes of the disorder.

The recently developed cognitive behavioural conceptualisation of anorexia nervosa proposed by Fairburn and colleagues provides an interesting model of the maintenance of the disorder. This conceptual-isation could inform treatment of those patients who do not present with other disturbances and personality difficulties, and who would be likely to benefit from this approach. It is worth noting that the developmental aspects of the disorder are not given primacy in this model, and the reasons for the choice of the body as the forum for the expression of self-control are not explored. Furthermore, the success of cognitive behavioural approaches in treating anorexia nervosa has not yet been determined and as such 'its efficacy remains in question' (Wilson, 1999:79).

The questionable efficacy of cognitive behavioural treatment of anorexia nervosa is in contrast to cognitive behavioural treatment of bulimia nervosa which has long been the treatment of choice and has proven efficacy (Wilson, 1999; Wilson and Fairburn, 1998). Cognitive behavioural treatment of bulimia nervosa has been demonstrated to be more effective in the short term than psychotherapies to which it has been compared. Earlier studies on the efficacy of behavioural modification (without the cognitive therapy component) in treating anorexia nervosa have demonstrated that while it can result in weight gain during the hospitalisation of patients, upon discharge from hospital they lose weight and relapse, leading to the conclusion by Garfinkel *et al.* (1977) that 'patients gain weight rapidly with this treatment and that, although not proving harmful, there is little evidence to suggest that it is superior to other conventional therapies. Not all patients with anorexia nervosa require or benefit from behavioural modification' (Garfinkel *et al.*, 1977:327).

In general, treatments for anorexia are required to be longer term than treatments for bulimia nervosa and cases with early onset and short duration have the best prognosis (Fairburn *et al.*, 1999). The low prevalence of anorexia nervosa, less than 1 per cent, makes it difficult to recruit participants for controlled studies and this has contributed to the absence of research relating to the comparative efficacy of various treatments of the disorder.

When anorexia nervosa occurs in conjunction with other manifestations of severe disturbance, such as other forms of self-harm, psychotic episodes or antisocial behaviour such as arson, it is one aspect of a constellation of difficulties, all of which require articulation, understanding and, ultimately, treatment. Isolating the anorexia nervosa or introducing a behavioural modification programme may be perceived as persecutory by the anorexic woman herself, and engender feelings of helplessness and loss of control in her only sphere of influence. Treating the anorexia nervosa is to work against the woman's conscious desire to remain thin at all costs, and conflicts with her needs. The treatment model proposed by Fairburn and colleagues aims to address this by focusing on the anorexic patient's sense of self-control and her thoughts about her need for extreme control over eating.

The cognitive behavioural model of anorexia nervosa proposed by Fairburn and colleagues has implications for treatment of the disorder. While respecting the value of this approach for certain individuals, I would argue that there are complex and symbolic uses of anorexia nervosa which cannot always be addressed or articulated through a cognitive behavioural approach. For patients who present with a constellation of difficulties, and for whom anorexia may be one among many forms of self-expression and acts of violence, a psychotherapeutic approach, in which earlier difficulties with containment and symbolic thinking can be uncovered, may be preferred. Clearly, empirical research exploring treatment efficacy and differentiating between those for whom cognitive behavioural treatment may be indicated, and those for whom psychotherapy is the preferred treatment option, would be invaluable.

Socio-cultural factors

It would be naive and inaccurate to deny the significance of the social context in which eating disorders develop, predominantly in women, in a culture which emphasises the aesthetic ideal of slimness and youth in women, to an unrealistic and unhealthy extent. While cultural factors have an important part to play in the development of eating disorders, they are clearly not the sole determinants of these disorders.

> The clinical as well as epidemiological findings that eating disorders are over-represented in women have been held as the most convincing support for the view that socio-cultural factors contribute to the expression of anorexia and bulimia nervosa . . . Since not all women are suffering from an eating disorder it would be naive to assume that cultural factors alone can 'cause' the development of anorexia or bulimia nervosa.
>
> (Weeda-Mannak, 1994:19)

Nonetheless, the central role of the tendency to evaluate self-worth in terms of shape and weight, particularly in Western cultures, is considered to be one of the distinguishing features of this disorder (Vitousek, 1996; Fairburn et al., 1999).

A feminist model

A feminist perspective on eating disorders and the social construction of beauty suggests that all women in Western societies are vulnerable to developing some degree of eating disordered behaviour, such is the emphasis on the cult of youth, slimness and beauty. While I have described extremes of behaviour, the women whose anorexia has taken over their lives, and threatened their very existence, it is important to acknowledge that such disturbed behaviour can be conceptualised as a continuum upon which we, as women, all lie:

> For Orbach, anorexia represents one extreme on a continuum on which all women today find themselves, insofar as they are vulnerable, to one degree or another, to the cultural constructions of femininity . . . the anorectic embodies, in an extreme and painfully debilitating way, a psychological struggle characteristic of the contemporary situation of women . . . in which a constellation of social, economic and psychological factors have combined to produce a generation of women who feel deeply flawed, ashamed of their needs and not entitled to exist unless they transform themselves into worthy new selves. (Read: without need, without want, without body.)
>
> (Bordo, 1993:47)

For women who present with anorexic symptomatology, in the absence of other disorders, cognitive behavioural therapy may be effective. This therapy would challenge the woman's accepted social constructions of beauty, and could replace these overvalued ideas with an emphasis on health and the strength, versatility and power of the mature female body. Similarly, a psychodynamic approach which helped the anorectic woman to explore the symbolic significance of her need to restrict her eating could help her to articulate her fears and accept her underlying impulses, enabling her to express in words the actions of her body. It is important to recognise that both therapeutic approaches would be in conflict with the powerful social message that equates extreme thinness with female beauty. Clearly, the more pervasive problem of oppressive social constructions of female worth, and its identification with slimness, requires powerful cultural re-evaluation. As Bordo states 'whether externally bound or internally managed, no body can escape either the imprint of culture or its gendered meanings' (Bordo, 1993:212). This pressure is inescapable and contributes to the obsession with the appearance of the female body, for both men and women, which in turn makes self-starvation, and other forms of self-harm, expressive forms of protest. Unfortunately, the cultural celebration of weight loss tends to disguise the extreme cruelty and violence of the anorexic condition.

THERAPEUTIC POSSIBILITIES

What kind of therapeutic relationship could possibly be established with an anorectic woman in the light of her intense and exclusive preoccupation with her own body, which precludes the possibility of intimacy with another? Hughes argues that the anorectic may exert a powerful affect on those around her, including her own family, and warns of the danger that the therapist will repeat these patterns, and be invited to engage in a strongly protective relationship in the countertransference:

> the anorectic is perhaps unique, however, in the way in which her flirting with death by starvation is both a prolonged and public act, and one in which family, friends and therapist are inexorably required to be witnesses to the self-destruction. This scenario is commonly complicated by the anorectic's lack of concern or even euphoria about her emaciation, and apparent indifference to the prospect of her possible premature death.
>
> (Hughes, 1995:49)

Psychotherapy with an anorexic woman will be fraught with difficulties as a powerful attempt will be made to kill off the therapist symbolically, through keeping her at a distance. This will conflict with dependence on the therapist and a desire for intimacy with her. This conflict is likely to mirror the central dilemma for the anorexic woman which is the desire to be fused with the mother and the terror of this fusion, and its feared annihilation of individuality. As well as being an assault on the actual body, anorexia is also an attack on bodily representations; in this case, the representation of the adult female body of the mother. It can coexist with purging, which may symbolise the inability, literally or symbolically, to digest experiences, out of an internal feeling of emptiness and the tendency to perceive anything which comes into internal or psychic space as an intrusion, to be defended against.

The therapist working with anorectics will face the difficult task of attempting to retain neutrality. She will struggle to avoid being drawn into the attempt to rescue the patient, and must not allow the therapy to be sabotaged by the anorectic's refusal to take anything into her internal world, even the help and understanding offered by therapist. The starving patient may also engender feelings of hopelessness, fear and impotent rage in the therapist, who is faced with the prospect of the patient's possible death, and is made witness to her ongoing self-torture. She is made to witness suffering which she is unable to prevent, and is therefore an indirect victim of the violence of anorexia. The nurturance offered by therapy may be experienced by the anorectic as a violation, an unwanted intrusion, as something good which she cannot take in. It is this 'no-entry' quality which the therapist must address with perseverance, sensitivity and respect, in the hope that eventually the anorexic woman will allow herself to engage in the therapy, and relinquish her relentless assaults on her own body.

CONCLUSION

Anorexia nervosa can be conceptualised as a woman's assault on her own body, particularly against her adult female sexuality, with its reproductive capacities. It can therefore be viewed as a dramatic expression of violence against the self, and against the mother, with whose body the woman identifies. It may reflect murderous feelings both towards the mother and towards the self.

I consider the model of female perversion illuminating in its exploration of the dynamics of anorexia: it emphasises the symbolic and unconscious meaning of the behaviour as an assault on the body of the mother as represented through the self. Anorexia may also symbolise the hope of the adolescent girl for immortality, as she attacks her reproductive capacity to defy ageing and death. The narcissistic immersion in the self, in the body as the source of all meaning is an essential aspect of the perversion evident in anorexia:

> The sickness occupies your every thought, breathes like a lover at your ear; the sickness stands at your shoulder in the mirror, absorbed with your body, each inch of skin and flesh, and you let it work you over, touch you with rough hands that thrill . . . Nothing will ever be so close to you again. You will never find a lover so careful, so attentive, so unconditionally present and concerned only with you.
>
> (Hornbacher, 1998:125)

Like other forms of self-harm, the meaning of anorexia for a particular woman needs to be understood: in its extreme form it signifies much more than simply the desire to conform to an accepted notion of beauty and desirability. It expresses a private and symbolic violence.

Part III

Violence against others

Chapter 7

Battered women who kill

INTRODUCTION

The notion of woman as killer is one which is abhorrent to cherished beliefs about femininity. The fact that women are more likely to kill within the family than to kill a stranger contributes to the horror and bewilderment which surrounds female homicides. In considering women who kill, psychodynamic questions emerge. These include the question of what is actually being split off and killed off through the murder, in terms of the killer's fantasy. Addressing unconscious issues in killing requires an understanding of how killing can be the enactment of a primitive defence mechanism whereby an aspect of the self, threatened with annihilation, retaliates through murder. The act of killing may be experienced as a temporary escape from this danger and may appear to ensure psychic survival. This apparent solution is short-lived, however, and the internal dangers return; the initial euphoria recedes and depression threatens.

Women who have disturbed early experiences may be more likely to enact this violence than others (Browne, 1987; Fonagy and Target, 1999) because of the difficulties which they have experienced in integrating their murderous feelings: first, their aggression is projected into others, their violent partners, and, when this becomes unbearable, they retaliate through violent action themselves. There are important social and psychological factors to consider in exploring the circumstances of domestic violence and revenge. Browne (1987) stresses that the background of the violent partners who are killed is a more significant predictive factor than the background of the women who kill, emphasising the role of the dynamics between the abused woman and her violent partner.

A central question of this chapter is why women, when they do kill, are more likely than men to kill intimate acquaintances and spouses or family members than strangers; this is in stark contrast to the male pattern of murder (HMSO, 1998). I address the psychological motivations and social situations of battered women who kill their abusive partners and their subsequent disposal by the Courts. In these cases I consider whether the plea of self-defence on the grounds of provocation offers a satisfactory alternative to the pleas of murder, or manslaughter on the grounds of diminished responsibility, and the response of the Courts to this plea. I do not provide an exhaustive account of female homicide, but focus on those cases where the apparent victim of violence, the battered woman, becomes the perpetrator of violence in an act of fatal retaliation.

This chapter provides statistics relating to the prevalence of the crime, various psychological models for understanding it, and illustrative case studies. In order to understand what leads battered women to kill, it is necessary to understand the dynamics between abuser and abused which characterise abusive relationships; a case study illustrates the difficulties of a woman abused by multiple violent partners and the psychological consequences of repeated abuse. A further case illustration describes a battered wife who killed her violent partner.

PREVALENCE

Statistical figures reveal that women are still much more likely than their male partners to be victims of fatal assault within the family (HMSO, 1993, 1998). When they are victims of homicide women are far more likely than men to be killed by their former partners and lovers:

> in 1997, just over half of male victims (54 per cent) and nearly four-fifths of female ones (79 per cent) knew the main or only suspect before the offence took place. While only eight per cent of men were killed by former partners or lovers, the figure was considerably higher for women (47 per cent).
>
> (HMSO, 1998:70)

Men were much more likely than women to be killed by strangers: 31 per cent of men were killed by strangers in contrast to only 12 per cent of women.

Analysis of the criminal statistics reveals that children are more likely to be killed by men than by women, that women are more likely to be killed by men than men are by women, but that when women do kill they are far more likely than men to kill their spouse, an intimate acquaintance or a family member. It is worth bearing in mind that the major proportion of violent crimes, including homicide, are perpetrated by men and that men are more likely to be convicted by a Court than women. In 1997 in cases of domestic homicide, 167 women were charged and 74 per cent were convicted, in contrast to 521 men who were charged with domestic homicide, of which 91 per cent were convicted. From 1991 to 1997 the Courts in England and Wales dealt with male and female suspects differently:

> males are more likely to be convicted than females, and the conviction is more likely to be for murder than for manslaughter. Furthermore males are more likely than females to be sentenced to immediate custody for manslaughter (immediate custody is mandatory for a murder conviction), and to be sentenced to a longer term.
>
> (HMSO, 1998:71)

The group most at risk of being killed were children under the age of 1, in which age group male victims comprised nearly 80 per cent. There were 57 infants per million under the age of 1 who were victims of homicide in 1997.

D'Orban (1990) reviewed the incidence, characteristics and patterns of female homicide, with special reference to England and Wales. He found that the male : female ratio for homicide offences was similar to the ratio for other offences of violence but that murder was almost exclusively committed by men. In the 1980s the annual average of female murder convictions was only 6.5 per cent of the total of murder convictions per annum. Wykes (1995) found that females committed relatively more homicide offences related to mental disorder (i.e. diminished responsibility, manslaughter and infanticide) than men, that they had a better chance of acquittal of murder, and that they were more likely to be dealt with by a probation order than by imprisonment. About 80 per cent of the victims of female homicide are family members; 40–45 per cent kill their children and about one-third kill their spouse or lover (Wykes, 1995).

THE TRAP OF VIOLENT RELATIONSHIPS

To what extent can it be said that a woman who 'chooses' a violent partner is aware of her actions and to what degree does she contribute to the violence? Does she have the option to leave earlier in the relationship or is she making a conscious choice to stay in a high-risk relationship? Is she implicitly condoning the violence through her apparent decision to stay? These questions relate to the extent to which women in violent relationships lose their capacity to make real choices or exercise their autonomy. There are important social and economic factors which are highly relevant to the continued dependence of some women on partners who may be violent and emotionally abusive.

LEARNED HELPLESSNESS AND DEPRESSION

A clear understanding of how victims develop particular responses to unpredictable aggressors over time, and how distorted their thinking may have become about the options available to them, is relevant to the current debate concerning legal defences for killing an abusive partner.

The development of learned helplessness and depression has been identified in the psychological literature relating to battered women who remain in abusive situations (Browne, 1987; Walker, 1984). The women who enter into relationships which are already violent, or which become abusive over time, may have certain vulnerability factors in their own backgrounds which, in combination with certain social stressors, make it more likely that they will have an unplanned pregnancy in adolescence and develop depression in adulthood (Harris *et al*. 1987). One highly significant vulnerability factor for depression identified by Brown and Harris (1978) in their seminal work on the social origins of depression was the experience of early maternal loss. Women who have been subject to parental violence often leave home early in an effort to escape the stressful situation. In the context of this need to escape from unhappiness their choice of partner may be somewhat indiscriminate. The person who appeared to offer sanctuary turns out to be an abusive or violent partner.

Once involved in a relationship these women may find it difficult to leave, even in the face of physical or emotional abuse, because of their lack of self-esteem, scarce financial resources, fear of letting others know about the abuse, and sense of dependence on their partner. Women who are repeatedly exposed to painful events over which they have no control and who have no obvious means of escape may develop the classic symptoms of learned helplessness as first identified by Seligman (1975) in laboratory animals: they become passive, lose their motivation to respond, and come to believe that they cannot take action that would allow them to escape from the painful stimuli, even when situations are introduced in which action could be taken by them to avoid the painful stimuli. This situation appears analogous with that of women who first attempt strategies to avoid their partner's anger but learn that, whatever they do, violence will result. Eventually, they lose faith in their own self-efficacy and become increasingly unable to take action, even when it could be effective. The experience of being mistreated further reinforces the low sense of self-esteem and the belief that they are powerless to alter their situation or take effective action. This 'learned helplessness' describes the powerful effects of prolonged exposure to uncontrollable aversive and painful stimuli and has cognitive consequences too; this sense of passivity and despair may be reflected in the way battered women appraise their situation and evaluate the avenues of escape available. Their perceptions of events may be very negative and their sense of their own power very impoverished; this attributional style is associated with depression.

The abused partner ceases to take action even in situations over which she *may* be able to exert an influence and becomes ever more dependent and unhappy. Her victimisation may result in a pattern of behaviour in which she is increasingly unable to defend herself against future abuse and a vicious cycle is established. Her attempts to alter the situation through reasoning with her partner are often ineffective and it may take third-party intervention or counselling to enable her to leave the situation. Leaving will not necessarily guarantee safety. Many women who leave will be hounded by their former partners until they are so intimidated that they return. Additionally, the socioeconomic and psychological problems which contributed to their attraction to the apparently strong partner in the first place will be unchanged and it is possible that, even if they leave one violent partner, they will be targeted by another, and feel unable to manage without a relationship at all. The pattern of victimisation may well be repeated.

THE DYNAMICS OF ABUSE

The violent partner expresses his dominance and asserts his identity through attempting to control and master every aspect of his partner's life. He uses patterns of coercive and violent behaviour to establish control and power over his partner (Dobash and Dobash, 1979). Through creating an illusion of omnipotence his own feelings of inadequacy and help-lessness are temporarily alleviated. This psychological process, projective identification, is a powerful means of attempting to rid oneself of unacceptable impulses through denying them in oneself and identifying them in another; the concomitant is that, having seen these projections in another, one is then able to despise and condemn them.

Klein (1946) described projective identification as an interactive process in which patients have a fantasy of evacuating unwanted parts of themselves on to the therapist, and this fantasy may be accompanied by behaviour intended to evoke feelings in the therapist corresponding to the fantasy, so that the other person begins to take on those characteristics. This dynamic not only occurs between therapist and patient but between partners in intimate relationships.

Projective identification serves an important function, particularly in those people who are unable to bear the fact that good and bad aspects of the self can coexist in the same person. An interesting feature of projective identification is the relation of the person on to whom badness has been projected to the person who has temporarily freed himself from unacceptable impulses; he is, in a sense, impelled to behave according to the projections that he receives. The person on to whom weakness has been projected may find herself feeling helpless, vulnerable, weak and useless. She relinquishes any feelings of self-esteem or control, feeding into her persecutor's distorted perceptions.

This dynamic is clearly evident in the battered woman who has essentially become the sponge for her partner's feelings of inadequacy and self-contempt. She absorbs these feelings, becoming increasing depressed and he, in turn, loses touch with his own feelings of vulnerability, finding his aggressive and sadistic feelings more acceptable, less frightening to acknowledge. The moment where the victim becomes aggressor, where the battered wife becomes the killer, can be seen as the moment of rebellion, of challenging the polarised and distorted roles which have been imposed. Just as the aggressive partner has denied his feelings of vulnerability through the battering, cruelty and intimidation, the abused partner has been allowed to deny her own feelings of murderous rage: this rage has been suppressed and her partner has enacted the feelings for her, until this moment. The fear of either murderous rage or complete vulnerability and the risk of unbearable abandonment are actually shared by both partners. The polarisation within the relationship has enabled each partner to deny an important and feared aspect of the self.

The relationship between abuser and victim is one in which both play an active part. The relationship cannot be established by one person alone and it is this interaction between the two parties, and the participation of the victim in the relationship, which is the most complex, and arguably the most difficult, issue for theorists to address. There is a fear that to explore the role of the victim or her participation in an abusive relationship is to blame her for the abuse that she has suffered. To ignore her role in the relationship would be to denigrate her and to assign her to a kind of incidental role in which she is wholly passive. I have attempted to explain the interaction between victim and abuser through the discussion of psychological defences like projective identification, and will now turn my attention to the sense in which the abuser perceives himself to be, and in some sense really is, wholly dependent on his victim. He must see himself through her eyes and his sense of manhood and power is derived from her devotion to and fear of him.

The victim is generally a highly significant person for her partner and she is aware of this. Initially, her partner may have been highly solicitous towards her, making statements of great love and dependence. Following the first violent incident he expresses profound feelings of remorse and regret, offering to do anything to make up for this behaviour and promising to change. These protestations of love and short-lived determination to change may be genuine, although very difficult, if not impossible, to enact. The victim is aware that her partner, at least in part, feels repentant and has other aspects to his character which are deeply at odds with this destructive and frightening side. She has projected her violent feelings on to him.

The victim may represent a powerful persecutory mother figure to the violent partner, whose separateness is a constant reminder that she may abandon him at any moment. It is as though the victim's sensitive understanding that her partner's violence stems from his own deprivation, and that he confuses her with other powerful and withholding women in his life, further prevents her from leaving him. The defence of identification is important here because those women who could identify with this deprivation may find it hardest to 'disappoint their partners' as to do so would be to recreate their own experiences of abandonment and rejection.

The unconscious representations of people, e.g. where a wife is seen as the mirror image of mother, is highly relevant to understanding how early experiences tend to be re-created in later life; the power of these associations is enormous. The abuser may be furious when faced with possible loss or abandonment because of his earlier experience of deprivation or betrayal. He may then displace his intense anger on his partner. He projects this blueprint of uncaring and rejecting women on to his partner and is hypersensitive to any perceived rejection or abandonment; he is looking for evidence that he is unlovable, often finding it impossible to accept if he is shown love and loyalty. He will often have had an early experience of witnessing parental violence and have learned that fathers beat mothers, that anger, concern and emotional involvement are all expressed through violence. He may perceive himself to be helpless and humiliated in relation to his partner, whom he views as virtually omnipotent, responsible for most things which happen to him.

The compulsive aspect of abusive relationships may be connected with the meeting of unconscious needs and the swapping of roles in that the abuser is actually dependent on his victim, who is, at some level, aware of this power. The abusive relationship thus has very strongly entrenched destructive dynamics which makes it very difficult to escape from or be able to leave.

VIOLENCE AND SADISM IN ABUSIVE RELATIONSHIPS

In violent relationships the abuser needs his victim to stay alive. The aggressive impulse is not to destroy her but to preserve her in order to control and hurt her, to make sure that she does not leave. It is a key feature of sadomasochistic relationships that the object needs to be kept alive to be tortured. The abuser needs his victim to be a living recipient of his torture, an available object into which to pour his self-contempt and feelings of helplessness, although at times of extreme rage he is capable of killing her. The violent man will often describe his partner as the 'ideal woman' whom he 'worships' but whom he is terrified of losing, and who he believes will eventually abandon and reject him. The use of sustained physical and emotional abuse and intimidation enables him to feel that he is in control of the situation and helps to enhance his sense of self-esteem, giving him a short-lived sense of efficacy and power.

DIFFICULTIES IN LEAVING VIOLENT RELATIONSHIPS

Browne (1987) points out that 'the question, "why don't battered women leave?", is based on the assumption that leaving will end the violence.' Her study consisted of forty-two female homicides and a comparison group of 200 victims of domestic abuse who did not kill. Fifty-three per cent of women in the group who did not go on to kill their violent partner had left the partner by the time of interview. She points out that these women will not easily be identified as battered wives because they have left after the first, or maybe the second, violent incident and often will not have discussed their experiences with anyone, out of shame, guilt or self-blame. In the homicide group in her study a significant proportion of women had left their violent partners in the past, and some had even been separated or divorced for several years before the fatal incident.

Browne (1987) outlines at least three important reasons why women do not, or cannot, leave their violent partners:

1   Practical difficulties in effecting separation.
2   Fear of retaliation.
3   The effects of severe abuse on the victim.

The practical difficulties of leaving a violent partner include the fact that most friends and relations are well known to the violent partner and this makes escape tricky. The woman cannot simply vanish without cutting herself off from friends and family just at the point when she needs their support most. The violent partner is often very jealous and possessive and he may be well aware of the possible refuges that she would seek in a crisis. While shelters for battered women and their families do exist, they are often oversubscribed and cannot offer protection for all women who seek it. Additionally, residence in a refuge or shelter carries, unfortunately, a degree of stigma and transience which may be particularly burdensome for children to bear. Arrangements for child-care and major disruptions to children's daily routines are also important considerations for any responsible and caring mother. The battered woman may be particularly vulnerable to feelings of guilt and self-blame and feel that, by leaving her partner and subjecting their children to disruption, instability and the loss of their father she is acting irresponsibly and selfishly. At the same time the desire to protect the children from violence may be a catalyst for her decision to leave.

1. Practical difficulties

When a woman has left her partner and entered a refuge or temporary accommodation with her children, she also runs the risk of a custody battle in which her husband uses the fact of her leaving him as evidence of her unstable mental state, lack of compliance with social norms and disregard for the well-being of her children. He may charge her with desertion. In a custody battle these are very grave allegations and could well jeopardise the woman's future care of her children. 'In many cases the abuser fights the woman for custody of the children, and sometimes wins' (Browne, 1987:111). This is more likely if there is no evidence of the partner's violence against the children. The abused spouse must rely on women's refuges or social services to house and support her.

Once social services are aware that a woman and her children are at risk of physical abuse they may refer the mother for psychological assessment which may conclude that, at the time of the evaluation, she is not able to offer adequate care and protection for her children. Once again the people to whom she turned for support, betray and abandon her and she may lose custody of her children. The fact of her environmental instability and current psychological distress following the separation may weaken her chances of retaining the care of her children. Social services have a statutory duty to protect the children. In cases of risk assessment child protection is the priority and the needs of the mother are secondary. The 1989 Children Act explicitly states that the needs of the children for welfare and protection are the paramount consideration of the Court and highlights the importance of keeping children within their biological families wherever possible. In cases where severe neglect or abuse of children has occurred it may be difficult for the professionals involved to avoid feeling punitive towards the parents, and they may become overly pessimistic about helping the family to stay together.

Rehabilitation may be the ideal but its success is not necessarily easy to envisage, particularly if the mother or primary caregiver has been guilty of serious neglect or abuse. There is a danger of polarisation between parents and child-care professionals. It may not always be possible to bear in mind that to help the mother psychologically and practically is to help the children; there is a risk that child-care professionals occasionally operate on the basis of a false dichotomy, i.e. only two options may be identified – helping the mother or helping the children – and these two are mutually exclusive. Where possible, attempts to 'parent the parents' should be made. In fact, there are many options available and care plans drawn up by the local authority can reflect this, identifying strategies for helping the mother to gain the necessary insight, skills and support so that rehabilitation of her children becomes possible. Sometimes psychological work is recommended as a precondition for rehabilitation, sometimes as an option to be undertaken once rehabilitation has occurred. One obvious difficulty with this is that psychotherapy then becomes a coercive activity, a means to achieving a goal, rather than something freely chosen. Much of forensic psychotherapy has this tension within it and there is an important sense in which this is viewed not as an obstacle to the work but as an acknowledged aspect of the therapeutic relationship; it is recognised that psychological change is sought, in part, to bring about an external change; in this case, to ensure that children are returned to a safe environment (see Chapter 3 'Maternal physical abuse').

The emotive nature of child protection work can create situations in which parents and social workers are polarised and a custody battle is fought out in the Courtroom in a way that is antithetical to the spirit of the 1989 Children Act. Parents may be split against each other or one parent may be essentially fighting the local authority for custody of the children. The fear of losing her children, through their abduction or death, or through a legal battle, may well deter an abused woman from leaving an apparently unbearable situation. She also knows that if she leaves she may be harshly judged by others, as a bad wife and callous mother, or told that she must have created the situation herself through provocation of her partner.

2. Fear of retaliation

This is a significant factor in preventing battered women from leaving violent relationships. Their partners have threatened to kill them and their children if they leave. Sometimes the violent man, who is genuinely desperate at the prospect of his own abandonment, threatens to commit suicide if his partner leaves him. This emotional blackmail taps into the woman's sense of overriding responsibility for her partner's mental state and frightens her. The fear of escalating violence following separation is grounded in fact and there is evidence that the most dangerous time for an abused woman follows attempted separation or its discussion (Glass, 1995).

If a woman has left, taking her children with her, and she is found by her partner, she believes that they will all be at greater risk of harm than previously, which thought terrifies her. Her partner has convinced her of his omnipotent control and that he will track her down wherever she tries to go, that she simply cannot escape from him. In Browne's study 98 per cent of the homicide group and 90 per cent of the comparison group believed that their abuser could and would kill them, and were convinced that leaving would not prevent this. Fears of being killed increase when the possibility of leaving is discussed with an abusive partner who may become homicidal, suicidal or deeply depressed; 'the point of, or even discussion of, separation is one of the most dangerous times in an abusive relationship' (Browne, 1987:115).

3. The psychological effects of severe abuse

The main effect of severe abuse is to heighten the victim's level of perceived helplessness. The vulnerability factors of some of the women, who formed relationships with men who became abusive, will still be present when those relationships become worse. While their vulnerability in terms of their background or lack of family and social support does not cause them to be abused, and cannot be held responsible for their partner's violence, it plays a role in increasing the likelihood that they will be victimised and also makes it more likely that they will be disadvantaged in terms of escape routes. If anything, their lack of self-esteem and feelings of helplessness will have been increased by the experience of violence in a relationship and they will feel even less able than previously to take effective action to leave. For those women who had strong social and family support the experience of trying to placate and subdue a jealous and possessive partner will often have meant weakening those links, becoming socially isolated and estranged from family, resulting in a loss of confidence and increasing dependence on the violent partner, who demands that he is the main, if not the sole, recipient of devotion and attention. The dynamics of abuse create a vicious cycle in which the victim becomes increasingly more passive and frightened and the abuser more able to control and terrorise; the more she gives up her external sources of support, the easier it becomes for the abuser to dominate her.

The emphasis on asking why women leave or stay in violent relationships also reveals the extent to which such action is framed in terms of individual choice and agency rather than as a product of social forces and the unequal distribution of power. The problem is framed in simplistic and individual terms. Mahoney (1994) discusses the notion of female victimisation and agency within violent relationships:

> Women live under conditions of unequal personal and systemic power. Violence at the hands of intimate partners, a relatively common event for women, is experienced in this context of love and responsibility . . . Social stereotypes and cultural expectations about the behaviour of battered women help to hide women's acts of resistance and struggle. Both law and popular culture tend to equate agency in battered women with separation from the relationship . . . 'Staying' is a socially suspect choice while 'leaving' is often unsafe. In fact, women often assert themselves by attempting to work out relationships without battering. Separation assault, the violent, sometimes lethal attack on a woman's attempt to leave the relationship, proves that the power and control quest of the batterer often continues after the woman's decision to leave. The prevalent social focus on leaving conceals the nature of domestic violence as a

struggle for control, pretends away the extreme dangers of separation, and hides the interaction of social structures that oppress women.

(Mahoney, 1994:60)

In the context of the practical problems of leaving, the fears of reprisal, the certainty that leaving will not necessarily mean safety, the paucity of alternative shelters, and sometimes the fact of previous failed attempts to leave, it is not surprising that battered women do not leave abusive relationships, and, even when they do, that they are not necessarily free from danger. The more profound question might be why the abusive partner is not requested to leave, or at least to seek help, by any agencies of social control. The dynamic in which the woman is held responsible for her partner's mental state, mood, social success, and blamed for any failure or distress is actually mirrored in the pervasive attitude which places responsibility for her own abuse on the victim herself, i.e. 'she should have left . . . she must have wanted it.'

This is a classic example of victim-blaming which can be explained by 'cognitive dissonance theory'. According to this theory, the belief that the world is just is such a cherished belief that events which suggest otherwise are reinterpreted so as to fit in with the 'just world hypothesis'. Rather than accept that a woman was severely abused emotionally, physically and possibly sexually, because of violence in her partner, it is more comfortable to identify characteristics in her which made such abuse understandable. If she can be held responsible for her own abuse, this makes it less likely that an 'innocent' person would also be victimised in the same way. This is known in social psychology as derogation of the victim. While it is undeniable that violence is the product of an interaction, it does not follow that the victim has caused her abuse, or that she bears responsibility for its beginning or end. The best predictive factors for violence are found in the backgrounds of the perpetrators, not the backgrounds of the victims. Although violence in childhood was a factor found in the majority of the partners of violent men, this factor was not nearly as significant in predicting future violence as the exposure of the abusers to parental violence in their own childhoods. While the repetition of patterns may be influenced by unconscious needs, this in no way exonerates the violent behaviour of the abusive partner but simply elucidates the way that a violent upbringing may enhance the likelihood of future violence.

The following study of a woman who was repeatedly involved in abusive relationships illustrates some of the reasons why battered women do not leave.

Case illustration: Jasmine: Multiple victimisation in a 22-year-old woman

Jasmine was referred to the forensic psychology services for assessment of her parenting skills. Her eldest four children, aged 7, 5, 4 and 3 years old, had been placed in long-term care under full care orders and were subject to adoption proceedings. They had three different fathers and all four had been severely physically abused by Jasmine's most recent partner. The two girls, aged 7 and 4, had been found to have been seriously sexually abused and there were suspicions that they had also been victims of physical violence. The boys had been found to have cigarette burns and bruises on their bodies indicative of severe and sadistic physical abuse. All four children had been very thin, pale and frail when the local authority had first investigated the situation, owing to concerns about the children being abused and neglected. The children described the cruelty with which they had been treated by their mother's most recent partner, who had frequently threatened to kill them and their mother, and who had frequently assaulted their mother in front of them.

Jasmine had recently given birth to a fifth child, whose father was the man who had sexually, emotionally and physically abused her other children. This child was the subject of the current care proceedings and Jasmine was applying for custody of him. He was 7 months old at the time of the assessment and was living in foster care. Jasmine had daily contact with him at a family centre, where she was taking part in cooking, budgeting and child-care groups. Her relationship with her most recent partner had ended and she was living on her own. She was extremely tearful throughout the interviews, expressing feelings of guilt and regret about having failed to protect her four eldest children from the serious abuse which they had suffered. She missed them badly and was frightened that her baby would also be placed for long-term fostering with a view to adoption. She had herself been the victim of violence by her previous partners. The central question of the assessment was the extent to which this vulnerable woman could protect a young baby in her care. The related issue of her capacity to protect herself was an essential consideration in this assessment.

There were factors in Jasmine's own background which appeared to contribute significantly to her parenting difficulties. These included her own experience of significant violence directed by her half-brother towards her mother; the lack of protection offered to her by her mother when she was a child, as demonstrated by her having been the victim of a sexually abusive relationship with an older, exploitative man; the disruption and discord that she suffered through parental separation when she was 12; and the lack of supervision and guidance throughout her childhood. Jasmine described her home life as difficult and unhappy after her parents' separation. She had run away from home at age 13, in an apparent effort to escape from a tense and fraught environment. Her mother seemed to have been unable to provide her with adequate support and supervision or to protect Jasmine or herself from physical abuse. At age 15 Jasmine's father died; he had been a source of some comfort and support to her and his death brought a profound sense of loss.

At age 14 Jasmine had been held hostage and repeatedly raped over a three-day period by her boyfriend to whom she had run to escape from an unhappy home situation. This violent incident clearly traumatised her. When I met her, eight years later, she still displayed symptoms of post-traumatic stress disorder including flashbacks to the rape and physical violence, nightmares about the experiences, intrusive thoughts about the sexual violation and violence, fears of being on her own with men, and a sense that the trauma was still taking place. Jasmine had been involved in sexual relationships with at least eight partners in the past seven years, all of whom had been physically abusive towards her. Her longest relationship had lasted just over one year. The pattern of these relationships was that the man would appear to offer Jasmine an escape from a difficult and violent relationship or an unhappy situation at home. She had little self-confidence and would only leave an abusive situation with his help. This new partner would then become violent himself, leaving her feeling trapped and helpless until yet another new partner would appear on the scene, apparently offering protection and a means of escape. Her desperation to leave a dangerous situation would affect the rationality of her judgements about the new partner and the decision to form a new relationship would be made in the context of anxiety and despair, without the necessary regard to potential risk to herself. Her children were with her throughout but their needs

were, unfortunately, neglected. These decisions were not in the best
long-term interests of the children in her care but appeared at the
time to offer short-term solutions to the threat of immediate
danger.

It appeared that Jasmine's early experiences affected her sense of
self-esteem and her internal model of parenting. Her mother was a
depressed woman who found it difficult to attend to her needs and
Jasmine, already vulnerable because of her experience of violence
and her own difficulties at school, where she was considered
'backwards', was left to find attention and affection where she could.
She had tended to seek out adults who she felt could protect her and
was unaware of the exploitative nature of their attention, which was
often sexual. She had few good objects in her internal world and a
confused notion of comfort and care. Her main feeling throughout
her early years was of being alone and unlovable and she hoped
that through having babies she could finally 'have something for
myself, someone that really loves me', reflecting both her sense of
deprivation and her narcissistic conception of children.

Her descriptions of violent encounters with men illustrate her
sense of resignation, powerlessness and fear. Her mother, to whom
she turned, was unable to offer real protection or refuge. Jasmine
described the physical violence inflicted on her by her previous
partner: 'I can remember one incident when he became violent
towards me. It was over money . . . he reckoned that I had spent
some of his wages when he was away. What he did to me then was
try to strangle me. He got angry and put his hands round my throat.
When he did this he would be under the influence of drink. He drank
quite a bit but later in our relationship it got worse. He got me
pinned to the floor and said, "I'm going to have to batter you, what's
you going to do to stop it?" He stopped, that time, but I don't know
why . . . I stayed at my Mum's after he had tried to strangle me. He
constantly tried to ring my Mum's that night and the phone had to be
unplugged. In the morning I was frightened to return to the house
and I asked for the police to come with me. I wanted to go back to
collect some of the kids' clothes . . . When I entered the house my
light bulb in the front room and the kitchen were smashed, two
windows were completely smashed. There was glass all round the
front room from bottles of beer which he had smashed into the wall.

I did not make a complaint on that occasion because he had already been arrested and I thought I wouldn't bother.'

She vividly described her sense of helplessness and her tacit acceptance that her evidence would be discounted and her maltreatment minimised if she were to make a further complaint against her violent partner. She had learned not to bother. This illustrates the psychological state of 'learned helplessness'. She believed that there was nothing she could do to avoid this terrorising and dehumanising treatment although she had taken the significant step of leaving her partner. The frightening consequences of having left him and the constant fear of his retaliation are demonstrated by Jasmine's experience of returning home to find a scene of devastation and destruction.

Outcome

Following my recommendations and those of the guardian *ad litem* for the baby, and the workers conducting the assessment at the family centre which Jasmine was attending regularly, it was agreed at a social services case conference that the local authority care plan would be to support gradual rehabilitation of the baby to Jasmine under a full care order. This would enable the local authority to retain shared parental responsibility with Jasmine and to remove the child and place him with foster parents should there be evidence that he was injured or that neglect had occurred. Jasmine was to be supported by the family centre, a family aide and the allocated social workers. She was also engaged in weekly counselling which enabled her to talk about her own experiences of sexual abuse, and her profound difficulties in asserting herself.

There was a positive outcome in this case in that one year after the care proceedings had been settled, Jasmine still had custody of her youngest child, and was coping well with the demands of child-care. She was also more assertive and confident in her own right, and seemed to feel contained by her individual counselling and the supportive system relating to the baby. The social worker had, however, frequently voiced concerns about her association with various male 'friends' but Jasmine maintained that she had not established a serious sexual relationship since the final hearing of the care proceedings case. Despite concerns about the nature of her involvement with these men, there was no evidence that either Jasmine or her baby was being physically, sexually or emotionally abused and therefore no need to change the care plan. She appeared to be supported by the help and attention of the local authority and, in particular, by the staff at the family centre, who took a maternal interest in her. The problems of her social isolation and poor self-confidence appeared to have been alleviated, in part, by the structure and support of the family centre. Additionally, her own mother was increasingly involved in her daily routine, which Jasmine greatly valued, feeling that her mother was finally making an effort to help her, through helping her with her son. She still found the loss of her older children, and her awareness of the abuse which they had suffered, distressing, and this sense of profound loss remained with her.

DISCUSSION

Intergenerational transmission of disturbed attachments

Violence and discord are often found in the backgrounds of adults who have failed to give their children adequate protection, or who have themselves abused them. This intergenerational transmission of abuse is partly explained by a social learning theory model which highlights the importance of early parental modelling on later parenting (Browne, 1987). Recent research from attachment theorists also provides empirical support for the intergenerational transmission of disturbed parenting and the development of individual psychopathology, such as borderline personality disorder (Fonagy, 1991; Fonagy et al., 1995). (See Chapter 1 for further discussion of attachment theory).

As described in previous chapters, an early experience of a mother who cannot provide the containment of the infant's projections, and cannot allow the infant to develop the capacity to mentalise, can result in a failure to think symbolically. This failure to mentalise predisposes an individual to violence; as painful mental states cannot be thought about and managed, they are externalised through behaviour. Disturbances in early attachment can lead to difficulty in developing the necessary confidence and sense of security which enable people to recognise and leave abusive situations or to lead an independent life. Jasmine appeared to have been deprived of stability and parental protectiveness in early life and seemed to be seeking compensation for this through her sexual relationships. The death of her father seemed to have deepened her need to have male sources of comfort and had left her with a fragile sense of confidence.

Like many victims of childhood traumas she repeatedly found herself in abusive situations where her apparent protector became her persecutor. One explanation for this is that she was trying to overcome the original trauma through re-entering the situation as an older and more competent person; this is known as 'mastery of trauma'. Another explanation is that this experience affected her so adversely that she was not able to distinguish between trustworthy and abusive partners or to pick up early warning signs of danger. The damage done to her self-esteem and confidence was so great as to make her needs for security and comfort override rational considerations about who would be able to protect and care for her children. She seemed to have been intellectually damaged by her traumatic experiences, which had left her with little capacity to plan for the future or to understand cause and effect. The effects of early traumatisation on mental development have been powerfully described by Sinason (1986) and are relevant to Jasmine's situation.

The description of mental handicap as a consequence of trauma given by Sinason (1986) suggests that cognitive deadening can follow emotional and sexual trauma as a defence mechanism for avoiding psychic pain. Thinking is attacked as a defence against remembering trauma. In Jasmine's case she appeared to have emotionally and intellectually shut down and shut out awareness. It was as though the only world that she could bear to inhabit was one in which confusion and chaos distracted her from recognising her own unhappiness and helplessness. Through blurring the harsh outlines of her world she achieved some kind of psychic survival. This unconscious defence had developed early in her life and remained her strategy for survival in adulthood but left her with profound difficulties in protecting either her older children or herself from sexual abuse and serious violence. Her own parenting of these children had appeared, at times, to reflect her needs for comfort and protection rather than theirs and her capacity to think about them was dramatically impaired.

BATTERED WOMEN WHO KILL

One of the most common victims of women who kill is the husband or partner. In a significant number of cases this partner has been violent to the woman over many years. I will address the psychological explanations offered for battered wives who kill their violent spouses. A substantial percentage of women who commit homicide of intimate partners have a history of being abused by them (Foster *et al.*, 1989; Barnard *et al.*, 1982; Daniel and Harris, 1982: Kirkpatrick and Humphrey, 1986). For women living under these conditions the possibility of killing their abuser becomes very real. But not all women who are abused (and a conservative estimate of spouse abuse in the United States estimates that 1.6 million women are beaten by their partners each year (Strauss and Gelles, 1986)) go on to kill and the reasons why some women do, and their psychological motivations, demand exploration.

Studies indicate that the presence of certain factors in the situations of battered women who killed distinguished them from those who did not go on to kill. These included the abuser's threats to kill, the abuser's alcohol abuse, the presence of a firearm or weapon in the house, and the woman's perception of experiencing severe psychological abuse. These seemed to be more important factors than the escalation and severity of violent incidents. This lends support to the notion that what is most important in determining what makes women kill their abusive partners is their own perception of the situation and their subjective experience of humiliation, degradation, isolation and terror imposed on them by their partners.

In her study Browne (1987) found that the factors which best predicted which women would kill their abusive partners were the severity of the woman's injuries, the man's alcohol or drug use, the frequency with which abusive incidents occurred, the man's threats to kill and the woman's suicide threats. Campbell (1986) administered the Danger Assessment to seventy-nine battered women in order to determine their risk of becoming either a victim or a perpetrator of homicide. The factors included in the assessment tool were threats to kill, a gun present in the home, drug or alcohol abuse by the batterer, sexual abuse, suicide threats or attempts by the woman, and the degree of control of the woman's life by the abuser. In a descriptive study of factors present when battered women kill, Foster *et al.* (1989) interviewed twelve women imprisoned for killing their abusive male partners and found that threats to kill made by the abuser and his daily alcohol use, and the presence of a firearm in the home, existed in most of these relationships. The women perceived the psychological abuse that they had experienced in the form of enforced isolation, humiliation and degradation to be more devastating than the physical abuse. Other factors present, but which the women themselves perceived as less important reasons for taking lethal action, included an escalation in the severity and frequency of violence, the occurrence of sexual abuse and the women's threats of suicide. Foster *et al.*, 1989, Browne, 1987 and Campbell, 1986 cited the presence of a firearm in the home as an important factor. The problems of substance and alcohol addiction may further contribute to the development of violence and other types of offending. There is evidence that alcohol abuse is a significant factor in the cases of women who kill their violent partners and alcohol dependence has also been found to be significantly associated with violence in a sample of female prisoners (Maden, 1996).

It is worth considering why the women's suicidal feelings should be an important factor in those women who went on to kill their partners. The link between suicidal and homicidal feelings has been well documented, particularly in the psychoanalytical literature (Hyatt-Williams, 1998; Zachary, 1997): the act of killing another person can be seen as a projection of murderous feelings which may be directed against an internal object, a part of the self. For women whose sense of self has been deeply disturbed, by their early experiences or by the traumatisation of living with a violent partner, or both, the intensification of feelings of self-loathing, fear, helplessness and worthlessness is highly probable. The reliance on primitive defence mechanisms like projection and projective identification becomes greater as the psychic and physical threats increase, and killing can be seen as the expression of these basic defence mechanisms.

A central explanation for why battered women kill is found in the notion of the 'battered wife syndrome' which has been used in Courts to plead for the charge of murder to be reduced to one of manslaughter on the grounds of diminished responsibility. It is important to consider the question of whether it holds up in a court of law as a self-defence plea rather than an attempt to argue for diminished responsibility. Related to this are the questions of whether it is psychologically valid and socially useful as a legal defence. Does the attempt to explain why the victims of abuse kill their abusers vindicate their action, or does it simply burden them with another social stigma and pathologise a simple act of self-preservation?

THE FAILURE OF PREVIOUS ATTEMPTS TO LEAVE A VIOLENT RELATIONSHIP

Why is extreme violence perceived to be the solution to the problem that a battered woman faces? It is ironic that the attempt to combat violence may produce in the 'victim' the motivation and commitment to kill in a moment of profound identification with the aggressor in order to defeat him. Why are other methods of escape or change unsuccessful? It is on this point that the notion of learned helplessness is particularly powerful as it describes how depression and the expectation of loss of control can result in failure to act and severe cognitive distortions in the appraisal of one's situation. This does not mean that the killing of a life-denying partner is necessarily irrational but it does clearly demonstrate how this may have seemed to be the only possible solution to a life-threatening problem.

This addresses Judges' queries about why other means of escape were not successfully attempted or even contemplated. There appears to be some suspicion that women who kill could actually have taken effective protective action first, that they could not be both helpless victims and cold-blooded killers. The confusion about how a victim can become an aggressor, and feel that there is no rational alternative other than killing, could be clarified if the effect of depression on thinking were better understood. Awareness of the practical difficulties faced by women who try to leave violent partners would also illuminate this area and dispel the myth that the women chose to remain in these relationships.

In fact women who killed *often* did take protective measures first, but these were revealed in time to be useless, feeding into the cycle of learned helplessness, and into the cycle of abuse and forgiveness which defined their relationships. In a sense these 'protective measures' could be viewed as the devalued currency of violent partnerships, the only means of communicating fear and anger by the victim, through the enlisting of third parties and the legal system. Only too often, however, these third parties and authorities had not offered the hoped-for power and protection and the victim was left even more desperate than before, with her partner more eager to assert his claim over her, in the face of threatened loss. He might also increase his efforts to restrict her movements and further frustrate her attempts to establish any form of independence.

Case illustration: Eve, a battered woman who killed

Eve, a 34-year-old mother of three, came to the attention of the forensic psychiatry services following the killing of her partner. She was admitted to the regional secure unit on remand for psychiatric assessment following her arrest for the killing. She had been trans-ferred from prison where she had been considered to be a suicide risk, following an attempted overdose, and had been diagnosed with psychotic depression. She had spent three weeks in the hospital wing of the women's prison before being transferred. She was pleading guilty to manslaughter with diminished responsibility.

Although she had been acutely depressed immediately following her arrest, at the time I met her, one month after her admission, she demonstrated no signs of mental illness. She still wept copiously when describing her feelings about being separated from her children, and her fears about their future. She was anxious about the impending trial and unsure whether the Crown Prosecution Service would accept the reduced charge of manslaughter. Although she appeared to be going through the stages of grief which would be expected in any case of a recently bereaved person, she did not seem to link this grief with feelings of guilt about killing her partner. She remained adamant that she had acted in a moment of intense fear about her partner's threats towards her and had been justified in killing him to protect herself and her children. She felt that the action reflected a moment of temporary insanity in that she would never normally behave in a violent way towards anyone, but that this impulsive and 'crazy' act had been brought about by years of sustained violence towards her, even while she had been pregnant with her youngest child, Kathy, aged 14 months.

The argument following which Eve had seized a knife and stabbed her husband was no different from the usual arguments in content, consisting largely of his accusations about her sexual infidelity. However, it followed a significant and potentially destabilising change in the relationship. She had recently taken on part-time work at a local pub and had been enjoying the freedom from home that it had given her. Eve was defending herself against her partner's accusation that she had been having an affair with a co-worker at the pub. She had not worked at any point during the twelve-year relationship but she had decided that, as Kathy was her last child, it would be important for her to rebuild a life outside the home.

The main difference on this occasion was that Eve had gained an insight into the possibility of another type of existence and some confidence that she could have an identity outside the home. The threat of losing the slight independence that she had gained, with which her partner had threatened her, appeared to her to be intolerable and a question of life and death. In her own background her mother had been kept a virtual prisoner in the house at the insistence of her alcoholic husband. The threat of repeating this pattern had been in her mind over the past few years and had become increasingly distressing to her as she saw a mirror image of her mother's life in her own. Her mother had died of cancer the previous year and this had caused frequent arguments between Eve and her partner who was even jealous of her visits to her mother, whom he perceived to be a threat to their relationship and an intrusion into their lives.

Until very recently she might have allowed the argument to proceed; however, on this occasion she felt that she could not stand the threats and abuse and was terrified that he might really kill her. She still suffered from deep feelings of grief related to her mother's death and had a strong sense of being an adult alone in the world as she had no contact with her father. Her partner threatened her with taking the children away while she was at work and accused her of 'whoring' behind the bar with her boss. He went up to the children's room and shouted to them that their mother was a 'slag' and a 'bitch'. They screamed at him to 'shut up' and Eve remembered her oldest child, her son, Gerry, aged 9, trying to hit and kick his father, resulting in him being pushed away roughly by his father.

Her partner came back downstairs and punched Eve in the face and then the stomach, choosing, as he tended to, those parts of her body which were most vulnerable. He had first assaulted her during her pregnancy with Gerry where he had seemed to perceive her pregnant stomach as a provocation. After he had punched her hard approximately seven or eight times in succession he pushed her on to the floor, leaving her to bleed and cry while he continued to shout at her about her supposedly deceitful and untrustworthy behaviour. When he eventually finished his tirade, he slumped in front of the television set and returned to drinking straight whisky, having already consumed approximately two-thirds of a bottle in the course of the evening.

Eve went up to check her children and found them crying in their shared bedroom and trying to comfort one another. Although she had gone to see the children with the intention of comforting them, when she saw how distressed they were she felt unable to say anything to them. She later said that her despair and horror were vividly reflected in theirs and that this realisation triggered the thought that the situation was completely unbearable – that she had to do something to stop it immediately. She remembered how terrified she had been that her father would kill her mother, and that she had often returned home from school with a sense of dread about what she might find when she entered the home. She was also reminded of her tremendous sense of relief when her father had eventually left her mother for someone else, when she was 13 years old.

On the way downstairs she had seen herself in the hall mirror, something she had learned to avoid doing following arguments, and she saw that her face was puffy and distorted, that her make-up had run all down her face making her look grotesque and mad. Her blouse, which had been washed and ironed for work that night, was covered with blood and foundation and several buttons had come off. She looked, she said, 'completely mad, like a crazy, slovenly woman' and her earlier confidence had been completely eroded. She felt full of resolve and rage. On entering the living room she saw that her partner had fallen into what seemed like a heavy sleep, a half-finished drink spilled on his lap and the glass on the floor by his feet. She felt a flash of elation when she saw him lying there, no longer capable of assaulting her. Her only thought had been to stop the misery and terror to which she and her family had been subjected and in order to do this she had to kill her partner, then, without hesitation, while he slept. The hysteria and fear had left her and she felt calm, determined and composed. She fetched a knife from the kitchen and stabbed her sleeping partner three times in the chest, puncturing his lungs and killing him almost instantly.

She had then phoned the police saying that she was sure she had killed her husband and asking them to come at once. When they arrived she was shaking, repeating phrases over and over again, and moving in a robotic manner. She manifested signs of post-traumatic stress disorder, in particular displaying emotional numbness and shock. Over the course of the next eighteen months she had flashbacks to the argument and the moment when the knife entered the body, finding herself shaking, sweating with a racing heart and rapid, shallow breathing, She was initially arrested and charged with murder.

The charge was later dropped to manslaughter on the grounds of diminished responsibility, to which she pleaded guilty. In her defence psychiatric reports were produced which emphasised the role of depression, which had developed after the birth of her youngest child, and had never been treated, intensifying in the days leading up to the offence. The killing, it was argued, reflected the actions of a deeply depressed woman, who had not had full awareness of the consequences of her behaviour, and who had not been able to make a fully rational decision because of the debilitating effects of her alleged depression. This account, although at odds with Eve's own recollection of events, had intuitive appeal to the Court and appeared to offer a satisfactory account of her assault on her husband. The positive action of taking on a job while in the throes of supposed depression was ignored and the possible justifications, grounded in rationality, for her killing this violent and abusive man were absolutely overlooked.

Eve had, in fact, consulted her general practitioner following the birth of her third child, explaining that she had fears about the baby's development. While this had been attributed to 'post-natal depression' Eve had not been able to say that her fears about the baby were grounded in the fact of her husband's assaults on her during her pregnancy. She had, quite reasonably, worried that her baby might be developmentally delayed as a result of blows inflicted upon her during the third trimester. She had also described some feelings of anxiety and depression, explaining that she had difficulty concentrating on even quite simple tasks, had no appetite and suffered from insomnia.

The reasons for killing

A central issue emerging from consideration of this case is the difficulty for the public in general, and the legal establishment in particular, of understanding the possible rational basis for killing. The gendered construction of killing makes it almost impossible to view Eve's action, in one sense a logical consequence of her experience of constant battering and abuse, as anything other than either mad or evil. The sympathy given to men who kill their unfaithful or 'nagging' wives is not extended to female killers (Kennedy, 1992).

Although Eve's understanding of her possible options was distorted by her abuse, her decision, in the context of her situation, had a rational basis. It appeared to her to be the only viable solution to an intractable and life-threatening problem. In order for such subversive behaviour to be explicable it had to be read as 'mad' rather than an act of self-preservation. It was therefore important to gather evidence testifying to her instability rather than lend credibility to her actions through attempting to enter into and understand her situation. While her consultation with a general practitioner for 'depression' was used as evidence for her mental instability during her trial, the rationality of her fears then, and the logic of her decision-making when she killed her husband, were not issues addressed in this trial, as if the possibility that a woman could kill her violent partner as a rational act of self-defence did not exist.

Eve was advised not to use the self-defence plea because the argument had ended by the time that she stabbed her husband. Although his assault on her had not endangered her life on this particular occasion, it had on others. On one occasion, when she had been heavily pregnant with their third child, he had kicked her down the stairs, and she narrowly missed the edge of a radiator at the bottom of the staircase. This assault could easily have caused her to miscarry, possibly causing the death of the unborn child. In the days leading up to the offence her husband's violence had intensified and was directed against their oldest child, who tried to intervene to protect his mother during one assault on her. She had not contacted social services to inform them about his violence towards her or the eldest child out of fear that the children would be removed from home.

This was a case in which the notion of 'psychological self-defence' could readily be applied, and indeed where physical self-defence was still a major consideration. Eve's rationale for the killing was that she could end the severe beatings which she had suffered on a regular basis (at least once every two weeks, sometimes more often) over the previous ten years, since her first pregnancy. Despite her resourcefulness and intelligence she had not found access to other ways of escape and had ended up killing the person who she feared would ultimately kill or destroy her.

The reservations surrounding the use of a battered woman's plea of self-defence in a case of domestic killing, compared with the familiarity and acceptance of a plea of 'diminished responsibility' demonstrate how much easier it is to locate murderous feelings outside, in the 'mad', rather than acknowledge that such rage is the likely consequence of systematic, degrading and debasing humiliation. It serves to distance the ordinary individual from those lunatic women who succumb to insane impulses apparently at random. It takes all responsibility away from the abuser despite his central role as the long-term aggressor in such cases. It also acts as a defence against recognising that everyone has the potential capacity to kill, and that to do so may, at times, reflect a decision which has a coherent internal logic. Accepting that possibility is not equivalent to excusing or condoning killing but is a crucial step in understanding that a battered woman *could* kill in self-defence, even though her immediate safety was apparently not in jeopardy.

In order for the plea of manslaughter on grounds of diminished responsibility to be acceptable, it is important that defence solicitors and psychiatrists emphasise the momentary and unpredictable nature of the madness at the time of the offence, that is, any suggestion that the behaviour is explicable in the light of the individual's background or situation will make it less likely that the plea of diminished responsibility will be accepted. This means that the legal objective, to enable a client to be found guilty of a lesser charge if she was 'out of her mind' at the time of the offence, is directly antithetical to the psychological and psycho-analytical task. The task of the psychologist or psychiatrist is to understand how the offence fits in with the person's history and current situation, how it can reflect her mind rather than simply reveal an aberration in her usual mental processes.

This case has parallels with that of Sara Thornton, a battered woman who was released from prison in 1996, following her appeal against her murder conviction for killing her violent husband, and her subsequent retrial. Sara Thornton had initially been refused the option of pleading manslaughter on grounds of diminished responsibility by the Crown Prosecution Service and had then been found guilty of murder (Wykes, 1995). At her retrial in 1996 she was found guilty of manslaughter on the grounds of diminished responsibility, related to an 'abnormality of mind' and her murder conviction was quashed (O'Hanlon, 1996).

It is essential to recognise the threat to psychic life which an assault, or a threat of assault, constitutes in the context of sustained and severe abuse. Psychological understandings of conditioned responses and the long-term effects of battering and emotional abuse can illuminate the processes by which an assault, which was not actually life-threatening, could be interpreted and reacted to as though it threatened fatal injury.

DEFENCES IN THE COURTROOM: LEGAL ISSUES

At present the charge of murder carries with it a mandatory life sentence. The battered woman who kills will receive a life sentence if she pleads guilty to murder. She may choose to plead self-defence or that she is guilty of the reduced charge of manslaughter, either on the grounds of provocation or of diminished responsibility. Currently, the only plea which has met with some success in reducing the murder charge to a lesser one of manslaughter is diminished responsibility, which can be founded on the basis of the 'battered woman syndrome'. The complete defence of self-defence, which would allow a killer to go free if accepted, has not been successfully used by battered women who have killed. The use of this defence rests on the notion of what force a 'reasonable man' could be expected to use in situations when his life was at serious risk. These actions have not been found to include those steps taken by women who believe their own lives to be severely threatened by their abusers.

The self-defence plea in relation to the notion of psychological self-defence

A central legal question in the area of female homicide is the acceptability of the plea of self-defence or manslaughter on the grounds of provocation for a battered woman who kills her abusive partner rather than the currently accepted plea of manslaughter with diminished responsibility. The notion of 'psychological self-defence' as valid grounds for killing has been proposed by an American author, Charles Ewing (1990), who argues that, in the case of battered women who kill, their very identity has been systematically eroded and that at the point when they kill they are struggling to retain psychic survival. The profound and sustained attack on their identity eventually results in a psychological, if not physical, life or death struggle. The perceived need to kill the aggressor can be justified by reference to the notion of psychological self-defence. Ewing bases his argument on the battered woman syndrome as defined by Walker (1984) and states that 'battered women who kill have invariably been both physically and psychologically abused by the men they killed. Many if not most of them have also been raped and/or sexually abused by their batterers' (Ewing, 1990:583). This argument has great relevance to battered women who kill in the UK, and who are also highly unlikely to plead self-defence on the grounds of provocation.

In what sense does the notion of psychological self-defence improve on the justification for homicide as the product of battered woman syndrome? Ewing argues that the battered woman syndrome helps to explain *why*, despite the claimed abuse, the woman did not leave her batterer before killing him but generally offers little evidence for the *reasonableness* of the woman's ultimate homicidal act. His aim is therefore to provide a rational basis for the decision to kill, arguing that what was under attack was the woman's psychological, if not actually her physical, survival at the moment of killing. He defines psychological self-defence as justifying the use of deadly force

> where such force appeared reasonably necessary to prevent the infliction of extremely serious psychological injury. Extremely serious psychological injury would be defined as gross and enduring impairment of one's psychological functioning that significantly limits the meaning and value of one's physical existence.
>
> (Ewing, 1990:587)

Ewing considers that the battered woman syndrome explanation offers a partial understanding of why women can predict the likelihood of future violence by their partners but states that this only really applies to those women who kill during a battering episode: the syndrome can be considered as a legitimate self-defence plea in those cases. In the majority of cases, however, where women kill their batterer while he is asleep or after an incident, the claim that their physical survival was at risk is not immediately relevant, therefore the self-defence plea is not acceptable. For the battered woman syndrome and the killing of a violent partner in self-defence to be acceptable, the notion of threat would need to be extended beyond the period of time of the actual violence, to explain why a woman killed, not at the time of the injury, but later or when the assault had abated, or, as Ewing argues, extended to encompass the notion of psychological self-defence.

Critique of the notion of 'psychological self-defence'

The notion of 'psychological self-defence' has been attacked, in particular by Morse (1990), on the grounds that it is the product of 'soft psychology' and represents bad law in which killing can be justified on subjective and flimsy grounds. The main argument against the acceptance by the Courts of such a defence appears to be the 'slippery slope' argument that, once one such case is accepted, there will be others which also fit the concept and that eventually everyone who kills will be able to offer legally valid grounds for murder; there seems no acknowledgement of the difference between *understanding* the motivations for fatal violence and *excusing* or justifying it.

The notion of extinction of self is vague and can even be considered inaccurate if a careful analysis of the dynamics of interpersonal violence is conducted. Ewing's account is somewhat simplistic and could benefit from psychological elaboration and theoretical precision. The role of the victim cannot be ignored; she changes in response to her aggressor's assaults and his emotional control over her. I would argue that battery does not erode the self but, in fact, creates a distorted, damaged and depressed self through the continued use of intimidation, threat and abuse. The underlying process through which the batterer attempts to rid himself of weakness, fear and self-contempt, by identifying them in the victim and then seeking to annihilate or destroy her (albeit temporarily), involves the psychological defence of projective identification and the victim herself takes on these characteristics; she is, in a sense, compelled to become weak, frightened, unable to placate or calm her partner within this highly circumscribed relationship. Ewing (1990) does not take into account the complexities of this process and the destructive interdependence between victim and aggressor which is established, and which perpetuates the cycle of battering, forgiveness, reconciliation, estrangement and battering. While he is right to highlight the fact that sustained violence results in psychological damage to the 'self', he ignores the nature of the self which is created, which can be viewed as exaggerations of certain aspects of the self and the neglect of others in a polarised dyad. That is, the victim takes on the despised parts of her aggressor and he loses, for an illusory moment, his weakness. She projects into him her own murderous rage.

Ewing's argument is that severe victimisation results in the loss of the capacity to function as an autonomous and integrated person to the extent that physical existence or life 'loses much of its meaning and value'. This describes the experience of many battered women accurately, but possibly overlooks the extent to which they have lost the capacity to retain even a notion of value or independence, as they have become so engaged with and psychically locked into the traumatic and destructive relationship. To have a sense of psychic threat demands that the victim can see what lies beyond the current state of assault. That battered women are often unable to protect their own needs or those of their children indicates that their perspective, the hold on values and priorities, has been so eroded that it could not really inform their decision to kill their abuser. This rational judgement about the relative value of life presupposes a state of integration and the capacity to think which has already been destroyed, or at least badly damaged. It also assumes the validity of the 'battered woman syndrome' which itself rests on a model of learned helplessness based on animal experimentation.

It can be argued that the theory of learned helplessness itself ignores the complexity of individual interpretations of events, i.e. the cognitive processes which mediate between the occurrence of painful stimuli and the individual's response to them. The 'battered woman syndrome' adopts this model and incorporates it into a description of a 'typical' response to sustained abuse in which the woman is perceived as very passive and victimised, losing her grasp on reason. The 'battered woman syndrome' ignores the active aspect of the female partner in a violent relationship and the significance of her unconscious and conscious choice to participate in the abusive relationship. Ewing (1990) has accepted these doctrines wholeheartedly and builds on them in an attempt to provide a sophisticated legal defence for battered women who kill. Despite the intuitive appeal of his notion, and its sympathetic description of psychic infiltration and defeat, it is ultimately untenable either as a legal defence or as a psychological analysis.

Like 'premenstrual syndrome' as a legal defence in Court the notion of 'psychological self-defence' is in danger of being patronising to women and pathologising their responses to extreme, systematic abuse. Careful analysis of individual situations should make the adoption of such theories, predicated on the notions of women's vulnerability and 'special' status, unnecessary. A legal defence which relies on the existence of a 'syndrome' is one in which pathology is central. The construction of a syndrome may have more utility as a legal defence in Court than as an empirically validated clinical entity. There is a danger that labelling a response to systematic abuse 'battered woman syndrome' without adequate reference to the social, cultural and political circumstances that allow this abuse to continue can contribute to stereotypes about women's inherent madness. Self-defence has been reconceptualised as hysteria.

Morse (1990) criticises Ewing's psychological extinction claim on the grounds that the scientific basis for this notion is weak and that even if it were stronger intense psychological misery does not justify killing. He also notes that 'even if the syndrome is valid there is no logical or empirically necessary connection between wife battering and severe extinction of self. He [Ewing] gives no reason or evidence to demonstrate either that battering is the only cause that can produce extinction of self or that all battered women suffer from severe extinction of self.' (Morse, 1990:601). Morse's criticism of Ewing's notion of 'psychological self-defence' fails to take into account the severity of the psychological damage caused by abuse sustained over years and the validity of psychological responses to such trauma, which may include distortions of perception and reasoning. The argument that such killing is never reasonable seems to miss the point that the consequence of such abuse is that notions of what is reasonable become irrelevant. The claustrophobic, trapping nature of domestic violence often produces a restricted set of stratagems in which violence is the only solution; it has become the common currency of communication in a situation where all other means of assertion or compliance have been rendered obsolete. For the former victim to take power and revenge on her partner she is compelled to use his methods of domination. Psychically, and even practically, violence may become the only option.

Provocation

The use of the provocation defence in cases of the battered woman syndrome has been accepted in the United States but has not been widely recognised in the United Kingdom.

> Women who kill have often been severely physically beaten and/or sexually abused over long periods of time by their male victims, whereas men who kill generally claim to have been provoked by nagging or promiscuity. Men regularly plea provocation on these grounds, claiming to have acted in the heat of the moment while women killers may have to seek a weapon or wait for abusers to be asleep or drunk, signifying premeditation.
>
> (Wykes, 1995:54)

Whether or not the provocation plea can be applied to women who kill violent partners is contingent on the definition of 'provocation'; it is currently described in law to be an immediate threat on the defendant. In cases of female homicide of an abusive partner, the killing does not necessarily occur at the moment of greatest threat, largely because women are generally not physically strong enough to overcome male assailants. The killing may occur minutes later when the woman has recovered from the immediate attack enough to equip herself defensively with a weapon. It may take place weeks or months later, in the face of a less serious assault which triggers the fatal attack. It has been argued in courts of law that the composure and degree of self-control required for the woman to equip herself with a weapon, at the point when the immediate threat to her own safety appears to be reduced, suggests a degree of intent, in a situation where she does not face a threat to her own life, which invalidates her plea of self-defence in response to provocation. Proponents of the self-defence plea argue that the battered woman's perception of what constitutes a threat to her own life has been shaped by her experiences in the past, and that she responds to cues of impending violence with a degree of fear which is entirely reasonable in the light of this. Her relationship to her partner is entirely relevant to her motivation for killing him. This is a valid and important argument, in which the psychological sequelae of systematic physical and emotional abuse are acknowledged without the victim herself being pathologised.

The type of reasoning and psychological defences which such victims develop are perfectly explicable and could reasonably be expected to inform their actions. The need to recognise the severity and horror of the psychological damage created by years of sustained abuse is essential. For the Courts to decide whether or not an abused woman can be said to have acted in self-defence, they need to understand clearly the long-term psychological effects of abuse and to retain a notion of how systematic abuse, sustained over years, can indeed be considered provoking factors in triggering a violent assault. The notion that only an immediate fight or threat can serve as a trigger to take self-preservative action rests on a simplistic and inaccurate understanding of psychological motivation, and on the consequences of repeated victimisation. The important work of human rights barristers, such as Helena Kennedy, has done much to challenge these notions and raise awareness in the courts of the dynamics of abuse.

TRANSFERENCE AND COUNTERTRANSFERENCE ISSUES IN TREATMENT

One of the most disturbing consequences of having killed is that the killer cannot trust themselves to differentiate between fantasy and reality. The ultimate and crucial barrier between thought and action has been broken and it becomes unsafe to acknowledge feelings of murderous rage in case they are re-enacted. In working therapeutically with killers, one is struck by the degree of fear which they experience as they project their own destructive and murderous feelings on to others, creating a persecutory and predatory external world.

A central task for the therapist is to allow reintegration of this anger into the self and the gradual reconstruction of the capacity to distinguish between fantasy and reality, to acknowledge impulses without enacting them. In analytic terms this can be likened to the development of symbolic thinking. There may be deep-seated issues of grief related to the offence of killing, e.g. feelings of loss related to the victim and the associated guilt, anger, despair and shock that accompany any bereavement. The guilt in the case of a killer may be much more profound than in an ordinary bereavement and may provoke a complicated grief reaction, which makes recovery slow and difficult.

The female killer will be incarcerated, whether in prison or in a psychiatric secure unit, and will be faced with separation from her children and other family members. This may appear intolerable and produce a profound depression. The stigma of having killed and the continuing feelings of anger towards the victim may pose intractable problems for the killer, who may be unable to face up to what she has done and retreat instead into a remote world where she denies what has happened. The relationship with the victim will often be characterised by ambivalent feelings, which in turn cause a complicated grief reaction. The realisation that the apparent solution to abuse and threats has failed to leave the killer with her family, but has resulted in her separation from them, may be very distressing for her and confirm her fears that she is a hopeless failure, who cannot ever escape from misery.

On an unconscious level the powerful defence of projective identification which killing involves, in which all bad is located in another person who is then annihilated, only evacuates these feelings temporarily, and is ultimately destined to fail. Although an initial feeling of euphoria and exhilaration may follow the killing, this is only transient and the killer will become depressed when unacceptable feelings are once again acknowledged in herself. She will see that her attempt to rid herself of these feelings through splitting them off, locating them in someone else and then killing him off, has failed, and that she must face the task of reintegrating them into herself. This exactly parallels the experience of the abuser, who used battering as a way of ridding himself of unacceptable feelings by projecting them into his partner and then attacking her. His defence against unwanted feelings is also destined to fail, offering only temporary relief from self-loathing, guilt and fear of abandonment; once these feelings return, so too does the need to batter again.

The therapist may become involved in a very powerful transference in the patient where she becomes the object of murderous rage or the highly idealised good object. It is essential that she receives ongoing supervision so that she avoids acting out these projections and becoming either a victim, like the client was, or a persecutor, like the abuser was, or the good object to whom no anger can be expressed because of the fears about the destructive power of anger. The person who has killed has relied on splitting as a defence mechanism and has been inextricably enmeshed in a heavily polarised relationship with her abuser. In order to enable this client to take anger, sadness, fear and helplessness back into herself, it is essential to avoid re-enacting the abusive relationship. It is also tempting to see the client as passive victim and to ignore the complexity of her relationship with her partner and the unconscious needs which it may have met for her. Such needs could include being able to split the anger off into her partner and not recognise it in herself. Ignoring these needs will collude with the client's denial of anger rather than helping her to integrate and manage it, tracing its origins. Forensic psychotherapy offers a sensitive model of working with people who have killed.

One way of avoiding moral censure for those involved with killers is to deny their aggression, viewing them solely as victims. This view is both psychologically inaccurate and therapeutically unhelpful; it is a product of denial on the part of the helper and requires close exploration through supervision. It is perhaps even more powerful when there are strong external similarities between therapist and client, for instance, age, gender and ethnicity, which enable an identification to be made easily. There may be strong reasons for a female therapist to work with a battered woman who killed but these should be examined carefully in each individual case.

CONCLUSION

Female homicide and the denial of female violence

As in so many cases of female violence, acceptance of the fact of female homicide requires a suspension of commonly held beliefs about violence and femininity, creating massive resistance to the notion that women can kill, and may, in some cases, have valid reasons for doing so. In the cases where battered women kill an abusive partner their previous role of victim makes such violence appear even more extreme and abhorrent. The incongruity of a beaten, submissive partner taking violent action in an attempt to annihilate her aggressor contributes to the difficulty that others have in making sense of her action, or reconciling the image of victim with that of killer. The fact of her rationality is perhaps even more difficult to bear and she is thus perceived as a mad or evil woman, who could have found other ways out of her situation if she had only tried. The evidence of such rationality in the planning of a killing, which may take place in the case of a battered woman who kills, suggests to the Courts that the action could not have been one of self-defence; the woman had time to plot and plan and therefore was not, at the moment of killing, under threat for her life. To see the woman as a calculating killer, one who has killed gratuitously, as it were, in that she was not in immediate danger at the time, is to deny the history of violence, intimidation and cruelty towards her and her children. What is also denied is the threat to her psychological survival and the desperation with which she responds to this psychic danger. The struggle is one of life or death psychically as well as physically as Ewing's notion of 'psychological extinction' attempts to highlight.

The wider context

Domestic violence is such an emotive and distressing phenomenon that it is tempting to simplify its dynamics, disregarding its complex nature and the role of each partner in maintaining the destructive interaction. To view the woman as only a passive victim is to deny female agency, but to ignore the social forces which create restricted choices for her is dangerous. The refusal to recognise psychic conflict and ambivalence in both the male abuser and the woman who kills him is striking. Until the complexity of the individual, interpersonal and social dynamics which contribute to the maintenance of violent relationships is recognised, the motivations of women who kill their violent partners will continue to be simplified and misunderstood. The woman who kills will either be vilified or glorified. In either case she will be removed from the realm of the ordinary and seen as extraordinary, which unfortunately overlooks the fact that she inhabits a world shared by many female victims of domestic violence, many of whom do not go on to kill.

While it is undoubtedly important to identify those factors distinguishing between battered women who kill their violent partners and those who do not, it is equally important to identify and address those factors, both internal and external, contributing to the situation of many more women who are subjected to domestic violence for years. Psychological intervention can and should take place within a context of social support and an understanding of the wider concerns of oppression, sexism and injustice.

Conclusion

My aim in this book has been to present a range of cases of female violence and to offer a model for understanding these cases. Although primarily informed by a psychodynamic perspective I have also drawn from other models, including attachment theory and a feminist understanding of the causes and manifestations of female violence; the latter was especially relevant to the discussion of self-harm as a form of communication and to the understanding of abused women who kill their violent partners. Each act of violence that I have discussed has a particular meaning and can be read as a communication of psychic conflict and distress.

The link between depression and violence should not be overlooked as many acts of violence, whether targeted against the self, others or children, are linked to severe depression. The strong connection between homicidal and suicidal urges is evident in the extreme acts of violence which occur within the context of depression. This is illustrated in Sylvia Plath's semi-autobiographical work, *The Bell Jar*, in which dying objects, images of death and killing are central motifs. She describes the torment of depression, and the subsequent violence which the central character inflicts on herself through various suicide attempts. Plath also explores the traditional medical response to attempted suicides, the manifestation of aggression, turned in on the self, and vividly describes the violence of this response, which itself mirrors the homicidal urges inherent in the suicidal acts. She presents a powerful account of the violence which psychiatric treatment in the form of shock therapy, known as electro-convulsive treatment, can inflict. This presents psychiatry at its worst, in what Plath perceives to be its brutal and objectifying treatment of depressed patients:

> Doctor Gordon was fitting two metal plates on either side of my head. He buckled them into place with a strap that dented my forehead, and gave me a wire to bite.

I shut my eyes.

There was a brief silence, like an indrawn breath. Then something bent down and took hold of me and shook me like the end of the world. Whee-ee-ee-ee-ee, it shrilled, through an air crackling with blue light, and with each flash a great jolt rubbed me till I thought my bones would break and the sap fly out of me like a split plant . . .

At least at Belsize I could forget about shock treatments. At Caplan a lot of the women had shock treatments. I could tell which ones they were, because they didn't get their breakfast trays with the rest of us. They had their shock treatments while we breakfasted in our rooms, and then they came into the lounge, quiet and extinguished, led like children by the nurses and ate their breakfasts there.

(Plath, 1963:151, 217)

This moving description of helplessness and fear serves as a powerful message for therapists to attend to their clients' experience of treatment. The therapeutic task is surely to help women articulate and express unhappiness and anger, so that they can effect change in their lives, not to silence or extinguish them.

THERAPEUTIC RESPONSES TO FEMALE VIOLENCE

As a clinical psychologist I draw from a range of models, depending on the particular difficulties with which clients present. I offer psychotherapy, often in conjunction with psychotropic medication which is prescribed by psychiatric colleagues. While I recognise the need for psychotropic medication in the treatment of what can be considered major mental illnesses, medication alone cannot resolve underlying psychological difficulties, and women who have committed violent acts, whether or not they are diagnosed with major mental illnesses, must be given a voice and empowered to understand and articulate their experiences in order to exert control over their lives. I see forensic psychotherapy as a central tool in achieving this task.

It is important to acknowledge that women often present at the forensic psychiatric and psychological services for multiple reasons, and enter these services with dual diagnoses; the existence of these diagnoses in female offender patients is described in the clinical audit conducted at the regional secure unit where I am based (Turcan and Bercu, 1999). The existence of dual diagnosis points to the complexity of difficulties with which violent women present in the psychiatric services and underlines the need for clinicians to approach them with a range of therapeutic models for understanding and managing their violence.

The psychiatric needs of women in prison have been well documented (Allen, 1987; Maden, 1996; Carlen, 1996, 1998) and it is clear that these mental health needs are not best addressed within the custodial services. In the case of psychotic women who kill, their mental state at the time is a key consideration in judicial decisions. If such women are 'sentenced to treatment' rather than custody it is essential that their psychotherapeutic needs are not subsequently overlooked so that they are confined within a hospital rather than a prison. Specialist services must be designed to address the specific needs of women in the psychiatric system, including facilitating contact with their children, and protecting them against sexual abuse and harassment. Carlen (1998) recommends that 'women-wise' practices be developed in the criminal justice system, which applies equally to the psychiatric services.

NEED FOR FORENSIC PSYCHOTHERAPY WITH VIOLENT AND PERVERSE WOMEN

In order for the violent client to be engaged in a model of psychological treatment informed by psychodynamic thinking, the ideal psychoanalytic model requires radical modification. It is generally not possible to treat patients in more than once-a-week therapy within the forensic services, and these patients may be incarcerated, or attending therapy as a condition of treatment attached to their probation order. The motivation of the patients to attend for psychological treatment may include the desire to avoid custodial sentence, the hope of retaining custody of their children in the face of care proceedings, or the fear of losing a significant relationship because of violence. The Portman Clinic model of psychoanalytic psychotherapy with offender patients (forensic psychotherapy) accepts these as valid reasons for wanting to understand and change behaviour. This approach makes it possible for violent individuals, some of whom may feel coerced into undertaking treatment, to become engaged in long-term therapeutic work in which the link between early experiences and current difficulties and between unconscious motivations and conscious behaviour can become explicit.

The integration of therapeutic services is crucially important in the areas of child and family psychiatry and the forensic psychiatric services; in these areas working with victims and perpetrators of abuse is often highly polarised and communication between the two specialities can be fragmented and poor. This failure of integration in the systems can only be detrimental to the common aim of reducing the risk of violence to children. Many abusive parents were themselves abused children who find themselves re-enacting their own traumatic experiences with their children. In the case of maternal violence this task may pose particular difficulties for professionals, who must question and eventually relinquish preconceptions about motherhood in order to engage and work with violent women.

The intergenerational transmission of violence, which is described throughout, is one of my central concerns. In order to understand violence it is essential to trace its origins and development. Psychotherapy is an invaluable tool for addressing the development and manifestation of violent impulses, and aims to facilitate the violent woman's understanding of her internal world and help her to manage the external expression of her distress and anger. By offering violent and abusive parents treatment aimed at addressing unresolved psychological issues, the risk of re-enactment of earlier trauma with their own children can be reduced. In order for this work to be effective, it is essential that the various mental health agencies co-ordinate their programmes and work together to help parents improve their understanding of child protection and child welfare, and to implement this.

WOMEN IN CUSTODY: THE EXTERNAL REALITY

In studying the area of female violence I have focused on the internal realities of the women whom I have seen in the context of psychological assessment and treatment. I have not included an extensive discussion of the external realities faced by violent women when they commit offences and enter the criminal justice system. The work of Carlen has been invaluable in providing a thorough exploration and critique of the treatment of female offenders.*

* I refer the interested reader to her work, specifically to her 1998 text, *Sledgehammer: Women's Imprisonment at the Millennium*, which is an extremely thorough, forceful and informative study of the treatment of female offenders and an argument for the abolition of imprisonment altogether. She presents criminal statistics relating to the high proportion of first-time female offenders who are incarcerated and whose children are therefore also punished through this enforced and unwanted separation. Maden's 1996 book, *Women, Prisons and Psychiatry: Mental Disorder Behind Bars* also provides a fascinating account of his study of the psychiatric conditions of incarcerated women and an exploration of how, if at all, the custodial services can meet these needs.

There is clearly a powerful interaction between social and psychological factors in the genesis of violence in women. It is evident that female violence is multiply determined and it would be wrong to minimise the importance of social factors, which can predispose individuals to criminality through the stresses of poverty, unemployment and racial and sexual discrimination.

The available research demonstrates that it is not possible to provide a simple formulation in which the relative weights of the various contributory factors are quantified. Specific types of violence, such as deliberate self-harm, have been studied in female prisoner populations and have been found to be associated with particular psychological experiences, such as a history of being in care, of violent offending and alcohol dependence (Cookson, 1977), and with arson, sexual abuse and violence within the home (Liebling, 1992). While these findings are of great interest, it is important to remember that they are associations between particular experiences and behaviour, rather than proved causes of the behaviour.

The social factors which influence rates of female violence are not necessarily fixed, in that attitudes about the acceptability of female aggression are changing, the social circumstances of women are also changing, and powerful role models for young girls have shifted. There has been an increasing rate of female violence since the 1970s, and in 1997 the number of violent crimes committed by women had doubled since the 1970s (HMSO, 1998). While the number of violent crimes committed by women is still far behind the number perpetrated by men, e.g. 8,600 compared to 49,600 in 1997, the increasing rate of female violence is still significant. The recent case of a 71-year-old widow who was murdered by two adolescent girls prompted media interest in the increase of female violence and in possible explanations for what has been dramatically termed 'this horrifying new trend' (*The Independent on Sunday*, 1 August 1999). Dr Sue Bailey, an adolescent forensic psychiatrist suggested that girls are now less inclined to express their anger through self-mutilation but will lash out at others, taking an active part in violent activities rather than simply accompanying a violent male in luring victims. It could also be suggested that the rising recorded number of violent crimes by women is indicative of an increasing acceptance of the possibility of female violence, and a willingness to prosecute female offenders. It is worth noting too that the violence which is now considered to be a 'horrifying new trend' is the violence towards others, rather than self-directed violence, or violence towards children, which, as I have argued, has been largely overlooked, despite its potential danger.

Nonetheless, the growing awareness of female violence, and particularly sexual violence, may indicate that some aspects of the denial and taboo of female violence are gradually being challenged.

THE DANGERS OF SENTIMENTALITY

A central thesis of this text is that female violence is often ignored or denied, because to accept it, particularly in relation to maternal abuse, would be too threatening to traditional and idealised notions of motherhood and femininity. I consider this to be a fundamentally danger-ous social attitude, which can lead to vilification of those women who do display violence to the extent that they are considered inhuman and 'evil', and, at the other extreme, a massive denial of risk to children who may remain under the unsupervised care of abusive mothers and carers. Ultimately, this denial of female violence, and specifically maternal abuse, results in the failure to recognise and design comprehensive and sensitive treatment programmes for women whose violence results from psycho-logical difficulties, with roots in their own early experience of deprivation and abuse.

Sentimentality can both engender and disguise violence. A sentimental attitude is one in which an abstracted conception of someone as part object is maintained, such that a denial of imperfections must be preserved. This attitude requires a suspension of objectivity or recognition of the conflicting qualities within the idealised person. It is a feature of a senti-mental relationship that it is an inauthentic one in which the flaws in the person are redescribed as benign or even desirable. Sentimentality requires idealisation, which can quickly lead to denigration. The cherished object can easily become an object of disappointment, engendering anger and contempt when it fails. The object may then need to be contemptuously dismissed or attacked, to rid the subject of its sense of anger and dis-appointment; the container of idealised projections now becomes the 'poison container' (deMause, 1990).

The move from idealisation to denigration can be seen in the senti-mental regard with which women and children are held, and the rage which is evoked when their aggressive or sexual impulses appear to become out of control or dangerous. There is then a punitive backlash which has a ferocity that may alarm those who attempt to understand aggressive behaviour. It can be seen in the public fury when mothers display aggressive or perverse behaviour, and appears to be a manifestation of rage and disappointment that these women have failed to conform to powerful stereotypes of them as nurturing and gentle creatures. The backlash against these women reflects the depths of the disappointment and anger that they do not conform to these sentimental notions and reveals the strength of the taboos relating to maternal incest and violence.

This process has been vividly elucidated by Welldon in her exploration of the idealisation and denigration of motherhood, and further illustrated here. The sentimental attitude disguises the violence of objectification and dehumanisation – the treatment of young girls, and women, whether or not they are mothers, as part objects – and must be redressed through a thoughtful and sensitive understanding of female violence.

Bibliography

Adshead, G. (1997) 'Written on the body: deliberate self-harm and violence' in E.V. Welldon and C. van Velson (eds), *A Practical Guide to Forensic Psychotherapy*, London: Jessica Kingsley.

Ainsworth, M., Blehar, M., Waters, E. and Wall, S. (1978) *Patterns of Attachment: Assessed in the Strange Situation and at Home*, Hillsdale, NJ: Erlbaum.

Allen, H. (1987) *Justice Unbalanced: Gender, Psychiatry and Judicial Decisions*, Oxford: Blackwell.

Allen, N. (1996) *Making Sense of The Children Act*, Chichester: Wiley.

American Psychiatric Association (1994) *Diagnostic and Statistical Manual-IV* Fourth Edition, revised, Washington DC: American Psychiatric Association.

Anderson, R., Ambrosino, R., Valentine, D. and Lauderdale, M. (1983) 'Child deaths attributed to abuse and neglect: an empirical study', *Children and Youth Services Review* 5:75–89.

Bach-y-Rita, G. (1974) 'Habitual violence and self mutilation', *American Journal of Psychiatry* 131–9, September: 1018–20.

Bannerjee, A.K. (1991) 'Trauma and Munchausen's syndrome', *Archives of Emergency Medicine* 8(3): 217–18.

Banning, A. (1989) 'Mother–son incest: confronting a prejudice', *Journal of Child Abuse and Neglect* 13:563–70.

Barker, H.L. and Howell, R.J. (1994) 'Munchausen's syndrome by proxy in false allegations of child sexual abuse: legal implications', *Bulletin of the American Academy of Psychiatry and the Law* 22(4):499–510.

Barnard, G.W., Vera, H., Vera, M.I. and Newman, G. (1982) 'Till death do us part: a study of spouse murder', *Bulletin of the American Academy of Psychiatry and the Law* 10: 271–80.

Beck, A.T., Rush, A.J., Shaw, B.F. and Emery, G. (1979) *Cognitive Therapy of Depression*, New York: Guilford Press.

Beckett, R.C. (1994) 'Assessment of sex offenders' in T. Morrison, M. Erooga and R.C. Beckett (eds), *Sexual Offending Against Children: Assessment and Treatment of Male Abusers*, London: Routledge.

Bentovim, A. (1990) 'Family violence' in R. Bluglass and P. Bowden (eds), *Principles and Practice of Forensic Psychiatry*, Edinburgh: Churchill Livingstone.

Berg, B. and Jones, D.P.H. (1999) 'Outcome of psychiatric intervention in factitious illness by proxy (Munchausen's syndrome by proxy), *Archives of Disease in Childhoood.*

Bifulco, A. and Moran, P. (1998) *Wednesday's Child: Research into Women's Experience of Neglect and Abuse in Childhood and Adult Depression*, London: Routledge.

Bifulco, A., Brown, G. and Harris, T. (1994) 'Childhood experience of care and abuse (CECA): a retrospective interview measure', *Journal of Child Psychiatry and Psychology and Allied Disciplines* 35(8): 1419–35.

Bion, W.R. (1959) 'Attacks on linking', *International Journal of Psychoanalysis* 40: 308–15.

Birksted-Breen, D. (1997) 'Working with an anorexic patient' in J. Raphael-Leff and R.J. Perelberg (eds), *Female Experience*, London: Routledge.

Blos, P. (1967) 'The second individuation process of adolescence', *Psychoanalytic Study of the Child* 22:162–86.

Blount, W.R., Silverman, I.J., Sellars, C.S. and Seese, R.A. (1994) 'Alcohol and drug use among abused women who kill, abused women who don't, and their abusers', *The Journal of Drug Issues* 24(2): 165–77.

Bluglass, K. (1997) 'Munchausen's syndrome by proxy' in E.V. Welldon and C. van Velson (eds), *A Practical Guide to Forensic Psychotherapy*, London: Jessica Kingsley.

Bluglass, R. (1990) 'Infanticide and Filicide' in R. Bluglass and P. Bowden (eds), *Principles and Practice of Forensic Psychiatry*, Edinburgh: Churchill Livingstone.

Bluglass, R. and Bowden, P. (1990) *Principles and Practice of Forensic Psychiatry*, Edinburgh: Churchill Livingstone.

Bools, C., Neale, B. and Meadow, R. (1994) 'Munchausen syndrome by proxy: a study of psychopathology', *Child Abuse and Neglect* 18(9):773–88.

Bordo, S. (1993) *Unbearable Weight: Feminism, Western Culture, and the Body*, California: University of California Press.

Bordo, S. (1997) 'The body and the reproduction of femininity' in K. Conboy, N. Medina, and S. Stanbury (eds), *Writing on the Body: Female Embodiment and Feminist Theory*, New York: Columbia University Press.

Bourget, D. and Bradford, J.M.W. (1987) 'Affective disorder and homicide: a case of familial filicide theoretical and clinical consideration', *Canadian Journal of Psychiatry* 32:222–5.

Bourget, D. and Bradford, J.M.W. (1990) 'Homicidal parents', *Canadian Journal of Psychiatry* 35:233–8.

Breen, D. (ed.) (1993) *The Gender Conundrum: Contemporary Psychoanalytic Perspectives on Femininity and Masculinity*, London: Routledge.

Briere, J. and Zaidi, L. (1989) 'Sexual abuse histories and sequelae in female psychiatric emergency room patients', *American Journal of Psychiatry* 146:1602–6.

Brockington, I. (1996) *Motherhood and Mental Health*, Oxford: Oxford University Press.

Brown, G.W. and Harris, T.O. (1978) *The Social Origins of Depression: A Study of Psychiatric Disorder in Women*, London: Routledge.

Brown, G.W., Harris, T.O and Eales, M.J. (1996) 'Social factors and comorbidity of depressive and anxiety disorders', *British Journal of Psychiatry* 168 (suppl. 30):50–7.

Browne, A. (1987) *When Battered Women Kill*, New York: The Free Press, Macmillan.

Brownstone, D.Y. and Swaiminath, R.S. (1989) 'Violent behaviour and psychiatric diagnosis in female offenders', *Canadian Journal of Psychiatry* 34(3):190–4.

Bruch, H. (1973) *Eating Disorders: Obesity, Anorexia Nervosa and the Person Within*, New York: Basic Books.

Bruch, H. (1985) 'Four decades of eating disorders' in D.M. Garner and P.E. Garfinkel (eds), *Handbook of Psychotherapy for Anorexia Nervosa and Bulimia*, New York: Guilford Press.

Burrow, S. (1992) 'The deliberate self-harming behaviour of patients within a British special hospital', *Journal of Advanced Nursing* 17:138–48.

Busfield, J. (1996) *Men, Women and Madness: Understanding Gender and Mental Disorder*, Basingstoke: Macmillan Press.

Calam, R.M. and Slade, P.D. (1987) 'Eating problems and sexual experiences: some relationships', *British Review of Bulimia and Anorexia Nervosa* 2: 37–43.

Calam, R. and Slade, P.D. (1994) 'Eating disorders and unwanted sexual experiences' in B. Dolan and I. Gitzinger (eds), *Why Women? Gender Issues and Eating Disorders*, London: The Athlone Press.

Campbell, D. and Hale, R. (1991) 'Suicidal acts' in J. Holmes (ed.), *Textbook of Psychotherapy in Psychiatric Practice*, London: Churchill Livingstone.

Campbell, J.C. (1986) 'Nursing assessment of risk of homicide with battered women', *Advances in Nursing Science* 8(4):36–51.

Carlen, P. (1996) *Jigsaw – A Political Criminology of Youth Homelessness*, Buckingham: Open University Press.

Carlen, P. (1998) *Sledgehammer: Women's Imprisonment at the Millennium*, Basingstoke: Macmillan Press.

Chasseguet-Smirgel, J. (1981) 'Loss of reality in perversions – with special reference to fetishism', *Journal of the American Psychoanalytic Association* 29:511–34.

Cherland, E. and Mathews, P.C. (1989) 'Attempted murder of a newborn: a case history', *Canadian Journal of Psychiatry* 34:337–99.

Chipchase, H. and Liebling, H. (1996) 'Case file information for women patients at Ashworth Hospital: an explanatory study', *Issues in Criminological and Legal Psychology* 25:17–23.

Clark, S.A. (1993) 'Matricide: the schizophrenic crime?', *Medicine, Science and the Law* 33:325–8.

Coid, J., Wilkins, J., Coid, B. and Everitt, B. (1992) 'Self mutilation in female remanded prisoners II: a cluster analytic approach towards identification of a behavioural syndrome', *Criminal Behaviour and Mental Health* 2: 1–14.

Cookson, H.M. (1977) 'A survey of self injury in a closed prison for women', *British Journal of Criminology* 17:332–46.

Coombe, P. (1995) 'The inpatient psychotherapy of a mother and child at the Cassell Hospital: a case of Munchausen's syndrome by proxy', *British Journal of Psychotherapy* 12(2): 195–207.

Cordess, C. (1998) 'Munchausen by proxy syndrome: failures of boundaries and relations', paper given at the 7th Annual Meeting of the International Association of Forensic Psychotherapy, Copenhagen, Denmark.

Cordess, C. and Cox, M. (eds) (1996) *Forensic Psychotherapy: Crime, Psychodynamics and the Offender Patient*, London: Jessica Kingsley.

Cox, A. (1988) 'Maternal depression and impact on children's development', *Archives of Disease in Childhood* 63:90–103.

Cox, M. (1990) 'Psychopathology and treatment of psychotic aggression' in R. Bluglass and P. Bowden (eds), *Principles and Practice of Forensic Psychiatry*, London: Churchill Livingstone.

Craissati, J. (1998) *Child Sexual Abusers: A Community Treatment Approach*, Hove: Psychology Press.

Craissati, J. and McClurg, G. (1996) 'The Challenge Project: perpetrators of child sexual abuse in south east London', *Child Abuse and Neglect* 20: 1067–77.

Cremin, D., Lemmer, B. and Davison, S. (1995) 'The efficacy of a nursing challenge to patients; testing a new intervention to decrease self-harm behaviour in severe personality disorder', *Journal of Psychiatric and Mental Health Nursing* 2: 237–46.

Crisp, A.H. (1995) *Anorexia Nervosa: Let Me Be*, revised edn. NJ: Erlbaum.

Dalton, K. (1971) 'Prospective study into puerperal depression', *British Journal of Psychiatry* 118: 689–92.

Daniel, A.E. and Harris, P.W. (1982) 'Female homicide offenders referred for pretrial psychiatric examination: a descriptive study', *Bulletin of the American Academy for Psychiatry and Law* 10(4):261–9.

Davin, P.A., Hislop, J.C.R. and Dunbar, T. (1999) *Female Sexual Abusers: Three Views*, Vermont: Safer Society Press.

Day, D.O. and Parnell, T.F. (1998) 'Setting the treatment framework' in T.F. Parnell and D.O. Day (eds), *Munchausen by Proxy Syndrome: Misunderstood Child Abuse*, California: Sage.

Dell, S., Robertson, G., James, K. and Grounds, A. (1993a) 'Remands and psychiatric assessments in Holloway Prison I: the psychotic population', *British Journal of Psychiatry* 163:634–40.

Dell, S., Robertson, G., James, K. and Grounds, A. (1993b) 'Remands and psychiatric assessments in Holloway Prison II: the non-psychotic population', *British Journal of Psychiatry* 163:640–4.

deMause, L. (1990) 'The history of child assault', *The Journal of Psychohistory* 18(1):1–29.

Department of Health (1989) *The Children Act 1989*, London: HMSO.

De Zuleta, F. (1993) *From Pain to Violence: The Traumatic Roots of Destructiveness*, London: Whurr.

Dobash, R.E. and Dobash, R.P. (1979) *Violence Against Wives*, New York: Free Press.

Dobash, R.E., Dobash, R.P. and Noaks, L. (1995) 'Thinking about gender and crime' in R.E. Dobash, R.P. Dobash and L. Noaks (eds), *Gender and Crime*, Cardiff: University of Wales Press.

Dolan, B. and Gitzinger, I. (1994) *Why Women? Gender Issues and Eating Disorders*, London: The Athlone Press.

Dolan, B. and Mitchell, E. (1994) 'Personality disorder and psychological disturbance of female prisoners: a comparison with women referred for NHS treatment of personality', *Criminal Behaviour and Mental Health* 4(2):130–43.

D'Orban, P.T. (1979) 'Women who kill their children', *British Journal of Psychiatry* 134:560–71.

D'Orban, P.T. (1990) 'Female homicide', *Irish Journal of Psychological Medicine* 7:64–70.

Eminson, M. and Postlethwaite, R.J. (eds) (2000) *Munchausen Syndrome by Proxy Abuse: A Practical Approach*, Oxford: Butterworth-Heinemann.

Ewing, C.P. (1990) 'Psychological self defence: a proposed justification for battered women who kill', *Law and Human Behaviour* 14(6):579–94.

Ewing, C.P. (1997) *Fatal Families: The Dynamics of Intrafamilial Homicide*, California: Sage.

Fairburn, C.G., Shafran, R. and Cooper, Z. (1999) 'A cognitive behavioural theory of anorexia nervosa', *Behaviour Research and Therapy*, 37:1–13.

Faulk, M. (1988) *Basic Forensic Psychiatry*, Oxford: Blackwell Science.

Feldmann, T.B. (1988) 'Violence as a disintegration product of the self in post-traumatic stress disorder', *American Journal of Psychotherapy* XLII:281–9.

Finkelhor, D. (1984) *Child Sexual Abuse: New Theory and Research*, New York: Free Press.

Folks, D. (1995) 'Munchausen's syndrome and other factitious disorders', *Neurologic Clinics* 13(2):267–81.

Follingstad, D.R., Polek, D.S., Hause, E.S., Deaton, L.H., Bulger, M.W. and Conway, Z.D. (1989) 'Factors predicting verdicts in cases where battered women kill their husbands', *Law and Human Behaviour* 13(3):253–68.

Fonagy, P. (1991) 'Thinking about thinking: some clinical and theoretical considerations in the treatment of a borderline patient', *International Journal of Psycho-Analysis* 72: 639–56.

Fonagy, P. and Target, M. (1995) 'Towards understanding violence: the use of the body and the role of the father' reprinted in R.J. Perelberg (ed.), *A Psychoanalytic Understanding of Violence and Suicide*, London: Routledge, 1999.

Fonagy, P., Moran, G.S. and Target, M. (1993) 'Aggression and the psychological self', *International Journal of Psycho-Analysis* 74: 471–85.

Fonagy, P., Steele, M. and Steele, H. (1991) 'Maternal representations of attachment during pregnancy predict the organisation of infant-mother attachment at one year of age', *Child Development* 62: 891–905.

Fonagy, P., Steele, M., Steele, H., Leigh, T., Kennedy, R., Mattoon, G. and Target,

M. (1995) 'The predictive validity of Mary Main's adult attachment interview: a psychoanalytic and developmental perspective on the transgenerational transmission of attachment and borderline states' in S. Goldeberg, R. Muir and J. Keer (eds), *Attachment Theory: Social Developmental and Clinical Perspectives*, Hillsdale NJ: The Analytic Press.

Foster, L.A., Mann Veale, C. and Ingram Fogel, C. (1989) 'Factors present when battered women kill', *Issues in Mental Health Nursing* 10:273–384.

Freud, S. (1917) 'Mourning and melancholia', in *On Metapsychology: the theory of psychoanalysis*, vol. 11, Harmondsworth: Penguin.

Freud, S. (1940) 'Splitting of the ego in the process of defence', Standard edition 23, London: The Hogarth Press and the Institute of Psychoanalysis.

Fualaau, V. (1998) *Un Seul Crime L'Amour*, Editions Fixot: Paris. English extract published in *Marie Claire* February 1999: 49–54.

Garbarino, J. (1976) 'A preliminary study of some ecological correlates of child abuse: the impact of socioeconomic stress on the mother', *Child Development* 47:178–85.

Garfinkel, P.E., Moldofsky, H. and Garner, D.M. (1977) 'The outcome of anorexia nervosa: significance of clinical features, body image and behaviour modification', in R.A. Vlgersky, *Anorexia Nervosa*, New York: Raven Press.

Garner, D.M. and Bemis, K.M. (1982) 'A cognitive behavioural approach to anorexia nervosa', *Cognitive Therapy and Research* 6: 123–50.

Garner, D.M. and Bemis, K.M (1985) 'Cognitive therapy for anorexia nervosa' in D.M. Garner and P.E. Garfinkel (eds), *Handbook of Psychotherapy for Anorexia Nervosa and Bulimia*, New York: Guilford Press.

Garner, D.M and Garfinkel, P.E. (eds) (1985) *Handbook of Psychotherapy for Anorexia Nervosa and Bulimia*, New York: Guilford Press.

Gelles, R.J. (1980) 'Violence in the family: a review of research in the seventies', *Journal of Marriage and the Family* 42:873–85.

Gelles, R.J. (1982) 'Toward better research on child abuse and neglect: a response to Besharov', *Child Abuse and Neglect* 6(4):495–6.

Gibbons, T.C.N. (1971) 'Female offenders', *British Journal of Hospital Medicine* 6: 279–86.

Gibson, E. (1975) *Homicide in England and Wales 1967–1971 Home Office Research Study No. 31*, London: Her Majesty's Stationery Office.

Gil, D. (1970) *Violence Against Children*, Cambridge, MA: Harvard University Press.

Glass, D.D. (1995) *All My Fault: Why Women Don't Leave Abusive Men*, London: Virago.

Glasser, M. (1979) 'Some aspects of the role of aggression in the perversions' in I. Rosen (ed.), *Sexual Deviation*, Oxford: Oxford University Press.

Green, A.H. and Kaplan, M.S. (1994) 'Psychiatric impairment and childhood victimisation experiences in female child molesters', *Journal of the American Academy of Child and Adolescent Psychiatry* 33(7):954–61.

Green, C.M. and Manohar, S.V. (1990) 'Neonaticide and hysterical denial of pregnancy', *British Journal of Psychiatry* 156:121–3.

Greenwald, J.P., Tomkins, A.J., Kenning, M. and Zavodny, D. (1990) 'Psychological self defence jury instructions', *Behavioural Sciences and the Law* 8(2): 171–80.

Grubin, D. (1998) *Sex Offending Against Children: Understanding the Risk*, Police Research Series, Paper 99 Home Office Research Development and Statistics Directorate: London.

Harris, T.O. and Bifulco, A. (1991) 'Loss of parent in childhood and attachment style and depression in adulthood' in C.M. Parkes and J.S. Hinde (eds), *Attachment Across the Life Cycle*, London: Routledge.

Harris, T.O. and Brown, G.W. (1996) 'Social causes of depression', *Current Opinion in Psychiatry* 9: 3–10.

Harris, T.O., Brown, G.W. and Bifulco, A. (1987) 'Loss of parent in childhood and adult psychiatric disorder: the role of social class position and premarital pregnancy', *Psychological Medicine* 17: 163–83.

Heidensohn, F.M. (1985) *Women and Crime*, Basingstoke: Macmillan Press.

Heidensohn, F.M. (1991) 'Women as perpetrators and victims of crime: a sociological perspective', *British Journal of Psychiatry* 158(suppl. 10): 50–4.

Herbert, M. (1996) *Assessing Children in Need and Their Parents*, Leicester: The British Psychological Society.

Herjanic, M., Henn, F.A. and Vanderpear, R.H. (1977) 'Forensic psychiatry: female offenders', *American Journal of Psychiatry* 134: 556–8.

HMSO (1993) *British Crime Statistics England and Wales 1992*, London: The Home Office, Research, Development and Statistics Directorate.

HMSO (1995) *Criminal Statistics England and Wales 1994*, London: HMSO.

HMSO (1998) *Criminal Statistics England and Wales 1997*, London: The Home Office, Research, Development and Statistics Directorate.

Hodgins, S. (1992) 'Mental disorder, intellectual deficiency, and crime: evidence from a birth cohort', *Archives of General Psychiatry* 49(6):476–83.

Holmes, J. (1993) *John Bowlby and Attachment Theory*, London: Routledge.

Hornbacher, M. (1998) *Wasted: Coming Back from an Addiction to Starvation*, London: Flamingo.

Hughes, P. (1995) 'Tolerating the intolerable: the therapist's countertransference with patients with anorexia nervosa' in *Suicide and the Murderous Self: Hearing It and Bearing It*. Conference proceedings, London: St George's Hospital.

Hunt, J. and Goldring, J. (1997) 'The case of Beverley Allitt', *Medicine, Science and the Law* 37(3):189–97.

Hyatt-Williams, A. (1998) *Cruelty, Violence and Murder: Understanding the Criminal Mind*, London: Karnac Books.

Hyler, S.E. and Sussman, N. (1981) 'Chronic factitious disorder with physical symptoms (the Munchausen syndrome)', *Psychiatric Clinics of North America* 4(2):365–77.

Jason, J. (1983) 'Child homicide spectrum', *American Journal of Disorders in Childhood* 137: 579–81.

Jason, J.J., Carpenter, M.M. and Tyler, C.W. (1983) 'Under recording of infant homicide in the United States', *American Journal of Public Health* 73(2):195–7.

Jones, D.P.H. (1994) 'Editorial: The syndrome of Munchausen by proxy', *Child Abuse and Neglect*, 18(9):769–71.

Jones, D.P.H., Byrne, G. and Newbould, C. (2000) 'Management, treatment and outcomes' in M. Eminson and R.J. Postlethwaite (eds), *Munchausen Syndrome by Proxy Abuse: A Practical Approach*, Oxford: Butterworth-Heinemann.

Kalichman, S.C. (1988) 'MMPI profiles of women and men convicted of domestic homicide', *Journal of Clinical Psychology* 44(6):847–53.

Kaplan, L.J. (1991) *Female Perversions*, London: Penguin.

Kellerman, A.L. and Mercy, J. (1992) 'Men, women, and murder: gender-specific differences in rates of fatal violence and victimisation', *The Journal of Trauma* 33(1):1–5.

Kennedy, H. (1992) *Eve Was Framed: Women and British Justice*, London: Chatto and Windus.

Kennedy, R. (1997) *Child Abuse, Psychotherapy and the Law*, London: Free Association Books.

Kennerley, H. (1996) 'Cognitive therapy of dissociative symptoms associated with trauma', *British Journal of Clinical Psychology* 35(3):325–40.

Kirkpatrick, J.T. and Humphrey, J.A. (1986) 'Stress in the lives of female criminal homicide offenders', paper presented at *Second National Congress on Social Stress Research*, (June) University of New Hampshire, Durham.

Kirsta, A. (1994) *Deadlier Than the Male: Violence and Aggression in Women*, London: HarperCollins.

Klein, M. (1932) *The Psycho Analysis of Children*, London: Hogarth Press.

Klein, M. (1946) 'Notes on some schizoid mechanisms' in M. Klein (ed.) (1980) *Envy and Gratitude and Other Works 1946–1963*, London: The Hogarth Press.

Knauft, B. (1989) 'Hobbes, Rousseau, and the analytic abuse of children in simple societies', *The Journal of Psychohistory* 17(2):202–3.

Knowles, J. (1997) 'Women who shoplift' in E.V. Welldon and C. van Velson (eds), *A Practical Guide to Forensic Psychotherapy*, London: Jessica Kingsley.

Korbin, J. (1986) 'Childhood histories of women imprisoned for fatal child maltreatment', *Child Abuse and Neglect* 10(3):331–8.

Korbin, J. (1987) 'Incarcerated mothers' perceptions and interpretations of their fatally maltreated children', *Child Abuse and Neglect* 11(3):397–407.

Korbin, J. (1989) 'Fatal maltreatment by mothers: a proposed framework', *Child Abuse and Neglect* 13:481–9.

Kumar, R. and Hipwell, A.E. (1996) 'Development of a clinical rating scale to assess mother–infant interaction in a psychiatric mother and baby unit', *British Journal of Psychiatry* 169(1):18–26.

Kumar, C.R., Hipwell, A.E. and Lawson, C. (1994) 'Prevention of adverse effects of perinatal maternal mental illness on the developing child' in J. Cox and J. Holden (eds), *Perinatal Psychiatry: Use and Misuse of the Edinburgh Postnatal Depression Scale*, Gaskell: London.

Lacey, J.H. and Evans, C.D. (1986) 'The impulsivist: a multi-impulsive personality disorder', *British Journal of Addictions* 81(5):641–9.

Lake, E.S. (1993) 'An exploration of the violent victim experiences of female offenders', *Violence and Victims* 8:41–51.

Laplanche, J. and Pontalis, J.B. (1988) *A Dictionary of Psychoanalysis*, London: Karnac Books.

Lasley, J., Kuhl, A.F. and Roberg, R.R. (1985) 'Relationship of nontraditional sex-role attitudes to severity of women's criminal behaviour', *Psychological Reports* 56(1):155–8.

Laufer, M.E. (1982) 'Female masturbation in adolescence and the development of the relationship to the body', *International Journal of Psychoanalysis* 63:217–27.

Laufer, M.E. (1993) 'The female Oedipus complex and its relationship to the body' in D. Breen (ed.), *The Gender Conundrum: Contemporary Psychoanalytic Perspectives on Femininity and Masculinity*, London: Routledge.

Laufer M. and Laufer, E. (1984) *Adolescence and Developmental Breakdown*, London: Yale University Press.

Lester, D. (1992) 'The murder of babies in American states: association with suicide rates', *Psychological Reports* 72:1202.

Libow, J.A. and Schreier, H.A. (1986) 'Three forms of factitious illness in children: when is it Munchausen syndrome by proxy?', *American Journal of Orthopsychiatry* 56: 602–11.

Liebling, A. (1992) *Suicides in Prison*, London: Routledge.

Liebling, H. (1995) 'Draft guidelines for nursing staff care plans for women who self harm'. Unpublished document.

Liebling, H. and Chipchase, H. (1992) 'A pilot study on the problem of self-injurious behaviour in women in Ashworth Hospital', *Division of Criminological and Legal Psychology Newsletter* (October): 19–23.

Liebling, H. and Chipchase, H. (1996) 'Feminist group therapy for women who self-harm: an initial evaluation', *Issues in Criminological and Legal Psychology* 25:24–9.

Liebling, H., Chipchase, H. and Verlangi, R. (1997a) 'Why do people self-harm at Ashworth Maximum Security Hospital?', *Issues in Criminological and Legal Psychology* 27:10–22.

Liebling, H., Chipchase, H. and Verlangi, R. (1997b) 'An evaluation of nurse training and support needs: working with women patients who harm themselves in a special hospital', *Issues in Criminological and Legal Psychology* 29:47–56.

Liebling, H., Chipchase, H. and Wetton, S. (1994) 'A study of self-harming behaviour in women patients at Ashworth Hospital'. Unpublished research findings.

Linehan, M.M. (1993) *Cognitive Behavioural Treatment of Borderline Personality Disorder*, New York: The Guildford Press.

Livingstone, R. (1987) 'Maternal somatisation disorder and Munchausen syndrome by proxy', *Psychosomatic* 28: 213–17.

Lloyd, A. (1995) *Doubly Deviant, Doubly Damned: Society's Treatment of Violent Women*, London: Penguin.

Lloyd, H. and MacDonald, A. (2000) 'Picking up the pieces', in M. Eminson and R.J. Postlethwaite (eds), *Munchausen Syndrome by Proxy Abuse: A Practical Approach*, Oxford: Butterworth-Heinemann.

Lomas, M.J. (1986) 'Maternal filicide: a preliminary examination of culture and victim sex', *International Journal of Law and Psychiatry* 9:503–6.

McClure, R.J., Davis, P.M., Meadow, S.R. and Sibert, J.R. (1996) 'Epidemiology of Munchausen syndrome by proxy, non-accidental poisoning, and non-accidental suffocation', *Archives of Disorders of Childhood* 75(1): 57–61.

McDougall, J. (1989) *Theatres of the Body: A Psychoanalytical Approach to Psychosomatic Illness*, London: Free Association Books.

Maden, A. (1996) *Women, Prisons and Psychiatry: Mental Disorder Behind Bars*, Oxford: Butterworth-Heinemann.

Maden, A., Swinton, M. and Gunn, J. (1994a) 'A criminological and psychiatric survey of women serving a prison sentence', *British Journal of Criminology* 34:172–91.

Maden, A., Swinton, M. and Gunn, J. (1994b) 'Psychiatric disorder in women serving a prison sentence', *British Journal of Psychiatry* 164: 44–54.

Maguire, M. (1995) *Men, Women, Passion and Power: Gender Issues in Psychotherapy*, London: Routledge.

Mahoney, M.R. (1994) 'Victimisation or oppression? Women's lives, violence and agency' in M.A. Fineman and R. Mykitiuk (eds), *The Public Nature of Private Violence*, London: Routledge.

Malan, D.H. (1997) *Anorexia, Murder and Suicide: What Can Be Learned from the Stories of Three Remarkable Patients*, Oxford: Butterworth-Heinemann.

Masters, A.L. (1990) 'Infanticide: the primate data', *The Journal of Psychohistory* 18(1):99–108.

Mayhew, P., Elliott, D. and Dowds, L. (1988) *The 1988 British Crime Survey: Home Office Research Study*, No. 111, London: HMSO.

Mayhew, P., Maung, N.A. and Mirrlees-Black, C. (1992) *The 1992 British Crime Survey Home Office Research Study*, No.132, London: HMSO.

Meadow, R. (1977) 'Munchausen's syndrome by proxy: the hinterland of child abuse', *The Lancet* 13 August: 343–5.

Meadow, R. (1995) 'What is, and what is not, "Munchausen syndrome by proxy?"', *Archives of Disease in Childhood* 72: 534–9.

Menzies Lyth, I. (1959) 'The functioning of social systems as a defence against anxiety' in I. Menzies Lyth (ed.), *Containing Anxiety in Institutions*, London: Free Association Books.

Miller, F. and Bashkin, E.A. (1974) 'Depersonalisation and self mutilation', *Psychoanalytic Quartery* 43: 638–49.

Mills, M. (1997) 'The waters under the earth. Understanding maternal depression' in J. Raphael-Leff and R.J. Perelberg (eds), *Female Experience*, London: Routledge.

Milner, A.D. (1995) 'Practical concerns about the diagnosis of Munchausen's syndrome by proxy', *Archives of Disease in Childhood* 72: 528–30.

Milton, J. (1994) 'Abuser and abused: perverse solutions following childhood abuse', *Psychoanalytic Psychotherapy* 8(3): 243–55.

Mirrlees-Black, C., Budd, T., Partridge, S. and Mayhew, P. (1998) *The 1998 British Crime Survey England and Wales*, London: Research, Development and Statistics Directorate.

Mitchell, J. (1992) 'Foreword' in E.V. Welldon, *Mother, Madonna, Whore: The Idealization and Denigration of Motherhood*, New York: The Guilford Press.

Mogielnicki, R., Mogielnicki, N., Chandler, J. and Weissberg, M. (1977) 'Impending child abuse: psychosomatic symptoms in adults as a clue', *Journal of the American Medical Association* 237:1109–11.

Morley, C.J. (1995) 'Practical concerns about the diagnosis of Munchausen's syndrome by proxy', *Archives of Disease in Childhood* 72:528–38.

Morrison, T. (1977) (reprinted 1998) *Song of Solomon*, London: Vintage.

Morrison, T., Erooga, M. and Beckett, R.C. (1994) *Sexual Offending Against Children: Assessment and Treatment of Male Abusers*, London: Routledge.

Morse, S.J. (1990) 'The misbegotten marriage of soft psychology and bad law: psychological self-defence as a justification for homicide', *Law and Human Behaviour* 14:6:595–618.

Motz, L. (1997) *The Faces of the Goddess*, New York: Oxford University Press.

Nott, P.N., Franklin, M., Armitage, C. and Gelder, M.G. (1976) 'Hormonal changes and mood in the puerperium', *British Journal of Psychiatry* 128: 379–83.

Oates, M. (1994) 'Postnatal mental illness: organisation and function of services' in J. Cox and J. Holdon (eds), *Perinatal Psychiatry: Use and Misuse of the Edinburgh Postnatal Depression Scale*, London: Gaskell.

O'Connor, A.A. (1987) 'Female sex offenders', *British Journal of Psychiatry* 150:615–20.

O'Hanlon, K. (1996) 'Provocation: characteristics of reasonable person-battered woman syndrome. Regina v Thornton', *Criminal Law Review* August: 597–99.

Orbach, I. (1994) 'Dissociation, physical pain, and suicide: a hypothesis', *Suicide and Life-Threatening Behaviour* 24(1):68–79.

Parnell, T.F (1998) 'Defining Munchausen by Proxy Syndrome' in T.F. Parnell and D.O. Day, *Munchausen by Proxy Syndrome: Misunderstood Child Abuse*, California: Sage.

Parnell, T.F. and Day, D.O. (1998) *Munchausen by Proxy Syndrome: Misunderstood Child Abuse*, California: Sage.

Pattison, M.E. and Kahan, J. (1983) 'The deliberate self harm syndrome', *American Journal of Psychiatry* 140: 867–72.

Pearson, P. (1998) *When She Was Bad*, London: Virago.

Perelberg, R.J. (1999) *A Psychoanalytic Understanding of Violence and Suicide*, London: Routledge.

Pines, D. (1993) *A Woman's Unconscious Use of Her Body*, London: Virago.

Plath, S. (1963) *The Bell Jar*, London: Faber and Faber.

Puri, Basant K. (1988) 'A psychiatric trainee's experience of holding the burden', *Psychoanalytic Psychotherapy* 3(3):271–6.

Rand, D. (1989) 'Munchausen syndrome by proxy as a possible factor when abuse is falsely alleged' *Issues in Child Abuse Allegations* 1: 32–4.

Raphael-Leff, J. and Perelberg, R.J. (eds) (1997) *Female Experience*, London: Routledge.

Ray, M.C. and Smith, E. (1991) 'Black women and homicide: an analysis of the subculture of violence thesis', *The Western Journal of Black Studies* 15(3):145–53.

Reader, L. (1993) 'Evaluation of a psychotherapy service for women in the community', *Shanti: Final Report to the King's Fund.*

Reder, P., Duncan, S. and Gray, M. (1993) *Beyond Blame: Child Abuse Tragedies Revisited*, London: Routledge.

Redfern, S. (1999) Personal communication.

Resnick, P.J. (1969) 'Child murder by parents. A psychiatric review of filicide', *American Journal of Psychiatry* 126(3):325–34.

Resnick, P.J. (1970) 'Murder of the newborn: a psychiatric review of neonaticide', *American Journal of Psychiatry* 126(10): 1414–20.

Robertson, G. (1990) 'Correlates of crime among women offenders', *Medicine, Science and the Law* 30:165–74.

Rosenberg, D.A. (1987) 'Web of deceit: a literature of Munchausen syndrome by proxy', *Child Abuse and Neglect* 11:547–63.

Ryan, G., Lane, S., Davis, J. and Isaac, C. (1987) 'Juvenile sex offenders: development and correction', *Child Abuse and Neglect* 11:385–95.

Ryan, G., Miyoshi, T.J., Metzner, J.L., Krugman, R.D. and Fryer, G.E. (1996) 'Trends in a national sample of sexually abusive youths', *Journal of the American Academy of Child and Adolescent Psychiatry* 35(1):17–25.

Sabo, A.N., Gunderson, J.G., Najavits, L.M., Chauncey, D. and Kisiel, C. (1995) 'Changes in self-destructiveness of borderline patients in psychotherapy: a prospective follow-up', *Journal of Nervous and Mental Diseases* 183(6): 370–6.

Samuels, M.P., McLaughlin, W., Jacobson, R.R., Poets, C.F. and Southall, D.P. (1992) 'Fourteen cases of imposed upper airway obstruction', *Archives of Disease in Childhood* 67:162–70.

Sandyk, R. (1992) 'Postpartum psychosis and the pineal gland', *International Journal of Neuroscience* 62:101–5.

Sansome, R.A., Sansome, L.A. and Wiedernam, M. (1995) 'The prevalence of trauma and its relationship to borderline personality symptoms and self-destructive behaviours in a primary care setting', *Archives Family Medicine* 4(5):397–400.

Saradjian, J. (1996) *Women Who Sexually Abuse Children*, Chichester: Wiley.

Schreier, H.A. and Libow, J.A. (1993) *Hurting for Love, Munchausen by Proxy Syndrome*. London: Guilford Press.

Schuler, R.A., Smith, V.L. and Olson, J.M. (1994) 'Jurors' decisions in trials of battered women who kill: the role of prior beliefs and expert testimony', *The Journal of Applied Social Psychology* 24(4):316–37.

Scott, P.D. (1973) 'Parents who kill their children', *Medicine, Science and the Law* 13: 120–6.

Seligman, M.E.P. (1975) *Helplessness: On Depression, Development and Death*, San Francisco: Freeman.

Sellars, C. and Liebling, H. (1988) 'Section 3 patients: the "non-offenders"', *Division of Criminological and Legal Psychology Newsletter*, 30–5.

Shengold, L. (1999) 'Foreword' in J. Perelberg (ed.), *A Psychoanalytic Understanding of Violence and Suicide*, London: Routledge.

Sinason, V. (1986) 'Secondary mental handicap and its relationship to trauma', *Psychoanalytic Psychotherapy* 2(2):131–54.

Sommers, I. and Baskin, D. (1992) 'Sex, race, age and violent offending', *Violence and Victims* 7(3): 191–201.

Stern, E.S. (1948) 'The Medea complex; mother's homicidal wishes to her child', *Journal of Mental Science* 94: 321–31.

Stewart, D.E., Addison, A.M., Robinson, G.E. *et al.* (1988) 'Thyroid function in psychosis following childbirth', *American Journal of Psychiatry* 145: 1579–81.

Stoller, R.J. (1975) *Perversion: The Erotic Form of Hatred*, New York: Random House.

Strauss, M.A. and Gelles, R.G. (1986) 'Societal change and change in family violence from 1975–1985 as revealed by two national surveys', *Journal of Marriage and the Family* 48: 465–79.

Strom, C. (1992) 'Injuries due to violent crimes', *Medicine, Science and the Law* 32:123–32.

Stuart, E.P. and Campbell, J.C. (1989) 'Assessment of patterns of dangerousness with battered women', *Issues in Mental Health Nursing* 10:245–60.

Sullivan, W.C. (1924) *Crime and Insanity*, New York: Longmans and Green.

Trowell, J. (1997) Paper given at 6th Annual Meeting of the International Association of Forensic Psychotherapy, London: Regent's College.

Turcan, M. and Bercu, S. (1999) 'Co-morbidity in female inpatients in a regional secure unit'. Unpublished document.

Ussher, J.M. (1989) *The Psychology of the Female Body*, London: Routledge.

Ussher, J.M (1997) *Fantasies of Femininity: Reframing the Boundaries of Sex*, Harmondsworth: Penguin.

van der Kolk, B., Perry, C. and Herman, J. (1991) 'Childhood origins of self destructive behaviour', *American Journal of Psychiatry* 148:1665–76.

Vanezis, P. (1991) 'Women, violent crime and the menstrual cycle: a review', *Medicine, Science and the Law* 31:11–14.

Vitousek, K.M. (1996) 'The current status of cognitive-behavioural models of anorexia nervosa and bulimia nervosa' in P. Salkovskis (ed.), *Frontiers of Cognitive Behaviour*, London: The Guilford Press.

Walker, L.E. (1984) *The Battered Woman Syndrome*, New York: Springer.

Warner, M. (1998) *London Review of Books*, 1 January.

Weeda-Mannak, W.L. (1994) 'Female sex role conflicts and eating disorders' in B. Dolan and I. Gitzinger (eds), *Why Women? Gender Issues and Eating Disorders*, London: The Athlone Press.

Weiner, P. (1998) Personal communication.

Welldon, E.V. (1991) 'Psychology and psychopathology in women – a psychoanalytic perspective', *British Journal of Psychiatry* 158(suppl. 10):85–92.

Welldon, E.V. (1992) *Mother, Madonna, Whore: The Idealization and Denigration of Motherhood*, New York: The Guilford Press. Originally published: London: Free Association Books, 1988.

Welldon, E.V. (1993) 'Forensic psychotherapy and group analysis', *Group Analysis* 26:487–502.

Welldon, E.V. (1994) 'Forensic psychotherapy' in P. Clarkson and M. Pokorny (eds), *The Handbook of Psychotherapy*, London: Routledge.

Welldon, E.V. (1996) 'Women as abusers' in K. Abel, M. Buscewicz, S. Davison, S. Johnson and E. Staples (eds), *Planning Community Mental Health Services for Women: A Multi-professional Handbook*, London: Routledge.

West, D.J. (1965) *Murder Followed by Suicide*, London: Heinemann.

Wilczynski, A. (1995) 'Child-killing by parents: social, legal and gender issues' in R.E. Dobash, R.P. Dobash and L. Noaks (eds), *Gender and Crime*, Cardiff: University of Wales Press.

Wilkins, J. and Coid, J. (1991) 'Self-mutilation in female remanded prisoners: I. An indicator of severe psychopathology', *Criminal Behaviour and Mental Health* 1:247–67.

Williams, G. (1997) *Foreign Bodies and Other Internal Landscapes*, London: Duckworth.

Williams, K. (1989) Factors associated with self mutilation. Unpublished thesis for M.Clin. Psychol. cited in H. Liebling and H. Chipchase (1992) 'A pilot study on the problem of self-injurious behaviour in women in Ashworth Hospital', *DCLP Newsletter*:19–23.

Wilson, G.T. (1999) 'Cognitive behaviour therapy for eating disorders: progress and problems', *Behaviour Research and Therapy* 37: 29–52.

Wilson, G.T. and Fairburn, C.G. (1998) 'Treatments for eating disorders' in P.E. Nathan and J.M. Gorman (eds), *A Guide to Treatments that Work*, New York: Oxford University Press.

Winnicott, D.W. (1964) 'The concept of the false self' in C. Winnicott, R. Shepherd and M. Davis (eds) *Home is Where We Start From: Essays by a Psychoanalyst*, Harmondsworth: Penguin.

Winnicott, D.W. (1949) 'Hate in the countertransference', *International Journal of Psychoanalysis* 30:69–74.

Wisdom, C.S. (1989) 'The cycle of violence', *Science* 24:160–6.

Wykes, M. (1995) 'Passion, marriage and murder: analysing the press discourse' in R.E. Dobash, R.P. Dobash and L. Noaks (eds), *Gender and Crime*, Cardiff: University of Wales Press.

Yaryura-Tobias, J., Neziroglu, F. and Kaplan, S. (1995) 'Self-mutilation, anorexia, and dysmenorrhea in obsessive compulsive disorder', *International Journal of Eating Disorders* 17(1): 33–8.

Yeo, H.M. and Yeo, W.W. (1993) 'Repeat deliberate self harm: a link with childhood sexual abuse?', *Archives of Emergency Medicine* 10: 161–6.

Zachary, A. (1997) 'Murderousness' in E.V. Welldon and C. van Velson (eds), *A Practical Guide to Forensic Psychotherapy*, London: Jessica Kingsley.

Index

AAI (Adult Attachment Interview) 29
abandonment 90, 106, 118, 120, 122,
    158, 223, 226; fear of 43, 251;
    nurses' feelings of 166; pain of
    119; therapy used to explore sense
    of 203
abuse *see* emotional abuse; physical
    abuse; psychological abuse; sexual
    abuse
acting out 75, 156, 197
active abusers 91–2
active inducers 62–4
adolescence 33, 43, 119; anorexia
    182, 193, 197–200, 201, 205, 206;
    criminal convictions 64;
    self-harm 152, 154, 165;
    somatisation 75; unplanned
    pregnancy 220
adoption 54, 230
Adshead, G. 61, 65, 76, 151, 155,
    158, 182
affection 29, 31, 40, 44, 133;
    avuncular 35; sexual 30, 35–6
affective disorders 139, 146, 159,
    160, 161; endogenous and reactive
    163; symptom relief from 162
age 30, 43, 252
aggression 18, 55, 65, 75, 76, 81, 109,
    125, 145; active 142; anorexia and
    195; denial of 252; fuelled by
    anger 158–9; immediate stimulus
    to 141; impulsive 83, 87, 153;
    madness' outside the realm of 82;
    male 42, 99; physical 96; primitive

fantasies 86; projected 217;
    punitive 179; rape and 131;
    self-harm and 152, 156; sexualised
    153; turned inwards 203
Ainsworth, M. 29
alcohol 99, 100, 134, 177, 236–7, 240
alienation 96, 121, 171
allegations 50, 51, 79, 225; false
    79–80
Allen, N. 92, 93, 256
Allitt, Beverley 59–60
altruistic motives 140, 143, 145
ambivalence 24–5, 38, 76, 77, 102,
    106, 198; cultural 197; leaving a
    violent partner 110; pregnancy
    142
amenorrhoea 145, 194
Anderson, R. 92
androgyny 194
anger 27, 51, 90, 107, 121, 138, 168,
    251, 252
aggression fuelled by 158–9;
    channelling 155; control of 161;
    coping with 151, 174; denial of
    252; displaced on partner 223;
    enacted 172; expression of 153,
    154, 174, 177–8, 202, 208;
    managing 157, 180; murderous
    122; need to discharge 97; relief
    from 160, 190; residual 103;
    self-injury as expression of 177–8;
    splitting off of 15; stifled 119;
    therapy used to explore sense of
    203